EDUCATION AND THE REPRODUCTION OF CAPITAL

Marxism and Education

This series assumes the ongoing relevance of Marx's contributions to critical social analysis and aims to encourage continuation of the development of the legacy of Marxist traditions in and for education. The remit for the substantive focus of scholarship and analysis appearing in the series extends from the global to the local in relation to dynamics of capitalism and encompasses historical and contemporary developments in political economy of education as well as forms of critique and resistances to capitalist social relations. The series announces a new beginning and proceeds in a spirit of openness and dialogue within and between Marxism and education, and between Marxism and its various critics. The essential feature of the work of the series is that Marxism and Marxist frameworks are to be taken seriously, not as formulaic knowledge and unassailable methodology but critically as inspirational resources for renewal of research and understanding, and as support for action in and upon structures and processes of education and their relations to society. The series is dedicated to the realization of positive human potentialities as education and thus, with Marx, to our education as educators.

Renewing Dialogues in Marxism and Education: Openings
Edited by Anthony Green, Glenn Rikowski, and Helen Raduntz

Critical Race Theory and Education: A Marxist Response
Mike Cole

Revolutionizing Pedagogy: Education for Social Justice Within and Beyond Global Neo-Liberalism
Edited by Sheila Macrine, Peter McLaren, and Dave Hill

Marxism and Education beyond Identity: Sexuality and Schooling
Faith Agostinone-Wilson

Blair's Educational Legacy: Thirteen Years of New Labour
Edited by Anthony Green

Racism and Education in the U.K. and the U.S.: Towards a Socialist Alternative
Mike Cole

Marxism and Education: Renewing the Dialogue, Pedagogy, and Culture
Edited by Peter E. Jones

Educating from Marx: Race, Gender, and Learning
Edited by Shahrzad Mojab and Sara Carpenter

Education and the Reproduction of Capital: Neoliberal Knowledge and Counterstrategies
Edited by Ravi Kumar

Education and the Reproduction of Capital

Neoliberal Knowledge and Counterstrategies

Edited by

Ravi Kumar

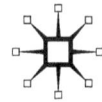

EDUCATION AND THE REPRODUCTION OF CAPITAL
Copyright © Ravi Kumar, 2012.

All rights reserved.

First published in 2012 by
PALGRAVE MACMILLAN®
in the United States—a division of St. Martin's Press LLC,
175 Fifth Avenue, New York, NY 10010.

Where this book is distributed in the UK, Europe and the rest of the world, this is by Palgrave Macmillan, a division of Macmillan Publishers Limited, registered in England, company number 785998, of Houndmills, Basingstoke, Hampshire RG21 6XS.

Palgrave Macmillan is the global academic imprint of the above companies and has companies and representatives throughout the world.

Palgrave® and Macmillan® are registered trademarks in the United States, the United Kingdom, Europe and other countries.

ISBN: 978–1–137–00686–8

Library of Congress Cataloging-in-Publication Data

    Education and the reproduction of capital : neoliberal knowledge and counterstrategies / edited by Ravi Kumar.
      p. cm.—(Marxism and education)
      ISBN 978–1–137–00686–8
      1. Education—Economic aspects. 2. Education and globalization.
    3. Capitalism. 4. Neoliberalism. I. Kumar, Ravi, 1975–

LC65.E3165 2012
338.4′7374013—dc23   2011048627

A catalogue record of the book is available from the British Library.

Design by Newgen Imaging Systems (P) Ltd., Chennai, India.

First edition: August 2012

For Rama
For her companionship and camaraderie

Contents

Series Editor's Preface   ix

Acknowledgments   xv

Chapter 1
Neoliberal Education and Imagining Strategies of
Resistance: An Introduction   1
Ravi Kumar

Chapter 2
Social Class and Rebellion: The Role of Knowledge
Production in Capitalist Society   15
Curry Stephenson Malott

Chapter 3
How Shall We Live as Lambs Among Wolves?
Reason—Passion—Power and Organization: What to Do?   41
Rich Gibson

Chapter 4
Class, Neoliberal Capitalism in Crisis, and the Resistant and
Transformative Role of Education and Knowledge Workers   63
Dave Hill

Chapter 5
Rethinking Schools and Society/Combating
Neoliberal Globalization   101
David Hursh

Chapter 6
Education Toward War   113
Faith Agostinone-Wilson

Chapter 7
Neoliberal Politics Impacting Education: Imagining
Possibilities of Resistance 135
Ravi Kumar

Chapter 8
The Struggle and Its Generalization: The Case of
the University 153
Paresh Chandra

Chapter 9
Learning Truth Telling: Beyond Neoliberal Education 171
Savyasaachi

Chapter 10
Twenty-First-Century Socialism and Education in
the Bolivarian Republic of Venezuela: An Alternative to
the Neoliberal Model 189
Mike Cole

Chapter 11
Being, Becoming, and Breaking Free: Peter McLaren and
the Pedagogy of Liberation 209
Peter McLaren in conversation with Ravi Kumar

Notes on Contributors 241

Index 245

Series Editor's Preface

Writing this preface in November 2011—things are moving fast; interesting times, indeed for the reproduction of capital. We are witnessing the unfolding of the most severe crisis of capitalism since the 1930s and it is displaying tensions and contradictions across the structures of globalized neoliberal capitalist systems. What emerged as a banking crisis in 2008 has now morphed into developing sovereign debt problems, threatening to trigger recession once again and the prospect of it spiralling into stagnation and global depression looms large. The atmosphere of crisis is expressed in myriad contexts across the full range of social, political, moral, philosophical, scientific, rational, and analytical dimensions. Simultaneously, prospects for left progressive critique, strategic analysis, and action are encouraging as the whole edifice of corporate finance capitalism is demonstrably under severe strain and, in some contexts, on the brink of collapse. There is little likelihood that the global elites will be able to patch together a swift enabling strategy for renewing their own forms of "growth" without adjustments, reform, and tactical regulation. Bank bailouts, sovereign debt crises and deflationary austerity policies serve to clarify once again the inequalities in the system, along with highlighted accompanying chaos and apparent intractable complexity in the management of finance capital's necessary risks in pursuit of shareholder value maximization. Nationally, democratic forms once again disconnect with global markets and democracy itself seems to be out of sync with financial and economic institutional mechanisms. This is graphically illustrated in the US, for instance, where the constitutional system of checks and balances is in political logjam, while at the center of the European turmoil the ramifications of popular resistance to Greek "bail-out" proposals triggers political and economic managerial inertia with intractability of broader coordinated responses across the European Union. Makeshift "solutions" are promulgated, entailing state sponsored socialism for the rich and capitalism for the rest.

The chronic systemic contradictory nature of economic, financial, and political crises incipient to capitalism are resurfacing, ever more visible, and proliferating. Forms of popular resistance targeting sites and spaces of capital abound, not least as outrage at the deepening of social contrasts highlighting social insecurity profiled against conspicuous elite greed. Social and political "unrest" is the prospect for the foreseeable future.

Recognition of such issues can be formative for emergent radical will to power for remaking social relations of expansive human possibility following and developing Marxist analysis. The guiding thread must be the contradictions of capitalist political economy, the structures, forms, and processes of the ways in which value is created through routine exploitation, demutualization, and concomitant devaluing of the creators, while empowering property and accumulated value for corporate and individual *haves* at the expense of the *have-nots*, thereby devaluing humanity in general. Contradictory as ever, the system disempowers consumers *even as consumers* and is undermining the assumed liberal necessity and essential expansiveness of capitalism's circuits of production even for possibilities of trickle down "redistribution." The promulgation of austerity policies mean that, for instance, significant proportions of young people and their parents' hope in the future is becoming ever more fragile. Thus, despite the expansion of access to higher education, whereby each new cohort of students has become distinctly better *credentialed* than the immediately previous generation, they can no longer aspire to the guarantee of social and economic well being and security of the standard of living in relation to that of their own parents. They face unemployment as well as devaluation of the credibility of their educational qualifications. Indeed, many parents themselves will be denied the comfortable old age they had come to expect as their social right. This is occurring not only in the heartlands of erstwhile prosperity, progress, and affluence but also ever more keenly in disadvantaged regions. In these contexts the fetishist mantra of social mobility is ever more readily exposed as an ideological charade, a myth of expansive equality through educational opportunity, while in reality a cloak for deepening social inequality and systemic social class consolidation. Such processes set the conditions of the possibility of anticapitalist class formation and political struggles across all areas of segmented social inequalities. However, such critical developments have yet to break *decisively* through and articulate across the terrains of neoliberal local, regional, national, and global hegemony. Anticapitalist, democratic socialist morale, while growing in many forms of actions and debates, has yet to emerge on a sufficiently large scale for radical social movements to significantly reset social, political, economic, and moral agendas to effectively challenge the status quo and underpin progressive transformations at each level of state forms. That said, radical social, moral, and political energy has surfaced across the globe, in a complex array of struggles for human rights, political freedoms, and forms of democracy, not least in emergent peripheral regions, most notably the Arab Spring in North Africa and the Middle East. Coercion and acquiescence give way to nonacceptance, to street protest, taking through occupation material and symbolic spaces, extraordinarily courageous nonviolent actions, and, more rarely, armed struggles. However, it is vital to keep in mind that for each of these contexts, shock and crisis can and often do consolidate reaction, too. Among the dramatic crisis dynamics of social relations that capitalist production necessarily generates will be compliance and acquiescence as well as resistance. Not that resistance, as such, equates directly in Marxist terms to progressive class formation and class action. Creative resistance and modes of capitalist adaptation, appropriation, and cooptation can readily go hand in hand. Liberal repressive tolerance is ever available in multiple forms. Educational institutions, for instance, are rarely simply *ideological* state apparatuses free of directly repressive aspects (in Althusser's terms). Punitive legal and physical enforcement and *repression* often hovers over and flows through such forms. For instance, rights to education and social welfare can be transformed into disciplinary mechanisms and effective top down strategies of domination in class struggle. These are powerful tactical and strategic devices operating directly and indirectly in, for and through the state and corporate power structures, constituting effective armories of demoralization and repression on behalf of the well-placed in this system of top down reinforcement of structures for capital accumulation.

Nevertheless, crisis developments serve as contexts and potential catalysts for democratic struggle. They help to clarify that capitalist progressive expansion of commodification has entered and thrived in all corners of human capacities and desires. Capitalism's negative logics have put paid to conventional consumer aspirations in the cosmopolitan and globalized heartlands, reversing the processes of its expansion through embourgeoisification of the "middle" social layers. Proletarianization is potentially more visible but widely and simply misrecognized as evidence merely of reduction of relative expansion of life chances and consumption possibilities, whose significance is taken to threaten prospects for "growth" rather than being identified as a fundamental systemic issues, and symptoms of deep contradiction. Thus, connections have to be made to understand and expose the essential dysfunctionality of the structures of capitalism and a key task is to show and popularize the weakness of its modes of dependence upon *expansive profitability*. A straw in the breeze, perhaps, but an encouraging cultural shift and polemical resource, nevertheless, may well be that the term "capitalism" has reentered common parlance and is being held up for critical scrutiny and debate in popular contexts and media beyond specialist academic and marginalized radical discourses. Capitalism is thereby less securely empowered in culture as the unspoken silent signifier for political economy of *the-way-it-is*, the TINA dispositional default which cancels possibilities for recognition or thinking through alternatives. This widens critical spaces for taking seriously the possibility for anticapitalist sentiments, analyses, actions, and movements and fundamental rethinking of what makes sense. There is a long way to go and it is foolhardy to rule out the manifold possibilities whereby the significance of critical economic and political manifestations may well give rise to funnelling more power to international globalized corporate capital, national elites and reactionary state powers. Expansive neoliberalism has shown few signs of serious atrophy or moving off the dominant policy agendas concerning social welfare, workfare, or all manner of public health and educational developments. Nor has attention to the ongoing consequences of climate changes and fundamental dimensions of social relations with the natural environment been progressed significantly. It is "on hold" at national policy levels due to preoccupation with apparently more pressing issues around financial and economic crises.

In their many guises and complexities, these considerations form a collective backdrop to this volume and its contributions to Marxist pedagogies of critique aimed at revitalizing the politics of resistance and anticapitalist class struggles *in and as education*. It assembles essays, analyses, personal testimony, and reflective commentary, providing materialist intellectual energy and analytical resources for identifying the potentially united powers of workers in all manners and at all levels of production in opposition to the structures of capitalist relations, institutional mechanisms, media, and outcomes. Such oppositional powers require integration for collective action, not least through coordinated social movements and broad based alliances, ever more effectively networking through internet resources. This includes artistic forms and fun, too, as materialist playful critical pedagogy of critique in which radicalizing *situationist* expression, for instance, in creative street and other expressive forms and productive disruption are important as Marxist education, none of which is to be confused with ludic escapism and/or superficial self recrimination and identity work. All such tactics are working toward integrating strategies for generating political and cultural challenges to the dominance of capital. The logic and coherence in diversity across these chapters support struggles in and for a transformed democratic and socialist public sphere. In these terms, and deploying a variety of Marxist critical forms, each chapter provides valuable resources for reporting and critically seeing through the empirical manifestations of the dominant mode of capitalist production. Topics and focuses include neoliberal experience in India; pedagogy, curriculum, structural reform in and around education and its devaluation into *schooling*; radical organization and practices of educational workers; academic production as radical commitment, including autobiography and rearticulating the personal and the political; possibilities and limits of digital technology for decommodified critical education; ongoing revolution in and through education in Latin America; education/military complex in the United States; the UK and US neoliberal heartlands and threats to ensuring a sustainable and just future; reason and passion harnessed in radical educational work, and more. They recognize, illuminate, and critique the creative destructive powers and exuberance of capitalism (celebrated, indeed, by Marx, himself), now deeply embedded globally in *turbo-capitalist* mode. They thus contribute to the continuous and developing legacy of the Marxist educative traditions addressing materialist immanent, ideology, and explanatory critique of the dominance and legitimacy of the capitalist mode of production. Put in Gramscian terms, they provide analyses, illustrating practices and possibilities in cultural and economic struggles in and for progressive hegemony. As such, these themes are united in and constitutive of radical *educative praxis*. They are formative, supportive of working through capillary forms, across multiple cultural layers and spaces and enabled through a variety of media. Thus, anticapitalist momentum is enhanced through critique, engagement, and confrontation, supportive of stubborn resistance, making connections and spreading confidence in productive discontent for building potential energy and resources for democratic socialist reconstruction. They serve to underpin pedagogic action in the organizing processes and oppositional structure building for what Marx referred to as *educating the educators* (Marx, 1845). They express critical praxis, not just as moments of cultural representation, nor simply as methodologically "interesting" and intellectually engaging epistemologies for alternative ways of thinking the world, but as formative practices in creating critical and transformative reality, too. They are simultaneously instantiating performative ontology and counterpoints to grim fatalisms. In dialectical mode, the agenda of anticapitalist class formation *in itself* is thus emergent in the work of these authors through moments in dialogue they constitute as structures and dynamics of anticapitalist ontology, all material to conditions of possibility for realizing formation of *class for itself*.

Finally, it is important to recognize that radical hope, while vital, if relied on alone, is hopeless. So far as Marxism and education is concerned, *Marxism as education*, educating the educators in and through socialist struggles, the practical business of dialectics requires occupation and labor movement coordination, street work, workplace and community organizing, articulated with political activism *in production to transform the dominant relations of production, distribution, and exchange*. Such is the broad agenda in all its complex ramifications for achieving progressive changes attuned to the breaking waves of the ongoing present. Each of the moments of this work contributes to the objective of empowerment as a renewal of the spirit and practices of the *commons* in which the condition for *individual liberation* requires the fulfilment of *emancipation of all* through open-ended democratic socialist practices. This book is a very welcome contribution to advancing these *educative* struggles in and for disrupting and transforming the reproduction of capital.

ANTHONY GREEN
November, 2011

Reference

Marx, K. (1845–1974) Theses on Feuerbach, in K. Marx and F. Engels. 1845. *The German Ideology,* London: Lawrence and Wishart.

Acknowledgments

This volume emerged out of a concern that has constituted the focus of my work for quite some time. My activities at *Radical Notes* led me to further explore new dimensions of the debate and I owe this work to my engagements at *Radical Notes*. My comrades Pratyush and Pothik have helped me further sharpen the arguments.

This endeavor was impossible without the involvement of contributors. I owe special comradely gratitude to them. Mike Cole needs a special mention. His chapter came from him when he was in deep personal shock after his son's sudden demise. Dave Hill, Rich Gibson, David Hursh, Faith Agostine-Wilson and Savyasaachi were very helpful in revising their chapters at a short notice. Conversations with Peter McLaren were very important to understand the politics of resistance not only within educational discourse but in general condition of politics of capital.

Special thanks to Paresh for his chapter on University as a possible site of resistance because there have been very few works on students movements and much fewer on understanding the politics through the structures and dynamics of university system. I would also thank Bhumika for the photograph that adorns the cover of the book.

Anthony Green as the series editor thought that this volume would fit in the *Marxism and Education* series and had set the ball rolling for this work. Gerstenschlager Burke and Kaylan Connally at Palgrave were of immense help and understood my difficulties and gave time to handle them.

Finally, this volume could be possible only at the cost of spending less and less time with Ayan and Rama.

Chapter 1

Neoliberal Education and Imagining Strategies of Resistance: An Introduction

Ravi Kumar

Capitalism is about the perpetual destruction of human creativity and bringing into the ambit of capital circulation every possible aspect of our life, and neoliberalism represents the most callous and aggressive form of this capital-on-offensive. It takes the labor-capital conflict to a new phase where the consensual politics of the ruling class, combined with its mantra of *everything is possible to achieve*, goes hand in hand with the project of homogenizing our very mode of living and thinking. Hence, what we get initially is a farcical hope that capitalism would provide everything that we need—it will usher in prosperity and happiness, and so on.

At different stages of history, liberal bourgeois intellectuals have argued that the prosperity of capitalism has rendered the need to transcend the rule of capital useless. There are possibilities, within capitalism, to improve the condition of the masses. Eduard Bernstein's framework furthered this idea in his debates within German social democratic politics. For sociologists like Talcott Parsons, the system remained unproblematic because the problems within it could be rectified through slight tweaking of its "units." Parsons wanted us to believe that "equilibrium" and "order" are important and suggested ways through which this could be done. Daniel Bell, in the post–World War II phase, was arguing for a similar kind of framework. Critiquing the idea that class-based antagonisms have paved the way for other different kinds of determinants of conflict and inequality, he wrote that "capitalism is not only, as Marx saw it, an economic system with employer-worker relations and classes formed on strictly economic lines but a social system, wherein power has been transmitted through the family and where the satisfactions of ownership lay, in part, in the family name...by which the business enterprise was known" (Bell 1958, 246–247). Property relations were no longer the determinants of inequality for him because there were other sources of power, and power became an important factor determining inequality. And, these forms of inequality no longer required establishment of a socialist system over the debris of capitalism.

Similar arguments have found echoes in works of liberals talking about "multiple subjectivities," "radical and plural democracy," and so on. There has been an inherent appeal to look for possibilities within capitalism, because it has still-unexplored aspects. Mouffe has been one such thinker who argued, concerned at the decline of the left, that the left needed to recognize the strengths of liberal democracy, while simultaneously revealing its shortcomings as well. "In other words, the objective of the Left should be the extension and deepening of the democratic revolution initiated two hundred years ago" (1995, 1)[1]. She believes that the liberal (bourgeois) democracy appears problematic because there has been a wide gap between their "professed democratic ideals and their realization." Rather "the general tendency on the Left has been to denounce them as a sham and aim at the construction of a completely different society" (Mouffe 1995, 1). Hence, for Mouffe, there has hardly been any problem with bourgeois democracy. If at all there is any problem, it has been that the principles have not been implemented properly. Democracy and institutions that came to symbolize it became significant instruments of change for a lot of thinkers. In other words, this has continued to be an important preoccupation within the Marxist/post-Marxist debate for over a century now.

There has been a host of theoretical discourse that has, through a concerted effort across history, tried to establish the inevitability and immutability of capitalism as a system. As indicated above, this came not only from the liberal bourgeois social science but also from a group of theoreticians who have been termed "post-Marxists." The postmodernists have been another group of theorists who vehemently negated the idea of a *system* (though ultimately subscribing to some semblance of it when they resorted to localized *systems*) by arguing how undemocratic and authoritarian is the idea of *universality*. Postmodernism went into complete denial regarding the possibility to "generate universal solutions or answers to problems and questions concerning contemporary forms of life from within, what might be termed, a conventional 'modern' problematic" (Smart 1992, 183). "Modern" and different ideas such as Marxism appeared to it as metanarratives whose "loss of credibility" it pronounced quite emphatically through works of different thinkers (Anderson 1999, 25).

Claiming to be an oppositional force, the postmodernists saw themselves "as standing in opposition to the powers-that-be, and one of the most frequently cited vindications of the postmodern sensibility is that it gives a voice to previously marginalised and subordinated subjects" (Thompson 2000, 65). However, the analysis of postmodern social thought, which targeted Marxism specifically, received varied responses from within the tradition of Marxism (and from trends that came to be called post-Marxist later on).[2] Some analysts have tried to collate these responses within four categories (Smart 1992, 184). For some others, postmodernism as a theoretical strand has taken in a number of theorists who would have otherwise resented it. McLaren and Farahmandpur (2000, 42) point how the radical theories of Paulo Freire and Antonio Gramsci are used to facilitate the sprouting of "the saplings of postmodernism." They recognize the way postmodern social theory contributed to understanding of "politics that underwrite popular cultural formations, mass media apparatuses, the technological revolution's involvement in global restructuring of capitalism, the ideological machinations of the new capitalism..." but in the end "its ability to advance (let alone sustain) a critique of global capitalism, corporate anorexia (downsizing and outsourcing) and the contemporary reign of money, has been severely compromised" (McLaren and Farahmandpur 2000, 42).

The significance of postmodernism lies in the way it has undermined the significance of class as a category that cuts across diverse forms of social divisions as well as the way it impacts and influences the systemic aspects of the world within which we live. It disconnects everyday human existence from the larger system where labor-capital conflict constitutes the basis of existence. Once such disconnections happen the classroom becomes an autonomous arena of transformative action for an educationist. Different forms of capital accumulation and possibilities of resisting those forms also get scuttled because capital does not appear as an all-pervading element in our existence. The discourse of the local ignores the continual presence of the capital-labor conflict/relationship, not only within its localized domain but also with the larger system, where rule of capital dictates the laws of our existence. It is largely this disconnection, which has allowed the intrusion of capital in every aspect of our life (and now in its most aggressive form under neoliberalism) to become normative. The arrival of neoliberalism has not only destroyed the possibilities of welfarism that one expected under one form of rule of capital but it has also brought all aspects of human existence under the rule of capital.

Here Comes Neoliberalism!!

Sometimes, one is compelled to go back to Marx and ponder whether he foresaw this stage when wrote that the bourgeoisie

> has pitilessly torn asunder the motely feudal ties... and has left remaining no other nexus between man and man than naked self-interest, than callous 'cash payment.' It has drowned the most heavenly ecstasies of religious fervor, of chivalrous enthusiasm, of philistine sentimentalism, in the icy water of egotistical calculation. It has resolved personal worth into exchange value and in place of numberless indefeasible chartered freedoms, has set up that single, unconscionable freedom—Free Trade. (Marx and Engels 2002, 222)

After all, what is outside the realm of circulation of capital? Nothing at all.

Neoliberalism has brought us to a stage where all aspects have been brought under the ambit of market. It is a system that functions on the principle of unregulated markets and brings all services within the ambit of market (McLaren and Farahmandpur 2000, 37; Giroux and Giroux 2006). There has been a shift in "political-economic practices and thinking since 1970s" in this direction. Today, there is hardly any place that can claim "immunity' from this tidal wave called neoliberalism. It has culminated in institutional reforms as well as created its own discourse, which appears hegemonic today" (Harvey 2002, 23). For Dumenil and Levy neoliberalism appears as "the expression of the desire of a class of capitalist owners and the institutions in which their power is concentrated, which we collectively call 'finance,' to restore—in the context of a general decline in popular struggles—the class's revenues and power, which had diminished since the Great Depression and World War II. Far from being inevitable, this was a political action" (2004, 1–2).

In some countries such as India, however, scholars myopically find it surfacing suddenly in the last decade of the twentieth century. It started working as a system that continually talks in the idiom of social justice and equality but is, in fact, shorn of such concepts because it advocates that these concepts can be realized in practice "by the maximization of entrepreneurial freedoms within an institutional framework characterized private property rights, individual liberty, unencumbered markets, and free trade" (Harvey 2007, 22). The state is only supposed to facilitate the creation and preservation of institutional frameworks that would allow such practices to flourish. The state ensures this by becoming an active (which is unabashedly overt unlike early stages) agent of capital. It resorts to aggression and physical violence, changes legislations, and brings about appropriate institutions required by neoliberal capital. One of the major areas has been the attack on labor, which has emerged at different locations across the world—be it France, England, or India. This phase of capitalism also produces serious issues for scholars to think about in terms of class formation and class alliances. For instance, Dumenil and Levy argue that "the dramatic social transformation realized during neoliberalism would have been impossible if an alliance had not been made between capitalist and managerial classes, in particular their upper fractions" (2011, 18). In fact, the role of such managers emerged during the recent recessions that hit economies across the globe. One aspect of this recession was how neoliberalism was about "a new high management or, equivalently, corporate governance." It provided an unbridled "freedom of enterprises to act" (Dumenil and Levy 2011, 18) and led to optimum possible commodification of social life, bringing everything in the domain of the market, which was then deregulated, and financial institutions and mechanisms of the ever-fluid and mobile capital had a field day. This has also been a phase of finance, which "has penetrated across all commercial relations to an unprecedented direct extent...finance is different today because of the proliferation of both purely financial markets and instruments and the corresponding ranges of fictitious capitals that bridge these to real activities" (Fine 2010, 13). Financialization also creates a situation of crisis for the economy because it becomes responsible not only for the "slowdown of accumulation" but it also creates "a dynamic in which real accumulation is both tempered and, ultimately, choked off by fictitious accumulation." It has undermined the role of the state as an "active agent of economic restructuring" and as an agent that would create propitious conditions for overall accumulation (Fine 2010, 19). In a certain sense the control over economic structures and processes goes out of the control of the state.

Neoliberal capitalism created an unprecedented polarization across class lines globally. The conflict between labor and capital had different dimensions—while labor was being impoverished, its ability to revolt and resist was also being blunted. On the one hand, one finds the state acting as a conduit for capital, trying to take away even basic rights such as the right to unionize, as has been happening in the factories of automobile company Maruti Suzuki in India; on the other hand there has been a weakening of resistance against capital on part of workers as well. There have been examples of how workers' unions contributed to the bail-out process during the recent recession. For instance, Ford and General Motors also "won agreements from the UAW union to delay contributions to a health trust fund for retirees and reduce payments to laid-off workers" (Amadeo 2011).

It is quite a characteristic of neoliberalism to target the rules governing the labor market and it "completely changed the conditions under which the capital markets function. There are many aspects to this—the centrality of the stock market and of capital in general, free international mobility of capital, and so on. Finally, neoliberalism is indeed the bearer of a process of general commercialization of social relationships, and that is one of its more shocking aspects" (Dumenil and Levy 2004, 2). These are the changes, which appear as indispensable if one has to ensure the growth of economy and prosperity of people. An ethnography of the debates concerning the labor law or privatization in name of efficiency and accountability largely emerged in the context of how important it was to bring about such changes to take an economy and society forward. Gradually, it became a normative condition, something natural. The voices of resistance will either invent new modes of expression or become silent and a part of the everyday normative processes within the process of surplus accumulation. In fact, social movements themselves have become problematic in the way they have distanced themselves from the class question and have directed the energies of protest towards localized processes that do not seek to question the processes of capital accumulation.

Neoliberalism and Education

There have been works that point to the inevitability of educational inequality within capitalism (Greaves, Hill, and Maisuria 2007) and also show how neoliberalism has affected education systems across the world (Hill 2007; Ross and Gibson 2007; Hill and Kumar 2009). There is hardly any aspect of our sociopolitical, cultural, or economic life that remains untouched by the rapacious campaign of neoliberal capital. "Neoliberalism has conquered the commanding heights of global intellectual, political, and economic power, all of which are mobilised to realise the neoliberal project of subjecting the whole world's population to the judgement and morality of capital" (Clarke 2005, 58). Given that education remains one of the most effective and influential ideological apparatus, neoliberal capitalism looks at it from two dimensions: (1) while it draws education into the marketplace and transforms it into a commodity that can be traded and thus make contribution to expansion of capital, (2) it also transforms the character (*content*) of education, which not only gets reduced to *skill development* and therefore creates a army of labor force required by capital at this particular historical moment, but also ensures that *criticality* remains a distant agenda of education. Social scientists have argued that "neoliberalism attempts to eliminate an engaged critique about its most basic principles and social consequences..." (Giroux 2004, 494).

Education under neoliberalism has been about control of students and teachers through implementation of different measures of standardization, and so on. This element of control also emerges from the fact that neoliberalism is about "reducing personal rights and the power of workers, and promoting economic growth and corporate profits" (Hursh, 2000). Raduntz argues that in the current phase of capitalism, education is at the center stage because of its crucial role in crisis management strategy. It has also become important "in terms of its role in research, in staff development and training in order to ameliorate the excesses and social stresses of constant organisational restructuring, and in assisting employees to adapt to the needs of their employers under these circumstances" (Raduntz 2006, 179).

Acknowledging that neoliberalism is actually about an unabashed advocacy of inequality, though it uses the rhetorics of justice and equality, educationists have looked at the need to resist this rule of capital. There have been different forms of resistance that have emerged globally against the ruthlessness of neoliberal capital. One such form was seen recently in the UK, where students and teachers were up in arms against the proposed hike in the cost of education and privatization of education. Not only was the fee hiked, but a second private university also came up in the UK. Along with these developments, the contractualization of teaching labor force took place (Finlayson 2010). Critics like Brissenden would argue that this is quite natural because, after all, "the neoliberalised university reflects this in the expansion of universities as a training resource for capital, while shifting the long term funding burden from public expenditure to the student, while minimising the upfront cost to the state" (Brissenden 2011). He would, however, argue that in such difficult times, when the crisis has forced people on streets, "the key challenge is to articulate the class nature of this crisis..." and to reimagine university as a space of critical enquiry "liberated from the stifling, deadly embrace of capital...." (Brissenden 2011). The shaping up of resistance on the streets that one saw in Britain, France, India, or the United States will have an impact only when the common thread running through the grievances of job cuts, contractualization, fee hike and consequent inaccessibility to education, and so on, is identified and a concerted effort is launched against it. In other words, the battle is against capital, which presents itself in different forms at different stages of its development.

While the resistance gets triggered in the streets and on different fronts, it is closely linked to the way resistance is imagined within the structures of education. When one refers to "structures of education" it is not about how the dominant discourse would transform education into a dissenting and resisting force but about how the struggle between labor and capital will be carried out within its confines. This resistance becomes necessary because "the neoliberal agenda for education means that teachers' role in capital's reproduction and development is now unambiguous...Teaching labour thus becomes directly value-producing and, inasmuch as they are productive of value, educators exist within capital" (Harvie 2006, 5). Rikowski shows how labor-power is part of the "personhood" of the laborer, unlike any other commodity, and, therefore, "it is also one that capital can never completely own in terms of the personhood of the labourer" (Rikowski 2006, 64). It is in this sense that the teacher as a laborer becomes a nightmare for capital—a potential source of rebellion. The role of the teacher as a catalyst in insurgency against the politics of capital becomes crucial in the same way as its role becomes crucial from capital's perspective as a tool for creating consensus about its politics. Generalizing McLaren's argument, resistance will involve creating a process that transforms the sites of learning/teaching as "sites for the production of both critical knowledge and socio-political action" (McLaren 2005, 105). Students must emerge out of these sites as "active agents for social transformation and critical citizenship" (McLaren 2005, 105).

The Volume

Given the situation where struggle between labor and capital is on at manifest as well as latent levels, this volume tries to bring together the different aspects of this struggle. A great amount of work has been done within the ambit of Marxism and education. These works have ranged from understanding the role of education in society to historically unravelling the linkages of polity, economy, and education. This volume is an addition to the vast literature on the subject but it looks at the issues of education from a different dimension. The chapters in the volume are reflections on the specific context in which they are located—and this context is that of neoliberal capitalism. However, they move beyond establishing the linkages between neoliberalism and education. Beginning with establishing the intersectionality of state, capital, and education, the chapters, in their own way, engage with possibilities of transcending the onslaught of capital. Cutting across different chapters, there is an analysis of how capital mutilates educational structures, shapes discourses to further its own interests, and is constantly engaged in thwarting possibilities of opposition. Contributors have made efforts through examples to demonstrate how this happens in different geographical locations—from the Northern Hemisphere to the Southern Hemisphere.

The different chapters, while being reflections on the politics of neoliberal capital, also suggest ways of resisting it. Though they are unravelling ways and means of resistance, their entry points are different. Curry Malott argues how capitalism used "highly complex ideological control mechanisms to perpetuate an inherently dehumanizing global capitalist system" and also ensures that rebellion is avoided. He looks at the processes that produce knowledge suitable to the system and even allow it to get out of the situations of crisis. He concludes that there are possibilities of resistance, and critical pedagogy can be the emancipatory educational practice that would facilitate emergence of a resistance.

Rich Gibson, in his chapter, argues about how the state pushes the agenda of capital in diverse forms and how this is reflected in the education system. Today is a situation of crisis for the "empire" and there are sufficient "ingredients for social upheaval" available. But, surprisingly, there are no signs of resistance emerging. There has been a weakening of the left. "The left has no analysis, no strategy, no tactics, no profound moral call for equality and freedom, and no succinct, easily grasped, ideology." Capitalism has made selling oneself appear natural to us and therefore makes class rule inevitable. There is a need to build resistance by connecting education, intellectual activities, and movements.

Dave Hill talks about transformative activism by education and other cultural workers such as teachers, lecturers, and so on; beginning with setting out the key characteristics of neoliberal global capitalism (and, more importantly, its accompanying neoconservatism) and its major effects on society and education, Hill highlights the obscene and widening economic, social, and educational inequalities both within states and, globally, between states. He shows how the detheorization of education and the regulation of critical thought and activists through the ideological and repressive state apparatuses have happened. The resistance to neoliberal politics through "viable solidaristic socialist counter-hegemonic struggles" has been weakened due to the "academic fashions" such as postmodernism and left revisionism.

David Hursh argues that we need to build a new educational system that does not focus on training individuals to be economically productive but rather aims to answer the essential questions of our time. Education in neoliberal times has been brought into the ambit of competitive markets, where students are assessed to become "entrepreneurial individuals" who are "productive" and are responsible only for themselves as individuals. They are taught not to think beyond the individual. There is a need to "reconnect the agenda of human welfare and the protection of basic human rights."

Faith Agostine-Wilson, in her chapter on the school-to-military pipeline, looks at the problems facing those interested in resisting militarism at its choke point—recruiting. Its reading of military documents and analysis of the trends in militarization and its relationship with the education system demonstrate how ideological and repressive state apparatuses work in tandem with each other without us, in fact, realizing that. She concludes by suggesting ways of challenging these trends within the school system and within the educational structure as a whole.

Ravi Kumar critically evaluates the voices of opposition to neoliberalism arguing that the battle is not for going back to welfarism but to establish a system that is outside the realm and control of capital. Beginning with a discussion on how neoliberalism has impacted education in India, he identifies the different strands of opposition to show how opposition to show how most of them end up being reformists who do not challenge capital do not challenge capital as the culprit and therefore make no effort to transcend it.

Paresh Chandra tries to look at the way neoliberal capitalism operates through institutional structures. He takes the example of the University of Delhi and analyzes how different constituents of the university space engage in politics. He argues that "the space to think freely must be defended at all costs. But the way to do it is not to try and save what space is already there, because it excludes too many, but to try and expand it". He uses the principle of generalization to understand the class struggle.

Savyasaachi, on the other hand, argues how the social sciences have been delegitimized as irrelevant disciplines, and how the construction of a singular framework suited to the designs of capital has percolated down to even those corners where resistance and dissent are supposed to emerge.

Mike Cole, in his chapter, makes a distinction between schooling and education, wherein the latter becomes "a more liberatory process" unlike the former, which is in the service of capitalism. He looks at the developments in education in Venezuela after the arrival of Hugo Chavez, and, as a case, picks up the revolutionary socialist educators who started an alternative school. While dealing with education, he takes up the unavoidable issues of participatory democracy, social movements, and the state in Venezuela and argues that the socialist education is "pivotal to the revolutionary process." Such a project generates the imagination that a different world outside capitalism is possible.

Peter McLaren, in his conversation, argues that exploitation is normalized institutionally when a small minority (the capitalists) monopolize the means of production, and workers must rely on wage labor at the behest of the capitalists. This inequity is preserved and reproduced by the state. The presence of the unemployed is used to pressurize employed workers, ensuring that they work unremittingly to produce for the capitalists. So, an anticapitalist curriculum begins with the struggle for morality, which can only occur outside of capital's value form. Equality is impossible under capitalism since under capitalism it is the quality of labor power that is paramount, not the equalization of labor power.

The volume stands different from the plethora of literature available till now because there are analyses represented from two different locations. They simultaneously demonstrate how they seem united insofar as facing the onslaught of neoliberal capital is concerned. Lastly, the contributors, while having different entry points to understanding the rule of capital and its manifestation in education, also offer ways and means of transcending it in their own different ways.

Notes

1. Laclau and Mouffe had written way back in 1985 that "the task of the Left therefore cannot be to renounce liberal-democratic ideology, but on the contrary, to deepen and expand it in the direction of a radical and plural democracy" (2001, 176).
2. Perry Anderson very compactly brings to us this debate among different trends within Marxism vis-à-vis postmodernism (Anderson 1999).

References

Amadeo, Kimberly. August 29, 2011. The Auto Bailout. Accessed on September 2, 2011 at http://useconomy.about.com/od/criticalssues/a/auto_bailout.htm

Anderson, Perry. 1999. *The Origins of Postmodernity.* London and New York: Verso Books.

Bell, Daniel. 1958. "The Power Elite—Reconsidered." *The American Journal of Sociology* 64(3): 238–250.

Brissenden, John. May 15, 2011. "The Academy is the Crisis". *New Left Project.* Accessed on June 10, 2011 at http://www.newleftproject.org/index.php/site/article_comments/the_academy_is_the_crisis

Clarke, Simon. 2005. "The Neoliberal Theory of Society" in *Neoliberalism: A Critical Reader* edited by Alfredo Saad-Filho and Deborah Johnston. London: Pluto Press, 50–59.

Dumenil, Gerard and Dominique Levy. 2011. *The Crisis of Neoliberalism.* Cambridge, MA: Harvard University Press.

Dumenil, Gerard and Dominique Levy. 2004. *Capital Resurgent: Roots of the Neoliberal Revolution.* Cambridge, MA: Harvard University Press.

Fine, Ben. 2010. "Neoliberalism as Financialisation." In *Economic Transitions to Neoliberalism in Middle-Income Countries: Policy Dilemmas, Economic Crises forms of Resistance* edited by Alfredo Saad-Filho and Galip L. Yalman. New York: Routledge.

Finlayson, Alan. December 9, 2010. "Britain, Greet the Age of Privatized Higher Education." *OpenDemocracy.* Accessed on January 11, 2011 at http://www.opendemocracy.net/ourkingdom/alan-finlayson/britain-greet-age-of-privatised-higher-education

Giroux, Henry A. 2004. "Public Pedagogy and the Politics of Neoliberalism: Making the Political More Pedagogical." *Policy Futures in Education* 2(3 & 4): 494–503.

Giroux, Henry A. and Susan Searls Giroux. 2006. "Challenging Neoliberalism's New World Order: The Promise of Critical Pedagogy." *Cultural Studies* <=> *Critical Methodologies* 6(1): 21–32.

Greaves, Nigel M., Dave Hill and Alpesh Maisuria. May 2007. "Embourgeoisment, Immiseration, Commodification—Marxism Revisited: A Critique of Education in Capitalist Systems." *Journal for Critical Education Policy Studies* 5(1). Accessed on July 15, 2009 at http://www.jceps.com/?pageID=article&articleID=83

Harvey, David. March 2007. "Neoliberalism as Creative Destruction." *Annals of the American Academy of Political and Social Science*, 610: 22–44.

Harvie, David. Spring 2006. "Value Production and Struggle in the Classroom: Teachers Within, Against and Beyond Capital." *Capital & Class* 88(Spring): 1–32.

Hill, Dave and Ravi Kumar. eds. 2009. *Global Neoliberalism and Education and Its Consequences.* London and New York: Routledge.

Hursh, David. Fall 2000. "Neoliberalism and the Control of Teachers, Students, and Learning: The Rise of Standards, Standardization, and Accountability." *Cultural Logic* 4(1) Accessed on May 10, 2011 at http://clogic.eserver.org/4-1/hursh.html

Laclau, Ernesto and Chanatal Mouffe. 2001. *Hegemony and Socialist Strategy: Towards a Radical Democratic Politics.* London: Verso Books.

Marx, Karl and Frederick Engels. 2002. *The Communist Manifesto.* London: Penguin Books.

McLaren, Peter and Ramin Farahmandpur. 2000. "Breaking Signifying Chains: A Marxist Position on Postmodern" in *Marxism Against Postmodernism in Educational Theory* edited by Dave Hill, Peter McLaren, Mike Cole and Glenn Rikowski. Lanham, MD; Boulder and New York: Lexington Books.

Mclaren, Peter. 2005. *Capitalists and Conquerors: A Critical Pedagogy Against Empire*, Lanham, MD: Rowman and Littlefield Publishers, Inc.

Mouffe, Chantal. 1995. "Preface: Democratic Politics Today" in *Dimensions of Radical Democracy* edited by Chantal Mouffe. London: Verso Books.

Rikowski, Glenn. 2006. "Education and the Politics of Human Resistance". *Information for Social Change*, 23(Summer): 59–74.

Ross, E. Wayne and Rich Gibson. eds.2007. *Neoliberalism and Education Reform.* Creskill, NJ: Hampton Press.

Smart, Barry. 1992. *Modern Conditions, Postmodern Controversies.* London and New York: Routledge.

Thompson, Willie. 2000. *What Happened to History?* London: Pluto Press.

Chapter 2

Social Class and Rebellion:
The Role of Knowledge Production in Capitalist Society

Curry Stephenson Malott

Since at least the Great Depression, the use of highly complex ideological control mechanisms to perpetuate an inherently dehumanizing global capitalist system, however crude and uncivilized, has been highly successful in maintaining basic structures of imperialist and neocolonialist power and keeping working-class / human rebellion at bay. However, there are times when the contradictions of capital, especially during times of crises, become so exaggerated that traditional forms of population control no longer serve their hegemonic functions. The current trend of global rebellion is arguably one of these times, when the frustration and anger of indigenous, settler-state, and formerly enslaved peoples burst to pieces normal relationships between the ruled (i.e., wage workers as well as those excluded from the treadmill of neoliberal production) and their often diverse rulers (i.e., capitalists and the governments that serve their elite interests). Because we are interested here in understanding and contributing to the current global movement (from Egypt, Libya, Syria, Greece, London, the United States to Venezuela, Peru, and Cuba) that, at its best, democratically subverts neoliberal capitalism, it is important to focus on the tenuous ideological role of knowledge production (i.e., compulsory schooling) in creating widespread consent for the accumulation of wealth through abstract labor. What follows is therefore a brief historical discussion of the debate about how social class is defined and understood. This history is important because it provides the lens through which we view the contemporary context. The last part of this chapter explores the present moment and possibilities for critically transgressing class and therefore capitalism as part of the process of getting to some sort of radically democratic global socialism (Cole 2011).

Competing Conceptions of Social Class

What defines capitalism more than any other characteristic is that it is a class-based system. At its most basic level, social class can be understood as the hierarchical grouping of people based on similar economic and occupational characteristics giving way to the collective experience of social rank and caste, such as lower/working class and upper/ruling class, and the manifest relationships between and within such stratum that define this system. Associated with the notion of class, and especially with caste, is the idea that it is predetermined by government power or noble authority, who loosely determines, by birthright, what occupations are available to what groups.

Because occupation is not judicially determined by birthright in North America—the United States, Mexico, and Canada, among much of the world—the ontological perspective that differences in wealth and power exist *not* because of social class, but, rather, are indicative of the division of labor that roughly represents the natural distribution of intelligence and drive, represents the dominant, hegemonized perspective, which tends to not be overtly stated in the knowledge production process, but, rather, is implied. From this largely Weberian perspective, *socioeconomic difference* becomes no more or less important to human diversity than eye color or body type, that is, one of many *neutral* differences that are entitled to universal respect and dignity. Class *difference* is therefore not something to be resisted, but, rather, *tolerated*. Within this interpretative framework, through which praxical knowledge about *being* in the world is produced, the concept of social class, to reiterate, is rarely discussed or included. In other words, within the knowledge production process of the bosses / the ruling class, social class is constructed as nonexistent. When social class is discussed in the social universe of capital, it is typically done through a Weberian sociological lens that focuses on categories (i.e., working class and middle class) at the expense of conflict and relationship (Curry 2011; Cole 2002; Kelsh, Deb, and Hill 2006). This has served an important function in keeping social movements (i.e., the civil rights movement) and the education left in particular focused on equity and equality within capitalism and therefore abandoning the larger, more permanent, goal of resisting capitalism and the ideological and material construction of abstract labor—or labor, generally speaking, disconnected from any single person with both use and exchange value, and thus a commodity consumed and traded by capital the same as any other commodity. Labor therefore becomes abstracted in this process because its presence in all other commodities is hidden through the use of money (Marx 1967). Put another way, abstracting labor is a necessary ideological and material tool of capital because it allows the tendency toward suffering, abuse, and extreme poverty, which characterizes the process of extracting wealth from human labor power and vital ecosystems, to be hidden and disguised in the glossy flash of high-powered and super-funded marketing campaigns.

As the vast majority of humanity, with varying levels of severity, are oppressed as wage workers by this hierarchal system of neoliberal capitalism, it should be no surprise that there exists an ancient tradition of knowledge production from working-class / subjugated perspectives, which, in different ways, has argued that the unequal relationship between what we might call bosses and workers is not the natural outcome of genetically determined endowments and deficiencies but is the result of a long legacy of abuse. We might begin naming this *legacy* as coercive, brutal, and manipulative, manifesting itself in highly concentrated accumulation of wealth and power that is as nearly deterministic as birthright in reproducing class structure and social relations, more generally affirming the central role class plays in capitalist society. Within this paradigm, the concept of social class is most fundamentally represented in the relationship between the vast majority, divested from the means of production, therefore possessing only their labor to sell as a commodity, and the few who hold in their hands the productive apparatus, land, and resources, and the vast fortunes accumulated from purchasing the labor power of the landless multitudes at a price far below the value it generates. In short, this antagonistic relationship between social classes represents the heart of what capitalism *is*.

Drawing on the insights of Adam Smith, Noam Chomsky (Chomsky 2007), summarizing what we can understand to be the ontological perspective of the profiteer or capitalist, notes that "the 'principle architects' of state policy, 'merchants and manufacturers,' make sure that their own interests are 'most particularly attended to,' however 'grievous' the consequences for others" (pp. 41–42). Similarly, outlining the primary self-serving invention of the capitalist, *the corporation*, Joel Bakan observes that "corporations have no capacity to value political systems, fascist or democratic, for reasons of principle or ideology. The only legitimate question for a corporation is whether a political system serves or impedes its self-interested purposes" (Bakan 2004, 88). Because safety and environmental regulations are a cost to production and thus encroach on margins, they are frequently violated as corporations sacrifice the public to satisfy their own self-interests.

Since The Great Depression of 1929, it has been increasingly difficult in North America to externalize these costs to those who rely on a wage to survive. For example, to appease an increasingly rebellious underclass, the Bretton Woods system was established in 1944, which, among other things, limited the mobility of capital, and, as a result, weakened the deadly grip of capital. However, with the assistance of an intensified emphasis on the propaganda machine, including schools and the corporate media, which have been designed to manufacture the consent of the working and middle classes to support their own class-based oppression as normal and natural, Bretton Woods was dismantled in 1971, which gave way to an era of unrestricted capital movement, and, consequently, the massive redistribution of wealth upwards (Chomsky 2008). This focus on the use of consent / the control of ideas / hegemony has resulted in the production of knowledge taking on a renewed importance within American and Canadian settler societies. The struggle over the purpose and goals of the education system has consequently become one of the primary battlegrounds where the working classes and ruling class vie for political power to determine the course of history.

From this epistemological perspective, as long as social class exists, that is, as long as there are two antagonistically related groups, workers and bosses, rich and poor, or oppressed and oppressors, there will not be consensus on what explains the basic structures of society, because what tends to be good for one group tends not to be beneficial for the other. For example, the idea that social class does not explain the inequality rampant in capitalist societies, but is the result of natural selection, is good for the beneficiaries of market mechanisms. At the same time, the notion that the violent class relation, which can only offer cyclical crises and perpetual war, is at the core of capitalist society, has provided much fuel against capitalism. In short, the class struggle that is indicative of capitalism itself is represented in the "fact" that higher wages are good for workers because they increase their standard of living, but hurt the bosses by encroaching on margins/profits.

From here, a smart place of departure might be to observe the current post–Bretton Woods economic structure of North America. A look at the data indicates that in the last ten years, in the United

States, the wealth of the ruling class has exploded while the middle class has simultaneously experienced a steady period of decline as the offshoring trends of the 1980s and 1990s have dramatically affected not just blue collar manufacturing jobs, but white collar service sector employment as well. As a result, the ranks of the poor and excluded have continued to swell. No longer able to finance a middle-class lifestyle, consumer debt also skyrocketed during this period. Setting off a system-wide pandemic of foreclosures, the bosses assured the public that the economy was fine, largely ignoring the high cost the public was paying. According to Greider and Baker (Greider and Baker 2008):

> In the long run, the destruction of concentrated wealth and power is always good for democracy, liberating people from the heavy hand of the status quo. Unfortunately, many innocents are slaughtered in the process. As the US manufacturing economy was dismantled by downsizing and globalization, the learned ones (Alan Greenspan comes to mind) told everyone to breathe easy—ultimately this would be good for the workers and communities who lost the foundations of their prosperity. Now that "creative destruction" is visiting the bankers, we now observe they are not so accepting of their own fate. (http://www.alternet.org/story/988)

Reflecting on this quote in a personal communiqué, Joe Kincheloe observed, "now that 'creative destruction' is reaching the corporate elite, they are not so sanguine about the situation," which is to be expected because, from the boss' perspective, "the pain of structural adjustment for the privileged is more distressing than it is for the poor." It was only a matter of time before the megabanks collapsed into their own self-made house of cards constructed of worthless defunct mortgages. This crisis and the government's attempts to "bail out" the capitalists with an unprecedented 700 billion dollar "bill," which increased to nearly a trillion dollars before it passed both the Senate and the US House, has exposed the self-destructiveness embedded within the logic of capital.

The knowledge that was produced about this bailout and aired through the corporate media focused on the ways it will benefit "mainstreet," that is, the workers of capital, which, in a way, has some element of truth to it because the financial capitalists cannot operate on their own. That is, they depend on other capitalists involved in industry, commercialization, real estate, and so on, to borrow money and invest in human labor as a commodity. It is the human labor who actually do the work and produce the wealth that is then appropriated, reinvested, gained, or lost. It should therefore not be surprising that the majority of representatives of the House and US senators, in making their case for the bill, stressed, over and over, the benefits that the "small people" will receive, as justification for their "yeah" rather than "nay" votes. But using that indirect "benefit" to obscure the basic antagonistic relationship between labor and capital, which, as long as it remains in tact, the majority of humanity will suffer, can be viewed as nothing short of an apology for the inevitable injustices of capitalism.

Since this bailout, or the redirecting of wealth upwards, corporate profits have reached record highs as more and more wealth is appropriated by the super rich. The knowledge produced about this trend paints a picture where out of control government spending, fueled by welfare socialism, has created massive debt thereby choking American workers to death. The implicit racism here assumes it is hard working white Americans who are being exploited by liberal politicians like Obama by giving undeserving lazy minorities their money. The call is therefore for a debt ceiling and massive cutbacks to reduce the deficit. However, rather than cut the largest most wasteful and destructive spending (i.e., the military and corporate welfare and bailouts), the call has been to cut the social programs that benefit working people, but are only a small fraction of the total spending. The goal must therefore not really be to reduce the debt or to help working people. While people want jobs, critical workers want to cease to be workers in order to be in control of one's labor power because a worker is, by definition, a subordinate position directed and manipulated by a boss or manager.

The global neoliberal trend of cutting spending on social programs while further lining the pockets of the super rich with the wealth created by the labor and suffering of the world's peoples (at least those not excluded from global capitalism), has led to revolutionary uprising from Egypt, to Greece, to the UK, to the US. Of course, the corporate media consistently characterizes the people's struggles against oppression as the actions of thugs and out-of-control kids. What is reinforced through the propaganda machine is the inevitability of capital and the equation of capitalism with freedom and democracy. However, despite the bombardment of these persistent messages, the global movement for a radically new world freedom from the irrational laws of capital and perpetual war is thriving. This trend reinforces the idea that while people can be conditioned to support a system set against their own class and human interests, we cannot be programed or predetermined because we always remain endowed with the capacity to self-reflect and become conscious of our conditioning.

We might therefore say that the mere existence of capitalism, its ruling classes in particular, represents the constant risk of an uprising, and the more powerful the bosses, the greater the inequality between the oppressors and the oppressed, and therefore the greater the probability of an uprising or frontal assault designed to seize control of state and private power. The bosses tend to have this awareness, and it is for this *ruling class class-consciousness* that the hammer is always in the background. However, the elite are more interested in avoiding *disruption* because that kind of *instability* is not good for business. The ruling class perceives those who rely on a wage to survive as a constant potential threat because their existence as labor is structurally, by definition, set against their own creative human impulse.

From this perspective, labor is always instinctively operating at some level of uprising in their struggle to relieve themselves from the chains that bind them. The objective of the capitalist is therefore to keep working class resistance at the lowest possible level through the combined use of force and consent, placing special emphasis, for obvious reasons, on consent, that is, the control of ideas. It has been argued by mainstream progressive sources that the slight hesitation to pass the recent trillion dollar bailout "bill" represents a victory for democracy because of the public's overwhelming disapproval and the swelling "crisis in confidence."

This crisis in confidence does not merely refer to the reluctance to spend money, as the corporate media would have us believe, but runs to the very core of capitalism as a viable economic system. US president George W. Bush alluded to this reading of the world in a special television appearance where he reassured his audience, the "small people," that "democratic capitalism is the best system that ever existed." Similarly, White House press secretary, Dana Perino, offered similar reassurance arguing that the United States is "the greatest capitalist country in the world" and that the public only needs to be willing to suffer for a short time so "we" can, once again, "enjoy prosperity." Barrack Obama and his administration has been no different, performing the same hegemonic role ensuring the public capitalism is strong and inevitable. As suggested above, because elite capitalists would never offer workers a choice in what economic system they preferred, more and more people are taking action on the insight that humanity and the natural world will suffer unless people fight back and challenge policies that treat the well-being of the public and the environment as incidental. That is, as long as the basic structures of power remain intact and wealth is flowing to the elite, the well-being of the public is not a concern.

Let us now situate in an historical context the ways in which knowledge is and has been constructed to explain and account for these trends and inequalities. The remainder of this chapter examines different approaches to these class-based issues. We end our discussion with critical pedagogy, which has recently begun to emerge as a leading force in emancipatory educational practice. We begin investigating the assumptions underlying the production of knowledge under capitalism in Europe because it was the European model of class society that was reproduced around the world through the process of colonization, which, in most regions, such as North America, continues to serve as the dominant paradigm.

Discourse Wars: Knowledge Production within Capitalism

Among the many scholars who have engaged an in-depth study of the innermost workings of Europe's model of class society, that is, capitalism, Karl Marx's has proven to be the most influential, resilient, relevant, and responded to (both positively and negatively). One of the most widely read constructions of knowledge of all times, the *Manifesto of the Communist Party*, by Karl Marx and Frederick Engels (1978), has touched, in one way or another, every major revolution around the world, rendering its conceptualization of social class particularly important for the study at hand.

By the end of the *Manifesto's* first sentence—a relatively short sentence—Marx and Engels have clearly broken with the idealist romanticism of bourgeois scholarship by firmly situating their analysis of class within an historical dialectics of antagonistically competing interests, noting that "the history of all hitherto existing society is the history of class struggles" (473), and, taken to its logical conclusion, underscores the tenuousness of the present moment. The duo continue, linearly and temporally, from a European-centered perspective, naming what they understand to be the stages of conflicting interests that define human social development, situating its beginning in ancient Rome and Greece, which would eventually give way to the modern, capitalist, bourgeois era.

Eurocentric, as suggested by the late Senegalese scholar and scientist, Cheikh Anta Diop, because there is evidence that suggests that capitalism is not, as Marx suggested, a relatively recent human construction because it existed in ancient Egypt. For example, Diop (1974) argues that in rural and urban centers during Egypt's Middle Kingdom (2160–1788 BC) there existed "marginal capitalism" as evidenced by the labor force being "free" and "contractual" and the existence of "a business class who rented land in the countryside and hired hands to cultivate it" motivated by the sole purpose of generating "huge profits" (p. 210). In the cities, Egyptian capitalists engaged in what seems to be very modern business practices such as "interest-bearing loans, [and] renting or subletting personal property or real estate for the purpose of financial speculation" (Diop 1974). While Diop (1974) argues that it was the "inalienable liberty of the Egyptian citizen" (p. 210) that prevented the development of "strong capitalism" with more power over the populous than the state or nobility, the contradictions within Egypt's hierarchical arrangements did lead to a series of unsuccessful internal revolutions.

Again, Diop's analysis, examined next to Marx and Engels's (1978) history of human social development, underscores the latter's European-centered perspective. That is, naming what they understand to be the stages of conflicting interests, beginning with ancient Rome, which transitioned into the Middle Ages, and finally giving way to the modern bourgeois era, Marx and Engels (1978) comment—"freeman and slave, patrician and plebeian, lord and serf, guild-master and journeyman, in a word, oppressor and oppressed" (p. 473). However, while Marx and Engels's timeline and family tree of humanity might be inaccurate, the conclusion that is drawn from the developmental concept remains highly relevant and instructive: the oppressors and the oppressed "stood in constant opposition to one another, carried on an uninterrupted, now hidden, now open fight, a fight that each time ended, either in a revolutionary reconstitution of society at large, or in the common ruin of the contending classes" (p. 474).

This observation is particularly relevant, as capital's current crisis, discussed above, has exposed, in stark relieve, that the very existence of capitalism is an elite class war continuously waged in a never ending quest to increase the bottom line, which can only come from more and more unpaid labor hours put to work grinding up more and more of the Earth's vital ecosystems. As part of the process of abstracting and distorting these class relations, the stock market is incorrectly presented as the producer of value. Challenging the assumption that the "profits and losses that result from fluctuations in the price of" stocks, represent "an index of genuine capital accumulation," that is, "reproduction on an expanded scale," Marx (1894/1991), in *Volume Three* of *Capital*, argues that they are "by the nature of the case more and more the result of gambling, which now appears in place of labour as the original source of capital ownership, as well as taking the place of brute force" (p. 607–609) or the exertion of labor power.

With the development of global capitalism, Marx (1894/1991) saw financial capitalists or bankers taking on a more central role as "imaginary money wealth" created on the stock market "makes up a very considerable part" of the money economy. As a result, bankers have become "intermediaries between the private money capitalists on the one hand, and the state, local authorities and borrows engaged in the process of reproduction on the other" (p. 609). Providing an analysis of how this system, with its built-in upward pulling gravity, without strict regulations, inevitably leads to an imbalance of commodities-to-consumer ratio, and therefore to a disruption in the actualization of value, Marx observes that "if there is a disturbance in this expansion, or even in the normal exertion of the reproduction process, there is also a lack of credit" creating a crisis in the confidence of the actual value of credit, which is indicative of "the phase in the industrial cycle that follows the crash" (p. 614).

Marx (with Engels), despite his shortcomings, therefore seems to offer what has proven to be a valid observation, that is, human society tends not to stand still—it is always in a stage of development—and as long as the old oppressed class become the new oppressors, society will remain pregnant with a new social order. Returning to the *Manifesto*, in making their case that the relations of production under capitalism will eventually be *burst asunder*, Marx and Engels (1848/1978) document the process by which Europe's (concentrating on France, England, and Germany) bourgeois capitalist class emerged "from the ruins of feudal society" (p. 474) playing "a most revolutionary part" (pp. 474–475) in that transformation.

The massive amounts of wealth extracted from the Americas by European powers led Marx and Engels (1848/1978) to the conclusion that "the discovery of America," as they called it, was one of the primary driving forces behind "the increase in the means of exchange and in commodities generally" and therefore to the "revolutionary element in the tottering feudal society, a rapid development" (p. 474). The argument is that the small-scale feudal arrangements were not equipped to organize the large armies of labor necessary for transforming the massive amounts of raw materials imported from the Americas needed to meet the exploding European demand for commodities, which was fueled by the influx of unprecedented resources. What is more, unlike Europe's nobility, whose power stemmed from their possession of land, the emerging bourgeoisie, without land, gained their advantage through the accumulation of capital due to the mercantile role they played in the extraction of American and African wealth. Summarizing the bourgeoisie's transformation from the oppressed to the oppressors, Marx and Engels unveil their most feared and celebrated prediction—that the bourgeoisie, who are still in power, like all of the oppressors before them, too will fall. A Marxist analysis might therefore view each new crisis of capital, such as the most recent one, part of capitalism's march toward its own inevitable demise. Consider Marx and Engels's description of the capitalist class:

> The bourgeoisie, wherever it has got the upper hand, has put an end to all feudal....relations. It has pitilessly torn asunder the motley feudal ties that bound man to his "natural superiors," and has left remaining no other nexus between man and man than naked self-interest, than callous "cash payment"...It has resolved personal worth into exchange value, and in place of the numberless indefeasible chartered freedoms, has set up that single, unconscionable freedom—Free Trade...The weapons with which the bourgeoisie felled feudalism to the ground are now turned against the bourgeoisie itself...The bourgeoisie forged the weapons that [will] bring death to itself; it has also called into existence the men who are to wield those weapons—the modern working class...(pp. 475–478)

While the broad strokes painted in the *Manifesto of the Communist Party* are useful for beginning to understand why knowledge produced by subjugated populations through the lens of Marx's work continues to be both feared and exalted, we must focus more centrally on his more elaborated work on the division of labor as a transition into the perspectives of his *pro-boss, nonsolidarity* critics, which continue to hold political sway in the contemporary context of global capitalism. In one of his major classic works, *Capital: Volume One*, Marx's (1867/1967) discussion of primitive accumulation as part of the historical development of the capitalization of humanity, which, as alluded to above, began in its "strong" form in England roughly a decade before Columbus set foot in present-day Haiti, is useful here in understanding Europe's engagement in the Americas in particular and global affairs in general. Because of the light it sheds on the discussion that follows, a sizable excerpt taken from *Volume One* of *Capital* (Marx) is presented here:

> The so-called primitive accumulation...is nothing else than the historical process of divorcing the producer from the means of production. It appears as primitive, because it forms the pre-historic stage of capital and of the mode of production corresponding with it.
> The economic structure of capitalistic society has grown out of the economic structure of feudal society. The dissolution of the latter set free the elements of the former.

> The immediate producer, the labourer, could only dispose of his own person after he had ceased to be attached to the soil and ceased to be the slave, serf, or bondman of another. To become a free seller of labour-power, who carries his commodity wherever he finds a market, he must further have escaped from the regime of the guilds, their rules for apprentices and journeymen, and the impediments of their labour regulations. Hence, the historical movement which changes the producers into wage-workers, appears, on the one hand, as their emancipation from serfdom and from the fetters of the guilds, and this side alone exists for the bourgeois historians. But, on the other hand, these new freed men became sellers of themselves only after they had been robbed of all their own means of production, and of all the guarantees of existence afforded by the old feudal arrangements. And the history of this, their expropriation, is written in the annals of mankind in letters of blood and fire....
>
> The starting point of the development that gave rise to the wage labourer as well as to the capitalist was the servitude of the labourer. The advance consisted in a change of form of this servitude, in the transformation of feudal exploitation into capitalist exploitation....
>
> The expropriation of the agricultural producer, of the peasant, from the soil, is the basis of the whole process. The history of this expropriation, in different countries, assumes different aspects, and runs through its various phases in different orders of succession, and at different periods. (pp. 714–716)

From Marx's work we can begin to *read* or *construct* the entire modern world as mediated and dictated by the Westernized process of value production through the capital–labor class relation. In other words, we can understand the entire process, from the ongoing need to primitively accumulate and expand, to the establishment of petrol-chemical industrialism, as a form of class struggle that began as a counterhegemony, but has since developed into perhaps the most oppressive, destructive, and irresponsible hegemony in recorded history. Put another way, capitalism was initiated by Western Europe's bourgeoisie against their feudal lords, some of the last remnants of Europe's "Dark Ages," but now rule with more barbaric force than ever before imagined. Ultimately, it has been the vast majority of humanity, disconnected from the soil and therefore from their indigenous culture, who have suffered from centuries of bourgeoisie pathology. In his examination of the historical development of class relations, Marx points to the division of labor as offering a place of origin.

That is, Marx argues that during the early stages of human development the division of labor was a naturally occurring by-product of age- and sex-based physical difference, and also, we would add, the result of the nonhierarchical creative diversity / multiple intelligences unique to human consciousness, as well as to the unpredictable nature of complex events, such as the establishment of purposeful economic systems. Within the division of labor, from this perspective, reside the most basic structural roots of organized society. Commenting on the *division of labor*, Marx (1867/1967) notes:

> Within a family, and after further development within a tribe, there springs up naturally a division of labor, caused by differences of sex and age, a division that is consequently based on a purely physiological foundation, which division enlarges its materials by the expansion of the community, by the increase of population, and more especially, by the conflicts of different tribes, and the subjugation of one tribe by another. (p. 351)

The issue of one tribe subjugating another will be taken up later. For now, I would like to focus on the context in which Marx situates this naturally occurring division of labor. Marx (1867/1967) hones in on the place-specific nature of tribal communities commenting that "different communities find different means of production, and different means of subsistence in their natural environment" (p. 351). In other words, the development of technology is informed by the specific characteristics of physical place or geography such as climate, terrain, arable land, game, waterways, distance, and accessibility to other human communities, and so on. As a result, human societies have developed vastly different technologies based on geography, which constitute the original source of commodities, that is, products produced in one context and consumed in another. For example, civilizations that emerged close to large bodies of water have tended to create ship-building technology, whereas those communities whose traditional lands are covered with ice, such as the Arctic, have developed technology conducive to more efficiently navigating the snow such as sleds and snow shoes.

In the following analysis Marx begins to break, however slightly, from his Eurocentric, linear analysis, acknowledging the persistence of ancient communities in the "modern" era. As an example, Marx (1867/1967) points to "those small and extremely ancient Indian communities, some of which have continued down to this day, are based on possession in common of the land...and on an unalterable division of labor" (p. 357). However, "each individual artificer" operates independently "without recognizing any authority over him" (Marx, 358). Marx attributes this independence, in part to the fact that within these arrangements products are produced for direct use by the community and therefore do not take the form of a commodity and thus avoid the value-generating process associated with it. As a result, the alienating division of labor engendered by the exchange of commodities is also avoided. Marx defines commodities as products consumed by others rather than those who produced them, and those who produce, under capital, are not independent craftsmen, but externally commanded.

Marx (1867/1967) quickly returns to Europe and goes on to argue that the guilds, who more or less labored independently, resisted the bourgeoisie's commodification of production and therefore "...repelled every encroachment by the capital of merchants, the only form of free capital with which they came into contact" (p. 358). Marx notes that the guild organization, by institutionalizing stages of production as specialized trades separate from one another such as the cattle-breeder, the tanner, and the shoemaker, for example, created the material conditions for manufacture, but "excluded division of labor in the workshop," and as a result, "there was wanting the principal basis of manufacture, the separation of the labourer from his means of production, and the conversion of these means into capital" (p. 359). Marx stresses that the process of value production is unique to capitalism and is a "special creation of the capitalist mode of production alone" (p. 359), and therefore not an original or natural aspect of the division of labor. Driving this point home, Marx critiques the "peculiar division" of manufacture, which "attacks the individual at the very roots of his life" giving way to "industrial pathology" (p. 363). Because of the forcefulness and accuracy of much of Marx's work, many proponents of capitalism have been forced to attempt to refute the idea that capitalism is a form of pathology, and that the capitalist relations of production, the relationship between what we might crudely call bosses and workers, is negative or harmful for those who rely on a wage to survive—the vast majority of humanity. What follows is therefore a brief summary of some of Emile Durkheim's pro-capitalist constructions that continue to dominate official knowledge production in the Western world, which, with slight variations, are all capitalist.

* * *

Widely influential French sociologist, Emile Durkheim, is considered to be one of the "fathers" and founders of sociology and anthropology. Through the late 1800s, Durkheim challenged much of Marx's analysis, setting out to demonstrate that the deep inequality between social classes that drew much attention from critics such as Marx—a central aspect of the Industrial Revolution that began in England—was a natural product of the development of human societies, and should therefore not be resisted, but encouraged through such sorting mechanisms as schools. Essentially, what Durkheim (2000) argues is that humanity (those relegated to the status of worker) would be wise to divest itself of any illusions of maintaining an independent existence and rather "equip yourself to fulfill usefully a specific function" (p. 39) because society requires us to bend ourselves to fit within the system that exists, to submit ourselves to the labor it requires. What Durkheim suggests is that the bourgeoisie, rather than a ruling class that embodies its own negation, represents the end of history and therefore the manifestation of the final and most advanced stage of human social evolution.

However, Durkheim could not ignore the class antagonism highlighted above by Marx, due, in part, to the intensity of the class struggle of his time and the recent memory of the workers' Paris Commune of 1871. Acknowledging the human need of not being made a slave or being externally controlled, while maintaining his belief that inequality serves a necessary function in advanced societies, Durkheim (2000) notes that "moral life, like that of body and mind, responds to different needs which may even be contradictory. Thus it is natural for it to be made up in part of opposing elements..." (p. 39). In effect, Durkheim tells us that "progress" has a price—a price that tends to cause distress within the individual—but that is the nature of the universe, and it is not wise to challenge laws of nature. Building the foundation for this "functionalist" approach to sociology in his dissertation, Durkheim (2000) theorizes:

> We can no longer be under any illusion about the trends in modern industry. It involves increasingly powerful mechanisms, large-scale groupings of power and capital, and consequently an extreme division of labor...This evolution occurs spontaneously and unthinkingly. Those economists who study its causes and evaluate its results, far from condemning such diversification or attacking it, proclaim its necessity. They perceive in it the higher law of human societies and the condition for progress. (pp. 37–38)

Again, Durkheim does not stop here in his analysis of *objective reality* as he reaches ever deeper into the grandiose, going on to argue that the division of labor does not just occur within the realm of economics, but can be identified within every aspect of life, and within all forms of life, rendering it a "biological phenomenon," and therefore a law of nature. By claiming that capitalism happened "spontaneously" and "unthinkingly" Durkheim effectively rewrites history, erasing the long struggle against the commodification of humanity that was anything but spontaneous or without thought. Essentially, Durkheim takes Marx's idea of the naturalness of the division of labor, divests it of its independent and communal nature, and replaces it with the notion that inequality and subservience to power are necessary manifestations of the advanced development of the division of labor.

This basic formula, with roots in Platonic epistemology that views intelligence as naturally and unevenly distributed, continues to exist in contemporary hegemonic discourses of the ruling elite—it is the presupposition informing the entire foundation of ruling class policy and practice. As a side note, the current crisis in confidence, discussed above, can, in part, be understood as stemming from the seeming incompetence and confusion emanating from the political bosses in Washington and elsewhere. Not only does Durkheim support this idea of a naturally-occurring hierarchical conception of class within societies, which undergoes intensified scrutiny during times of crisis, but he ranks civilizations/nations on a similar scale. Essentially, Durkheim argues that there is a tendency among societies that demonstrates that as they grow larger, the division of labor grows more specialized and entrenched, and as a result, they become more advanced. However, confronted with the existence of larger nonwhite nations, Durkheim argues that there are exceptions to this rule, which seems to stem from his belief in racial hierarchy. Consider:

> The Jewish nation, before the conquest, was probably more voluminous than the Roman city of the fourth century; yet it was of a lower species. China and Russia are much more populous than the most civilized nations of Europe. Consequently among these same peoples the division of labor did not develop in proportion to the social volume. This is because the growth in volume is not necessarily a mark of superiority if the density does not grow at the same time and in the same proportion... If therefore the largest of them only reproduces societies of a very inferior type, the segmentary structure will remain very pronounced, and in consequence the social organization will be little advanced. An aggregate of clans, even if immense, ranks below the smallest society that is organized, since the latter has already gone through those stages of evolution below which the aggregate has remained. (Durkheim 2000, 49)

Neither was Durkheim's implied white supremacy his own invention, nor was the idea of a natural hierarchy among Europeans represented within the division of labor new to him. However, it is beyond the scope of this essay to trace the origins of those ideas. What follows, rather, is an analysis of how hegemonic conceptions of the division of labor have influenced policy in the United States, situated in a more contemporary context looking at the work of Friedman. As we will see below, Milton Friedman (2002) argues that restrictions on the extraction and accumulation of wealth and the further entrenchment of class antagonisms only threatens the freedom of "progress," that is, capitalism, and of men and women pursuing it.

Milton Friedman and Neoliberalism

Milton Friedman, pro-capital, economist extraordinaire, received worldwide recognition in 1976, winning the Nobel memorial Prize in Economic Sciences, and has been touted as the world's most influential economist of the twentieth century. Friedman has drawn the attention of the likes of internationally renowned political analyst and activist Noam Chomsky (1999), who referred to him as a "neoliberal guru" while vociferously critiquing *Capitalism and Freedom* for hegemonically equating "profit-making" with being "the essence of democracy" and that "any government that pursues antimarket policies is being anti-democratic, no matter how much informed popular support they might enjoy" (p. 9).

Friedman's supposition that the surest way to freedom is through capitalism is informed by the ancient hierarchy of intelligence paradigm that views economic competition the playing field most conducive to fostering the environment that will encourage and enable the superior individuals to rise to the top and assume their place as leaders and decision makers, that is, capitalists. Attempts to legislate against exploitation and abuse to ensure a functioning democracy, from this approach to knowledge production, is viewed as an attack on freedom because it prevents the naturally endowed masters from assuming their biologically determined place within the hierarchy. This construction is an unquestionable aspect of *objective reality*. Informed by this logic, the primary responsibility of government is therefore to "preserve the rules of the game by enforcing contracts, preventing coercion, and keeping markets free" (Friedman 1955, 1). Connecting Friedman's philosophy to practice, Chomsky (1999) observes:

> Equipped with this perverse understanding of democracy, neoliberals like Friedman had no qualms over the military overthrow of Chile's democratically elected Allende government in 1973, because Allende was interfering with business control of Chilean society. (p. 9)

In order for government, and society more generally, to fulfill their scripted functions, reasons Friedman (1955), they require social stability, which is not possible without "widespread acceptance of some common set of values" and "a minimum degree of literacy and knowledge" (p. 2). Friedman (1955) reasons that the government should subsidize these *basic* levels of education because it "adds to the economic value of the student" (p. 4) and capitalists should invest in their labor just as they invest in machinery. The public is therefore viewed as a resource to be manipulated by the natural leaders for the *common good*. Making this point Friedman (1955) argues that education "is a form of investment in human capital precisely analogous to investment in machinery, buildings, or other forms of non human capital" and can be justified as a necessary expenditure because "its function is to raise the economic productivity of the human being" (p. 13). For Friedman (1955) then, knowledge production as an actively engaged endeavor is reserved for the elite, rendering the vast majority subject to the necessary "indoctrination" needed to ensure the widespread acceptance of "common social values required for a stable society" even if it means "inhibiting freedom of thought and belief" (p. 7).

As one of the world's leading theoreticians of free-market capitalism, it is not surprising that Friedman (1955) was a strong supporter of the privatization of, and thus the corporate control over, public education, masking it with a discourse of *choice*. In more recent times, Milton Friedman acknowledged that the testing-based No Child Left Behind act, touted as the surest path to increasing achievement was really designed to lend weight to the *choice* and voucher movement by setting schools up to fail and then handing them over to private managing firms such as Edison Schools (Kohn 2004). Critical educator Alfie Kohn (2004) has commented that "you don't have to be a conspiracy nut to understand the real purpose of NCLB" (p. 84). That is, NCLB is nothing more than a "backdoor maneuver" (Kohn 2004, 84) constructed around conceptions of *choice* allowing private for-profit capitalists to take over public education. Friedman's theory paved the theoretical pathway for these *neoliberal* tendencies of the public realm being handed over to corporations to be realized.

Friedman's theory is based on the assumption that the competition for education dollars would push, out of the necessity to survive, education investors to offer superior products to attract customers. Schools that offered a substandard product would not be profitable, and would therefore be forced to either improve or close. Again, The No Child Left Behind act of George W. Bush has served as a standards-based approach to usher in Friedman's desire to privatize public education, which has had disastrous results on the knowledge production process. As a result, a major blow was leveled against the practice of education as an active engagement designed to understand the world and transform it, taking aim specifically at the labor/capital relationship and its manifest hegemonies such as white supremacy and patriarchy.

These developments, however, are well documented. For the purpose of this discussion, we will turn our attention to the larger Eurocentric vision of Friedman's discourse, which is equally relevant as we approach a potentially new era in knowledge production in North America. That is, the potential Democratic presidency of Barack Obama, while pro-capitalist in principle on their homepage, claim to "believe" that "teachers should not be forced to spend the academic year preparing students to fill in bubbles on standardized tests" (Obama Biden). The manifestation of this desire would provide critical pedagogues much needed breathing room to engage in counterhegemonic knowledge production and critical praxis after this long period of Friedman-inspired privatization.

Friedman leaves little room for misinterpretation regarding his conceptualization of democracy and social class, which, we will see, is in many ways almost the exact opposite of Marxism, underscoring, in a sense, a testament to Marx's continued relevance in terms of directly and indirectly informing popular democratic movements challenging basic structures of power and therefore demanding a response by the architects of contemporary US public hegemonic discourse and policy. Within his paradigm Friedman (1962/2002) situates capitalism as the central driving force behind human evolution and therefore responsible for the "great advances of civilization" such as Columbus "seeking a new route to China" (p. 3), which consequently led to the emergence of vast fortunes generated by Europe's colonialist empire building, slavery, genocide/depopulation, and repopulation, and on a scale so massive, so horrendous and so utterly barbaric as to render comprehending its manifestation as a criminal act carried out by real living, breathing, feeling people, almost unimaginable (Malott 2008). Friedman, therefore, does not seem too different from his predecessors. That is, describing Columbus coming to the Americas as one of the great advances in civilization can only be understood as callous and thoroughly Eurocentric.

But again, Friedman draws on the example of Columbus for the "advances" that have resulted from the "freedom" to pursue private "economic interests," and therefore as evidence to support capitalism. Friedman (1962/2002) goes so far as to argue that free-market "capitalism is a necessary condition for political freedom" (p. 10). Friedman's thesis can be understood as a direct response to the popular support for nationalized economies designed to promote an equal distribution of the wealth generated by the productive apparatus arguing that "collectivist economic planning has...interfered with individual freedom" (p. 11). Individual freedom, for Friedman, stems from unregulated market mechanisms "stabilized" by a limited government whose function is to "protect our freedom both from the enemies outside our gates and from our fellow citizens: to preserve law and order, to enforce private contracts, and to foster competitive markets" (p. 2). Friedman points to the Soviet Union as an example of what he argues is the coercive tendency of government intervention in economic affairs. It is not surprising that Friedman does not mention the infinitely more democratic and egalitarian nature of Cuba's centrally planned economy compared to the US-supported free-market systems in the Caribbean and Latin America (Malott 2007).

The "law and order" referred to by Friedman can best be understood as the way in which "the descendents of European colonizers shaped...rules to seize title to indigenous lands" (Robertson 2005, ix) and to "enforce" these "private contracts." Similarly, the Monroe Doctrine, touted by Walter Lippmann (Lippmann 1927) as bounded by "law" and "custom," can be understood as extending the United States's "sphere of influence" to the entire western hemisphere. That is, to ensure that the resources and productive capacities of not only this region, but much of the world, would be controlled by US interests. These self-endorsed "commitments" of the United States have been upheld with deadly force explaining the United States's simultaneously open and hidden war against the Cuban Revolution and Castro's trouble-making in the hemisphere (Chomsky 1999; Malott 2007). While the hegemony of US power has seemed all but total, it has not been without critique and resistance from not only Cuba and Latin America, but within the US as well. At the heart of this counterhegemony has been the ongoing development of critical pedagogies, one of the primary philosophical influences of which can be traced to both Southern and Northern Native America.

Critical Pedagogy: Democratic Praxis against Class

Although he is certainly not the first critical pedagogue, the late Brazilian radical educator, Paulo Freire, is, however, the practitioner

SOCIAL CLASS AND REBELLION

credited with the founding of what we have come to know in North America as *critical pedagogy*, with his first book being published in Brazil in 1967. Freire's *Pedagogy of the Oppressed* (Freire 1970), initially published in the United States in 1970, is arguably the seed from which critical pedagogy in education in North America has sprouted. Freire and other critical theory trained, Latin American, critical pedagogues were highly influenced by liberation theologists such as Leonardo Boff (Boff 1978) and Leodardo Boff and Clodovis Boff (Boff and Boff 1987) of Brazil, Peruvian Gustavo Gutiérrez (Gutiérrez 1988), and world-renowned Archbishop Oscar Romero (Romero 2005) of El Salvador, who was assassinated in 1987 after becoming "known across the world as a fearless defender of the poor and suffering" earning him "the hatred and calumny of powerful persons in his own country" (Brockman 2005, xv). What is common among these leaders is that they all practiced (practice) and developed their theologies with the poorest and most oppressed sectors of their societies, who, wherever Indigenous peoples are found, tend to be Indigenous peoples. Within these theologies of liberation we can therefore find the democratic impulse that can be treated, risking romanticization, as a common characteristic among a diverse range of traditional Indigenous communities.

Critical pedagogy has always been concerned with challenging the discourse of hierarchy that legitimizes oppression and human suffering as indicative of the natural order of the universe. Rather than viewing intelligence as unequally distributed and therefore the practice of democracy extremely limited, critical pedagogy is based on an armed love and radical faith in people's ability to tend to their own economic and political interests in the spirit of peace and mutuality. In a recent series of interviews with David Barsamian, international activist Noam Chomsky (2007) describes the characteristics of what he understands to be the praxis of democracy, that is, widespread political participation

> There can't be widespread structural change unless a very substantial part of the population is deeply committed to it... If you are a serious revolutionary, you don't want a coup. You want changes to come from below, from the organized population. (p. 121)

This unyielding democratic impulse of Western-trained, North American critical pedagogy can be largely attributed to the generous philosophical gifts of not only Native South Americans but also Native North Americans such as the Haudenosaunee. According to Donald A. Grinde (1992) in "Iroquois Political Theory and the Roots of American Democracy" many of the "founding fathers" of the US, Benjamin Franklin most notably, rejected the antidemocratic European model, drawing instead on the brilliance of the Iroquois system of shared governance designed to ensure democracy and peace by putting power and decision making in the intelligent hands of the people united in a confederation of nations and not in the divine right or assumed superiority of a ruler. Grinde and others in *Exiled in the Land of the Free* (Lyons, Oren and Mohawk 1992) document, in great detail, the generosity of the Iroquois leaders in assisting Euro-Americans, before, during and after the American Revolution, in creating a unified Nation composed of the original thirteen colonies as the foundation for long-term peace, freedom, liberty, and democracy in North America. Putting the American Revolutionary war in a context foreign to traditional social studies instruction, Grinde (1992) notes that "the first democratic revolution sprang from American unrest because the colonists had partially assimilated the concepts of unity, federalism, and natural rights that existed in American Indian governments" (p. 231). It is abundantly clear that the gift of democracy received by the US government by the Haudenosaunee has all been but subverted. For examples of the democratic tradition in contemporary times, outside of Native communities themselves, we have to turn our attention to the highly marginalized critical tradition.

However, we might say that this democratic tradition, commonly associated with European critical theory (i.e., Marxism), is an appropriation because the Native American source of these generous gifts, in the contemporary context, tends not to be cited. For those already engaged in the life-long pursuit of knowledge, this is an easily amendable flaw—requiring of such Western-trained critical theorists/educators an active epistemological and material engagement with Native Studies and Indigenous communities the world over (Ewen 1994; Kincheloe 2008). We might say that the critical theoretical tradition, rooted in Indigenous conceptions of freedom and liberty, represents a rich history of opposition to antidemocratic, authoritarian forms of institutionalized power—private (corporate), federal (state), and religious (Clergy/Church)—for it is this unjust power that poses the greatest barrier to peace. The example of the Haudenosaunee is relatively indicative of this tradition, which stands in stark contrast to the antidemocratic model perpetuated by Durkhiem, Lippmann, Friedman, and the like.

Conclusion

Reflecting on the current crisis of capitalism, working people, as always, will bear the burden because the bosses will not pay the costs if they can defer it to "the simple people," as US Congressmen and women so often paternalistically refer to the *American people*. The role of knowledge production in capitalist society is to prevent popular uprising. However, these methods of indoctrination, while relatively successful over time, are threatened constantly by workers themselves and our indestructible potenial for social revolution. As we have seen in recent years, sometimes it takes events like a trillion dollar reward for systemic irresponsible deception—the loving touch capitalism has always afforded "the bewildered herd"—to waken the sleeping giant of those who rely on a wage to survive. The crisis in confidence *is* the sleeping giant waking up, which goes much deeper than the reluctance to spend/consume. That is, the questioning goes to the heart of the modern world—the process of value production and its dehumanized underlying driving force, which is the quest for profit, whatever the consequence. While the *sleeping giant* metaphor can be useful and powerful, the risk is that it is a form of reductionism. That is, reducing the infinitely vast diversity of consciousness to a single entity flattens out the richness of all the contributing parts. We must therefore be careful not to confuse the individual parts for the whole (Kincheloe 2005). To illustrate this point, we might say that while the left pinky toe seems to effectively stimulate the epistemological curiosity of many people, it alone cannot account for the complexity of the entire giant.

As critical pedagogues, it is within these instances of overt crisis that is our time to shine and do what we do: teach and engage with democratic principles, that is, help that big old giant stand up, become self-actualized, reach its full nondeterministic potential, and mature gracefully. Pedagogy is always critical at this juncture because the dominant paradigm does not recognize that we are all unique *free wills* and not things to be directed. If the system did, it would not be what it is. It would be something different, and that is what we want. What will life after capital be like? Who knows? Maybe we'll decide to call it Fun Style. Who is against fun? To be successful, we must continue to rigorously strive to name the world, as it currently exists. We might call this the struggle over *the meaning of our language*, and thus, the meaning of the world and ourselves.

For example, despite the central role social class plays in determining the conditions of human life in capitalist society, it is a concept that receives very little attention in corporate media outlets. On rare occasions when it is introduced, it tends to be treated as the objective state of falling within a particular income bracket and is therefore just one of the many ways people are diverse—no more or less special than being male or female, or short or tall, for example. What is implied is that inequality is the natural state of humanity, and that any centrally planned attempts to democratize the distribution of wealth is therefore *un*natural because it limits the individual's freedom to create his or her own economic destiny, allowing the cream to rise to the top, as it were. The entire history of coercion, propaganda, genocide, and conquest that paved, and continues to pave, the way for class society to exist, and the ongoing resistance against it, tends to be left out of these discussions, almost without exception. Making a similar observation Chomsky (1993) plainly states that "in the United States you're not allowed to talk about class differences" unless you belong to one of two groups, "the business community, which is rabidly class-conscious" and "high planning sectors of the government" (p. 67).

It is therefore not saying too much that the class-perspective found in the work of Durkheim, Lippmann, and Friedman has greatly influenced the business press, which tends to be "full of the danger of the masses and their rising power and how we have to defeat them. It's kind of vulgar, inverted Marxism" (Chomsky 1993, 67). What we find is that this self-serving perspective of those who benefit from class-based inequalities, in mainstream, dominant society, is presented as objective reality—as normalized and naturalized. However, because our humanity can be limited, but never completely destroyed, hegemony cannot be complete, and the less so, the more seriously we take the wisdom of those who counterhegemonically came before, and those who continue to generously contribute to the critical tradition.

References

Bakan, Joel. 2004. *The Corporation: The Pathological Pursuit of Profit and Power*. New York: Free Press.
Boff, Leonardo. 1978. *Jesus Christ Liberator*. Maryknoll, NY: Orbis.
Boff, Leonardo and Clodovis Boff. 1987. *Introducing Liberation Theology*. Translated by Paul Burns. Maryknoll, NY: Orbis.
Brockman, James. 2005. Preface to *The Violence of Love* by Oscar Romero. Compiled and translated by James R. Brockman. Maryknoll, NY: Orbis.

Chomsky, Noam. 1993. *The Prosperous Few and the Restless Many: Interviewed by David Barsamian.* Berkeley, CA: Odonian Press.
Chomsky, Noam. 1999. *Profit Over People: Neoliberalism and Global Order.* New York: Seven Stories.
Chomsky, Noam. 2007. *What We Say Goes: Conversations On U.S. Power in a Changing World: Interviews with David Barsamian.* New York: Metropolitan Books.
Chomsky, Noam. 2008. "Anti-democratic nature of US capitalism is being exposed." *Irish Times.* Accessed on November 20, 2010 at http://www.irishtimes.com/newspaper/opinion/2008/1010/1223560345968.html
Cole, Mike et al. 2002. *Marxism Against Postmodernism in Educational Theory.* Lanham, MD: Lexington Books.
Cole, Mike. 2011. *Racism and Education in the U.K. and the U.S.: Toward a Socialist Alternative.* New York: Palgrave Macmillan.
Diop, C. A. 1974. *The African Origin of Civilization: Myth or Reality.* Chicago: Lawrence Hill Books.
Durkheim, Emile. 2000. "The Division of Labor in Society" in *From Modernization to Globalization: Perspectives on Development and Social Change*, edited by Timmons Robert and Amy Hite. New York: Blackwell Publishers.
Ewen, A. ed. 1994. *Voices of Indigenous People: Native People Address the United Nations.* Santa Fe, NM: Clear Light Publishers.
Freire, Paulo. 1970. *Pedagogy of the Oppressed.* New York: Continuum.
Friedman, Milton. 1955. "The Role of Government in Education." Accessed on September 23, 2009 at http://www.schoolchoices.org/roo/fried1.htm.
Freidman, Milton. 2002. *Capitalism and Freedom.* London: University of Chicago Press.
Greider, W. and D. Baker. 2008. "Big Banks Go Bust: America's Financial System in Crisis." Accessed on September 16 at http://www.alternet.org/story/98863/
Grinde, Donald A. 1992. "Iroquois Political Theory and the Roots of American Democracy" in *Exiled in the Land of the Free: Democracy, Indian Nations, and the U.S. Constitution* edited by Chief Oren Lyons & John Mohawk. Santa Fe, NM: Clear Light Publishers.
Gutiérrez, Gustavo. 1988. *A Theology of Liberation: History, Politics and Salvation.* Maryknoll, NY: Orbis.
Kelsh, Deb and Dave Hill. 2006. "Class, Class Consciousness and Class Analysis: A Marxist Critique of Revisionist Left and Weberian Derived Analysis." Accessed on June 14, 2008 at http://www.jceps.com/index.php?pageID=article&articleID=59.
Kincheloe, Joe L. 2005. *Critical Constructivism Primer.* New York: Peter Lang.
Kincheloe, Joe L. 2008. "Critical Pedagogy in the Twenty-first Century: Evolution for Survival." In *Critical Pedagogy: Where Are We Now?* edited by Peter McLaren and Joe Kincheloe. New York: Peter Lang.

Kohn, Alfie. 2004. "NCLB and the Effort to Privatize Public Education." In *Many Children Left Behind: How the No Child Left Behind Act Is Damaging Our Children and Our Schools* edited by Deborah Meier and George Wood. New York: Beacon.

Lippmann, Walter. 1927. *The Phantom Public: A Sequel to "Public Opinion."* New York: Macmillan Company.

Lyons, Oren, and John Mohawk, ed. 1992. *Exiled in the Land of the Free: Democracy, Indian Nations, and the U.S. Constitution.* Santa Fe, NM: Clear Light Publishers.

Marx, Karl. 1867/1967. *Capital: Volume 1: A Critical Analysis of Capitalist Production.* New York: New World Paperbacks.

Marx, Karl. 1991. *Capital: Volume 3: A Critique of Political Economy.* New York: Penguin Classics.

Marx, Karl and Frederick Engels. 1848/1978. "Manifesto of the Communist Party" in *The Marx-Engels Reader: Second Edition* edited by Robert Tucker. New York: Norton.

Malott, Curry. 2007. "Cuban Education in Neo-Liberal Times: Socialist Revolutionaries and State Capitalism." *Journal for Critical Education Policy Studies* 5(1). Accessed on May 12, 2009 at http://www.jceps.com/?pageID=article&articleID=90.

Malott, Curry. 2008. *A Call to Action: An Introduction to Education, Philosophy, and Native North America.* New York: Peter Lang.

Malott, Curry. 2011. "Pseudo-Marxism and the Reformist Retreat from Revolution: A Critical Essay Review of *Marx and Education* by Jean Anyon." *Journal of Critical Education Policy Studies.* 9(1). Accessed on September 3, 2011 at http://www.jceps.com/?pageID=article&articleID=206

Robertson, L. 2005. *Conquest by Law: How the Discovery of America Dispossessed Indigenous Peoples of Their Lands.* New York: Oxford University Press.

Romero, Oscar. 2005. *The Violence of Love.* Compiled and translated by James R. Brockman. Maryknoll, NY: Orbis.

Chapter 3

How Shall We Live as Lambs Among Wolves? Reason—Passion—Power and Organization: What to Do?

Rich Gibson

I wrote the paragraph below for an essay in *Cultural Logic*, published on September 6, 2001:

> From time to time in the St. Clair River, which runs rapidly along the eastern coast of Michigan connecting Lake Huron with Lake St. Clair, a combination of high winds and atmospheric pressure causes the river to split apart, leaving a wet marsh between an onrushing tide of water headed south, and a trailing wave of great power. The locals call this a seiche, and the long moments that pass as the broken water surges to connect with itself, usually accompanied by dark purple skies, they call the seiche time. Perhaps this is the seiche time, the murky purple space between powerful waves, moments of great upheaval and crisis, the time when what is most sensibly linked appears to be forever disconnected: people from their work and the products they make, their love, and from one another; theory from practice, language from life, the parts from the whole, and social justice from equality, democracy, care, and inclusion. (http://eserver.org/clogic/4-1/introduction.html)

The Consummate Leader Cultivates the Moral Law (Sun Tzu)

The seiche time ended with the whirlwind five days later, the terrorist billionaire's attacks on the World Trade Center and the Pentagon, the empire's response invading Afghanistan, then Iraq, the bipartisan suspension of civil liberties, expansion of surveillance and force, and, finally, the economic collapse linked not merely to the dislocation of finance and productive capital, what Lady Astor called, "running off higgledy-piggledy," from industry, but also the bloated costs of war itself (*NY Times*, "100 Candles for a Darling of Society," March 30, 2002).

In US schools, a long seiche of slow preparation to regain full control of those who prepare the next generation of workers, teachers, following the war in Vietnam, swept into hyperspeed with the No Child Left Behind act, regimenting the curricula, replacing the minds of school workers with the minds of profiteers, enforcing with racist antiworking class high-stakes exams, invading the schools with divisions of militarists preaching witless nationalism.

Today, the empire stands exposed, or so it should be, as morally bankrupt, driven by greed alone, fully corrupt at every level, unwilling and unable to meet fundamental human needs—jobs to health care to education and all in between. The United States has been fought to a standstill in Iraq by an enemy with no long history of resistance, no internal defense industry of note, no definable external supply lines, no clear chain of command or central leadership. The US military is losing in Afghanistan, as did 300,000 Soviets before them. The best the United States could hope for would be a somewhat tamed Taliban rule, giving in to the madmen, and fully isolating the Al Qaeda terrorists. Then, in 2008, Russia invaded Georgia, a key US ally, and the United States did nothing. Next, a joint Israeli/US force attacked the imprisoned people of Gaza, killing hundreds, a horror the entire world recognized, laying waste to whatever post-Katrina and Iraq US reputation existed.

A nation of people who went shopping on the urging of President Bush, as trade-off for perpetual war, sees its rising expectations crushed with a foreclosure crisis, national and personal debt crises, while banksters at CitiGroup try to buy $50 million jets with federal bailout money. Inequality booms. 2.7 million people lost jobs in 2008 in the United States. A total of 600,000 people lost jobs in December 2008 alone, and 45,000 people lost jobs on January 26, 2009. Those jobs were in every key sector of the economy—demonstrating the acceleration and breadth of unemployment. The public sector threatens layoffs, payment in script, speed up, demands for concessions, and tax hikes while services—libraries to garbage pickup to health care and pensions, are eradicated. It's a world-wide collapse of the giant Ponzi scheme that operated in the international company store of capitalism. In some countries like Mexico, only drug money and remissions hold the economy together.

Elites are insulated, isolated. Their political campaigns are advertising campaigns, winners fixed by who spent most (Obama outspent

McCain three-to-one on TV ads; despite the wreckage of the Bush administration, the election was no landslide though turnout was the highest in 40 years; race remained key. A total of 55 percent of white people voted for McCain).

The REAL vote went on in regard to the bank bailouts; overwhelming public opposition, despite a full scale media assault to portray the bailout as a rescue. But the government, nothing but an executive committee of the rich and their armed weapon, is going to bail itself—the united banksters and their politicians, on the grounds that we are all in this together when we are not at all in this together. That today's voters do not recognize the nature of the government, yet they overwhelmingly oppose this transparent robbery, is indicative of the problem we face in pedagogy and practice—a gap that needs to be crossed.

City politicians and governors from New York to California queue up for jail cells, facing corruption and morals charges—hookers and toe-tappers. The last moral compass for the country is TV's Judge Judy, the second richest woman in the United States. And, clearly enough, this is all the work of people, not Nature, nor gods. It is class war, an international war of the rich on the poor.

These are the ingredients for social upheaval, revolution (Johnson 1982). But there is no rise of revolutionary analysis, action, or even talk in the United States. To the contrary, the population, fickle and hysterical, having turned on the once beloved George Bush to the favors of a father figure and demagogue, Obama, is at a loss about what is up, why things are as wrong as they are, what to do, why, and what would replace our multiple dilemmas. The election built nationalism, not reason.

All Morons Hate It When You Call Them a Moron (Holden Caulfield)

And why is that? There is no left. Following the largest world wide antiwar demonstrations in history, what claims to be the US left, squandered potential and set about developing tactics in the absence of strategy, dodged the responsibility of making a clear moral and ideological stand that all could hear, failed to teach people that we are responsible for our own histories (if not our birthrights), and today lies split between factions (The Communist Party USA's front, United for Peace and Justice, ANSWER, the National Assembly, etc.), all ducking terms like capitalism, imperialism, class struggle, and above all, revolution. The left has no analysis, no strategy, no tactics, no profound moral call for equality and freedom, and no succinct, easily grasped, ideology.

We are lambs among wolves. We do not have to live as lambs among wolves.

It would be easy to blame the postmodernists. Postmodernism, religion with an angry cloak, raised every narrow identity, every neurosis, every standpoint of what was really a tiny capital, to a central issue beyond critique, worthy of worship (Breisach 2003). Finally and predictably, it became ego over solidarity. Academic postmodernists became priests of a whine from the ivory tower, at base a whine about the vanishing of professorial protections and privileges. Postmodernism atomized academia even further than its usual state—minds crouched in little individual warrens hoping for a hint of notice, and it influenced the left, forming a kind of reincarnated right-wing Menshevism. But the very real promise of perpetual war is clearly upending the lofty dream of "changing the discourse," and, I hope, will have the hidden benefit of killing postmodernism which tried to disconnect past, present, and future; deservedly giving this Versace-clothed corpse a secret burial where it can never be found again—maybe in one of those mystical "spaces" or "interventions," it enjoyed so much.

Still, there is no left.

I blame the Bolsheviks, Lenin, Stalin, Mao, and the Communist Parties of the world who never understood Marx and his undying belief that people could be creative, passionate, caring, more or less free by living equitably in matters of production, reproduction, and decision making. Marx investigated not merely the capitalist system, but recognized the possibility that people could be whole, human, by demolishing it, retaining what was useful about it, and moving to a higher level, going beyond capital; becoming whole, transcending alienated life, in revolution. This sets up Marx's ethic of equality and mutual care that was quickly forgotten by Bolshevism and socialism in general, sacrificed on the altar of speeding production.

Nor did the Bolsheviks grasp Marx's maxim, "criticize everything." Behind a veil of internal discipline, they recreated the slavish belief: Do what you're told. Bolshevism lost interest in forging a mass base of class conscious people. The historical critique of tyranny, rule through deceit, custom, hierarchy, and assassination—and voluntary servitude—going back to the first slave and, in writing, back beyond the Greeks, vanished under Bolshevism (La Boetie et al. 1997).

The failures of Bolshevism (and its inheritor, Stalin) set up the failures of the last century, now spilling into both of today's antiwar movements and the educational justice movements, repeating the grotesque Bolshevik errors (mechanical materialism; reestablishing the values and production practices of the bourgeoisie; supporting bogus national movements that the Bolsheviks opportunistically pegged "the new subject," and thus inherently revolutionary when they were just nationalists; abolishing the idea of class struggle; propping up "good" bosses while they claimed to fight "bad" ones; claiming that truth lay within the central committee when truth is always slightly beyond us; promoting the idea that Bolshevism would have to create abundance in order to share it out and that abundance could only be fashioned by capitalism so socialism became capitalism with a party promising future benevolence which would never happen; personality cults; transforming inner party debate to invective and murder to the point it was impossible for the party to self-correct; abolishing the negation of the negation in philosophy and thus negating the idea of revolution; betraying what they set out to do and becoming what they claimed to oppose). And all that was repeated in school social movements like the sixties' Students for a Democratic society and is repeated today by the very same people, some—the self-proclaimed Weathermen like the infamous opportunist Billy Ayers—once liberals with bombs, now reformers, who say they can do school reform without engaging fundamental social change, or people who think they can reason and write their way out of capitalism. Now the antiwar movement, whose face is the Communist Party's United For Peace and Justice, is a funnel for the Democratic Party, and the education reform movement still thinks it can teach beyond the social relations required by capitalism.

First, those who agree with me that the greatest possibility in the United States and much of the world is the emergence of a mass, popular, fascist movement with millions of people marching to its tune, will have to forgive me for saying that I am not going to write about what would need to be done. Political conditions inside the fading US capitalist democracy and the Patriot Act today make that unwise. Like everyone who ever faced a true historical crisis, as we do today with economic collapse interacting with growing realities of endless war (economic collapse that may well be only resolved by endless war, popularized by a war-means-work mentality), what peers back at us from the future is something entirely new. Perhaps it is overblown, or a recognition of my own limits, to say I know of no historical precedent for our predicament. Hence, on the darker side of guessing that we may be surrounded by a hostile population for some time, I suggest studying the early days of the

Vietnamese revolution, Michael Collins, and Chinese perseverance in the Long March.

However, I bet against my better judgement and write here with greater hope on the chance we might help derail that ugly prospect with a four-legged project: *Reason, Passion, Power,* and *Organization,* in the context of saying, again, we are lambs among wolves. We face a real crisis in which our opposition, which I propose is mainly the US ruling class, which exists, has a determined central command, weapons, two centuries of experience with exclusion and deception, and the habits and traditions of everyday life on their side, and has demonstrated repeatedly that they are prepared to spill rivers of blood. They also stand naked as strategically incompetent, tactically inept—which may mean they are in the long term, weak, but in the short term, desperate and scary.

Even so, educators have phenomenal potential power. We are tasked to investigate ideas, we occupy key positions in society, connecting multiple communities, and we can quickly understand that a good part of social change is pedagogical, linking reason to power.

On the matter of *reason*, I want to apply Marx's maxim, "criticize everything," to capitalist democracy and the failure to follow Marx's path by nearly every reform group, and Bolshevik remnant, in the world. I also hope to apply reason to social analysis and the development of strategies and tactics. So, I will investigate abstract democracy, capitalist democracy, and the fetish the left has made of democracy in the United States.

Expanding on Che Guevara, who, when he witnessed the US sponsored violent overthrow of the democratically elected Arbenez regime in Guatemala, said, "It was then I left the path of reason," I say we must see more paths than reason alone.

On matters of *passion*, I want to investigate what it is that the left has failed to demonstrate to people about Marx's view about being whole, equitable, creative, caring, even friendly—and how we desperately need to build that into our organizations now, before the vision is lost in the thousand forms of selfishness that make class rule possible. I will suggest that one impact of the dramatic expansion of finance capital, dominating productive industrial capital, and the parallel deindustrialization, has been the acceleration of the collapse of the family, once central to inhibition against change, and, thus, the acceleration of the ruling class call to educators to fashion, not just fear of the outer cop, but to instill the inner cop, the inner priest, via the regimentation of the curriculum and high-stakes exams (Schneider 1975).

HOW SHALL WE LIVE AS LAMBS AMONG WOLVES? 47

Reason must be connected to *passion* if we are to change people's minds, carry out any pedagogical project, but especially the one at hand that connects the struggle in education to society.

On *organization and power*, or *organized action*, I want to quickly review where the Rouge Forum—which, I assert, is the core of the left in the United States—is and where I think we need to be.

Let us begin with *Abstract Democracy*, and quickly toss away the abstract pretense of democracy standing by itself.

Here are three telling quotes about Democracy:

> Democracy is the name we give the people whenever we need them.
> Marquis de Flers Robert and Arman de Caillavet
> (http://www.quotationspage.com/quote/856.html)

> The whole dream of democracy is to raise the proletarian to the level of stupidity attained by the bourgeois.
> Gustave Flaubert (1821–1880)

> Under democracy one party always devotes its chief energies to trying to prove that the other party is unfit to rule—and both commonly succeed, and are right.
> H. L. Mencken (1880–1956)
> (http://www.quotationspage.com/quote/856.html)

We can see how US democracy deals with popular Hamas, crushes democratically elected regimes it does not like as in Guatemala, Nicaragua, Haiti, and Chile, seeks to murder popular leaders like Castro, creates bogus democratic movements in accompaniment with the CIA as in Kosovo or Poland, promotes democracy in the USSR and calls the KGB leadership "democracy advocates," restores drug gang warlords in Afghanistan and calls that democracy, invades and Balkanizes Iraq for oil and regional control while waiving the democratic flag, and props up tyrants like the Saudis all over the world. Democracy is less than meaningless, actually inverted, in the outer reaches of the empire. The United States uses the National Endowment for Democracy as a front for the CIA all over the world, and inside the United States as well, to destroy indigenous movements that fight for equality.

Internally, US democracy, often with liberals in the lead, fashions the theft of the public treasury in maneuvers like Enron or the trillion dollar bankster bailouts, which involved every sector of government, demolishes the environment and gets the citizens to pay for the superfund sites, cheats at the ballot box, as in 2000; the rich use the sheer power of their money to deceive and exclude people in national elections that now measure, not so much vote counts, but who spends the most. Obama betrayed his own promise to rely on public funds.

Democracy relies on a tax system that forgives the rich their riches and punishes workers for having to work. Greek democracy and US democracy were stacked on slavery. US democracy is an untrustworthy privilege won through the plunders of vicious imperial violence, part of the buy off of the population of the empire's citizens, just as the nationalist loyalty of top union leaders is purchased by the CIA. US abstract democracy sits on the false idea that we are all in this nation together, when we actually writhe in the midst of class warfare, our side losing for now (Moore 1957).

In the one place where we might expect to see some kind of abstract democracy operating—the unions—we witness the most grotesque perversions of abstract democracy, as in the American Federation of Teachers or the United Auto Workers unions, both functioning with a caucus system that locks out nearly any dissent whatsoever, a system upheld by the democratic Supreme Court. Union democracy is a myth. The unions, decidedly a part of the system of capital, are reduced to capital's motive: chase the dues money (Gibson, 2006).

Governors, whoremongers and corrupt, line up for prison cells, from New York to Illinois. Every big city in the United States is polluted with political corruption, from Mayor Kilpatrick's disgrace in Detroit to Mayor Murphy's disgrace in San Diego, just as the cities were utterly corrupt 100 years ago, as Lincoln Steffens demonstrated in *Shame of the Cities*, but Steffens was never able to connect incidents of corruption and the necessary tie of a system of exploitation and buy offs, so he treated each city's rot as a fluke, just as Jonathon Kozol continues to do with education reform today, calling for "democracy."

When US antiwar activists in the Vietnam era wanted to organize a vote against the war, they arrogantly forgot about the Vietnamese vote taking place on the battlefield.

Plunkett of Tammany Hall begat Randy "Duke" Cunningham. The 2008 election spectacle has cost more than one billion dollars, for TV ads alone. The offer was with the Clinton versus Obama dog fight, two demagogues declaring they can outsuperstition the other and one war criminal, McCain. Such is abstract democracy in the US, serving at best as something of a warning signal to the ruling class (Szymanski 1978).

In philosophy, abstract democracy is religion, dialectics without materialism, the dead end of critique, a source of class rule. You suspend your critical thought, agree to one Imaginary Friend or another, enter an arena run by self appointed translators for the IF, pay them, accept the hierarchies they created before you arrived, take direction and adopt the rules of the translators for the IF, and since your IF has to expand or collapse, and since there is no way to resolve religious disputes, no way to offer proofs, others become enemies. Rivers of blood.

I do not want to hear about abstract rule of the people. Rather than vote in this system, the best move might be to turn the tables and, instead of buying a politician, get some pals and collectively sell your votes. I dismiss the abstraction of democracy.

I do want to address *capitalist democracy*, which Marx described as the best fit for the social system when under expansion. To grasp the relation of capital and democracy we must understand that they are not piled, one on the other, but fully imbued with each other. They developed together in history. It is like a mathematical fraction in which the numerator exists as a full partner with the denominator. But capitalism and democracy is a zipped up relationship that is ignored or denied in civics classes, and which can ebb and flow depending on power relations between classes. We know US democracy can vanish, fast, as in Detroit in 1967 when all laws were suspended and the military invaded the city. The same is true of Canada, with the War Measures act enforced in 1970.

"Capital Is the All-Dominating Power of Bourgeois Society" (Marx 2008)

What, then, is capitalism? It is, first, a *system of exploitation*, a giant sucking pump of surplus labor, a relentless quest for profits in which those who do not expand, die, as with the US auto industry. Capitalism is born in inequality and violence. Those who own, stole, and the rest, who must work to live, work under an unjust condition that claims to give us a fair day's pay, when in fact that day's pay begins with the violence of being dispossessed and ends with our being paid but a portion of what our labor creates—the source of profit. Over time, production becomes increasingly social, yet the value of that production is looted by those few who hold power and capital. Still, at least in theory, the revolutionary system of capital which demolished feudalism (then gave it new life in the Taliban) creates a world in which all people could live fairly well, if they shared.

So, capitalism is a system of exploitation in which those who must work to live must vie with each other for jobs, while nation based owners vie with each other for cheap labor, raw materials, and markets, often using militaries made up of workers who are sent off to fight the enemies of their real enemies: the rich at home.

Capitalism is a system rooted in *Alienation* and *Exploitation*: People who must sell their labor to live; that is, the vast majority of people, are drawn together in systems of production which, over time, are more and more socialized (bigger plants, more interconnected forms of exchange, technology, and communication, etc.).

However, the people who must work, who form a social class, are set apart from each other in competition for jobs and do not control the process or the product of their work. We see that as school layoffs prompt educators to point at one another, suggesting someone else should go first, while the curriculum and teaching methods are imposed from the top down. Kids really need more educators, not less, and corporate profits and CEO pay still boom.

While we have more control over our time as educators than most workers, we do not determine how the work will be done, nor do we choose what will be done with the product and don't own the profits gained (whether it is a Pinto of child or a chocolate). The more they engage in this form of exploited work, the greater the growth of difference between them and their employers. At the same time, the more workers labor, the more they enrich their rulers, and wreck themselves. Alienation is a loss of self, indifference to others, and a surrender to passivity. Each group forms, in essence, a competing social class, hence Marx says, "history is the history of class struggle." Alienated individuals, though, become increasingly isolated, while, simultaneously, they are driven together in ever more distinct, separated, classes. At the end of the day, the alienated person is split from him/herself; self-destructive.

Alienation and exploitation lead to Commodity fetishism: Capitalism is propelled, in part, by the sale of commodities for a profit (as in surplus value). Over time, both workers and the employer class relate more to things than they do to other people, indeed people begin to measure their worth by commodities, especially the chief commodity, money, which in many instances becomes an item of worship. Businesses no longer focus on making, say, steel for use, but on making money, for profits. Education becomes, not leading out, as from the Greek, but for domination, and test scores become the fetish.

Finance capital begins to dominate industrial investment, or such is the path in the United States. People who must sell their labor become commodities themselves, and often view themselves and their own children that way. How much you make determines who you are, who you meet, who you marry, where you travel. You are not what you are, but what you have. People then begin to see what are really relations between people, as relations between things (every human relationship mainly an economic one), which leads to the *connection of commodity fethishism and reification*. In discussing the stock market, most economists treat it as if it had a wisdom and life of its own (remember the religion metaphor). In schools, children have been routinely commodified, sold to companies like McGraw-Hill (textbooks) and Coca Cola—and most teachers would agree that this process has accelerated in the last decade. Commodification means that people become things, less human, less connected so Marx argued, "the more you have, the less you are."

Test scores remain a good example. No Child Left Behind sets up an appearance of equality, just like the myth of a fair day's pay for a fair day's work. The myth is that children enter the testing room as equals, the harder they prep, the better they will do. The reality is that the more their parents earn, the higher the scores. The more you are concerned about test scores, the less you are learning anything important; the more you are learning, for example, subservience. In school, the battle for profits meets the battle for social control.

As with capital, the more you concentrate on test scores, the more stupified you become. But, the politicians ask, "how else can we measure learning?" while masses of people forget we could just ask the kid. Or, if we are truly so concerned about testing and scores, why not give the kids the test on the first day of school and keep giving it, with reflective instruction, until all pass?

War, on one hand, and unconcern, on the other, are results of commodity fetishism. Greed, domination and fear are the underlying ethics, underpinned by indifference, the opposition of love.

Combined these three processes, exploitation, alienation, and commodity fetishism forge *reification*: All reification is a form of forgetting (Horkheimer and Adorno 2001). The relations of people, disguised as the relations between things, become so habitual that it seems natural. Things people produce govern people's lives. Commodity production and exchange are equated with forces of nature. "Natural laws," really inventions of people, replace real analytical abilities (as in seeing supply and demand, or scarcity and choice, as the centerpieces of economics, rather than seeing economics as the story of the social relations people create over time in their struggle with nature to produce and reproduce knowledge, freedom, and life—or in political science, discussing democracy as if it had nothing to do with social inequality).

Reified history is abolished, capitalism assumed to be the highest attainable stage of human development. Nothing changes. Normalcy in some capitalist countries is really store-bought assent to exploitation—masked as freedom. Test scores are good examples of reification in school. Measuring little but parental income and race, test scores are worshiped uncritically, influencing people's lives far beyond their real value. Real estate salespeople love test scores, churn the market.

Reification hides the system of compulsion and disenfranchisement, a push-pull from the powerful, that mystifies a social system of exploitation so thoroughly that it is able to seriously call itself a centripetal point of freedom, producing a mass neurosis so powerful that it encourages it subjects to steep in two decades of consumerist euphoria while their social superstructure, like schools, their social safety net, like welfare or health services, evaporates underneath them.

Their industrial base vanishes as well—a hangover from euphoria, the Golden Calf becoming the Trojan Horse—which is not wise for a nation promising to wage meat grinder perpetual wars on the world to have the steel industry owned by outsiders from India, Germany, and Japan. One has to worry about what happens when this population cannot use its play stations or get to the mall. They may be the most dangerous people in the history of the world.

These processes of capital give those who own an enormous machine for lying and deceiving, a massive propaganda machine extending from all forms of media into schools, throughout the military, etc.

This background sets up our look at *capitalist democracy* as the best system for capital as it expands. The capitalist state is an executive committee of the rich, not autonomous or neutral, but their debate forum, where they iron out their differences, they allow the vast majority of people to choose which of them will oppress best. The capitalist democracy is also an armed weapon in service to property rights. As the ruled far outnumber the rulers, and since coercion and force alone cannot sustain capitalist production, to pacify areas people must be turned into instruments of their own oppression.

We can see now how the one-person-one-vote mythology would appeal both to rulers who seek to divide and conquer, and to individuals isolated by the system of alienation, fooled by the atomizing deception apparatus that promotes individualism—voting promotes the lowest forms of opportunism, boils down to "what about me?"—and the false notion that a vote can bring fundamental social change. The vote count serves as a warning signal to ruling classes. People hide from one another in voting booths, wrongly thinking they are making real public decisions when they really have no control over the processes and products of the system—and most cynically know politicians always lie—yet they vote thinking they are exercising their only public or social power, when in fact they are just setting themselves off from others and the reality is that their real power lies in unity with other workers at work, to build solidarity to fight to control the value they create. The crux of capitalist democracy is revealed in the fact that nearly no one expects to have a vote on anything significant at work, unless they own the workplace.

Others, excluded, (by Jim Crow laws or chicanery) might be disgruntled, while those who don't vote can be attacked for being responsible for the bad choices voters make.

Fundamentally powerless student councils are practice areas for future political leaders, councils where all concerned pretend they have influence, when they are mere performers reading blank scripts. Student councils are sandboxes. When university presidents see the kiddies inching outside the sandbox, the presidents (or principals) abolish the vote and push the kids back in.

The rule of law, which appears to be natural law, law suspended above and apart from class struggle, is a form of reification. On the face of it, justice, but at base it is class rule and, moreover, the rule of law is key to commerce—mutual trust is hardly enough, indeed, laughable.

The masses of people are told this is the law, which is alienated law, "the will of the ruling class exalted into statutes," (Marx 1995), a sandbox of property laws overseen by millionaire judges that only incidentally considers people. The mythological rule of law is sheer class rule that shifts as class struggle and largesse or bankruptcy meet one another.

Within this law, as in religion, people deepen their alienation, choose, and pay others to think and act for them, others who operate behind the habits of hierarchy and the force of arms. When serious differences, collisions of interests, appear between the capitalists of a given nation, they conduct civil war. The base for capitalist law is the same as the capitalist ethic: Profits are good, losses are bad, keep a careful count. Capitalist law is the law of property, ownership, not humanity.

The religion metaphor works well with schooling in the industrialized world. In the abstract, as with abstract democracy, public schools are there for the common good. But they are capitalist schools, above all—granted, opposition exists in some ways like it does in a factory. Educators in capitalist schools are somewhat like missionaries for capitalism. Look at the hierarchies: men run the administration (Bishops), and women (Nuns) do the front line work. School workers, who have more freedom than other workers, have a clear choice—be a missionary for the system of capital, or not.

No one ever voted themselves out of what is, at base, a Master/Slave relationship. The Masters will never adopt the ethics of the slaves. The singular path of reason alone will not overcome the system of capital, though reason must be our light and beacon. Our choice today is between community or barbarism.

Marx was correct in seeing that capitalism is a giant worldwide company store, an international war of the rich on the poor, and most importantly that the dispossessed of the world, probably all of us, have a real interest in overcoming that system and, not replacing it with another form of dictatorship, but with an ethic and reality of reasonable equality.

The People's Insurrection Is Against Tyranny (Babeuf 1794)

The logic of the analysis of capitalist democracy leads directly to revolution. There is no other way out. While we should abhor violence, we should not reify it, treat it as if abstract violence stands on a plane similar to abstract democracy, beyond history, social conditions, or the legitimate arts of resistance. We should not celebrate hatred, nor shy away from it. The opposite of love is not hate, but indifference.

The logic of revolution against capital is true, especially now when finance capital in the United States, now in free fall yet continuing to expand, is challenged by capital in other nations like China, which has a well motivated, not exhausted, military and needs that oil just as much as the United States. Oil moves the military, which in turn is absolutely key to any empire's ability to flourish, which is why saving gas will do little or nothing about the perpetual oil wars. US finance capital is hit by the crises we are familiar with: the mortgage, personal debt, and national debt crises, the ghastly rise in food and transportation costs, and so on. Harsh times came fast following the collapse of Lehman Bank and we witnessed the merger of finance and government with the series of bailouts, welfare to the rich, as the usual privatization of profits melded with the socialization of losses.

It follows that capitalist democracy in the United States is not expanding with the Obama election, but rapidly contracting, and fascism emerges. As class antagonism grows, state power becomes an ever more national power over labor and reforms, with capital only increasing the power of its state. There are no more labor laws of any worth, no civil rights laws, habeas corpus, rights of privacy, free speech (remember, "watch what you say") are gone, through bipartisan legislative action as well as the courts.

The fight back to transform the system of capital needs to look carefully at the rise of fascism (merger of the corporate and political elites, suspension of common laws, racism, nationalism, a culture writhing in violence in search of a strong leader—all moving at hyper speed within the national election now). Saying "emergence of fascism," does not mean fascism has arrived, but it does mean that fascism exists for some people in the United States now, say a young black man in Detroit or Compton, while it is appearing before the eyes of others—volunteers drafted by the economy in Iraq.

The recent election should not only be studied as how to choose who will best oppress the majority of the people from the executive committee of the rich, the government, it should also be studied, more importantly, as how an element of capitalist democracy, the preposterous election, has speeded the emergence of fascism, that is,

- the corporate state, the rule of the rich,
- the suspension of civil liberties,
- the attacks on whatever press there is,
- the rise of racism and segregation (in every way, but especially the immigration policies),
- the promotion of the fear of sexuality as a question of pleasure (key to creating the inner slave), and the sharpened commodification of women (Sarah Palin to pole dancers),
- the governmental/corporate attacks on working people's wages and benefits (tax bailouts to merit pay),
- intensification of imperialist war (sharpening the war in Afghanistan sharpens war on Pakistan which provokes war on Russia, etc., and the United States is NOT going to leave Iraq's oil),
- the promotion of nationalism (all class unity by, especially, the union bosses),
- teaching people the lie that someone else should interpret reality and act for us, when no one is going to save us but us,
- trivializing what is supposed to be the popular will to vile gossip, thus building cynicism—especially the idea that we cannot grasp

and change the world, but also debasing whatever may have been left of a national moral sense,
- increased mysticism (is it better to vote for a real religious fanatic or people who fake being religious fanatics?), and
- incessant attacks on radicals (Bill Ayers is not a radical; he is a foundation-sucking liberal now, once he was a liberal with a bomb, but people see him as the epitome of a radical and he IS connected to Obama).

That is a litany of the acceleration of fascism (Gibson 2000).

Al Szymanski outlined the basic functions of the capitalist state three decades ago. This is a reminder:

1. Guarantee the accumulation of capital and profit maximization and make it legitimate.
2. Preserve capitalist class rule.
3. Raise money to fund the state.
4. Form and preserve capitalist class rule. (Szymanski 1978, 212)

But the left of the US antiwar movement, and the education reform movement, abandoned the critique of capitalist democracy, meaning they have no basis for analysis, no ability to develop strategies and tactics across a nation or even in unique communities—because they do not grasp how power works or why it is that the power of people who work lies, not in the voting booth, where odds are the voting machines are owned by their enemies, but at work where they can collectively win control of the processes and products of their work, in communities, or in the military where the working classes are already organized and armed.

At the same time, *the left has made a fetish of Abstract Democracy*, following the postmodernist coalitions where the notion of class struggle or the word "capitalism" is banished and people are urged to go off in narrow race/nation/sex/language "autonomous" grouplets, taking up their constricted issues, as did the 10,000 people meeting in Atlanta in 2007 at the World Social Forum (WSF), thinking this will somehow lead to real resistance to a ruthless enemy with a long history of rule and a centralized command. The WSF created no strategy at all. To quote America's last remaining moral compass, Judge Judy, "it doesn't make sense and it is just not true." It won't work. Judge Judy is a perfect example of the appearance of judiciousness, when it is really the application of the values of the bourgeoisie, and the sale of judiciousness, as the filler between commercials.

Inside the trap of Abstract Democracy, a tyranny with a thousand hierarchies and forms of selfishness, each uniting the individuals with the whole of capital, the left has shown it is unable to get its ideas to leap ahead of daily social practice, an absolute necessity if we are to envision a better world and set about creating it.

In order to make a fight, people must trust one another. That means they must meet with each other in integrated groups that recognize that class remains the key issue at hand, of course mediated by questions of race, language, sex, gender, nation.

That, coupled with its unremitting captivation with nationalism, is the main reason the US left has had no impact whatsoever on the last seven years of imperialist war, even though a million and more people hit the streets in the first week of the Iraq invasion. They evaporated into their semiautonomous worlds and have not exercised their potential power since. A somewhat similar thing happened to the school reform movement, which, other than parts of the Rouge Forum, simply refuses to address the connections of the system of capital, imperialism, war, the regimentation of school life and the curriculum, oversight through high-stakes exams, militarization, and privatization as well.

It is fair to say, I think, that the dominant elements of public life in the United States are opportunism, racism, nationalism, ignorance, and fear (surely that is true of the professorate) though we have to recognize that the sheer persistence of continuing to work, in our case on behalf of kids, has considerable courage built into it.

Anyone interested in confronting our conditions today must follow Hegel's dictum: "The truth is in the whole." The whole is capitalism. Some live in capitalist democracies, and most do not, but it is the whole that must always be addressed, like keeping the front sight aligned with the rear sight. Even reforms will not be won without both sights on the target. The failure to create a mass base of class conscious people, which is our life and death high-stakes test, remains the Achilles heel of nearly every social movement. It follows we need to openly talk about what capitalism is, why class struggle takes place, what can be done, and what a better future might be. We need to answer the question: What do we want people to know, and how do we want them to come to know it?—inside every action we take.

Let us soar on to *passion*. A great part of the school reform movement, of the antiwar movement, of the Marxist project, is pedagogical. Do people learn through reason alone? They do not.

The entire system of capitalist democracy is a system of deceit, misrepresentation, and, although it may seem as if anyone can see what is up, few do. What constructs mistaken consciousness, what underpins the indifference, "whatever" keeps the system going, or, what reveals the Man Behind the Screen, or, what causes some people to acquiesce while others resist, even knowing they won't soon win? Engels said there is no simple connection between being, the system of capitalist social relations, and consciousness, or class consciousness (Schneider 1975, 24).

Consider the impact of capitalist democracy on capitalist schooling, its purportedly public system that is, in fact, several segregated systems conducting education mostly along the lines of the race and class, a preprison program in Detroit, a pre-Walmart program in National City, a presocial worker program in LaMesa, a prelaw system in Lajolla, and a private system in Bloomfield Hills, where the rich send their kids—like Mitt Romney and George Bush. In Romney's school, youth learn the view, "this is our world and we will discover how we might make it act," while elsewhere, depending on the rung of the segregated ladder, kids learn, "tell me what to do and I will do it."

Capitalist schooling in the United States, since the multidimensional decay ushered in by the Vietnam war, has taken the place of the family in the social breaking in of the future work force through marching kids inside a system of inhibition, suppression, prohibition, in which society seizes control of childhood, and, I think significantly, tries at once to make kids asexual, fearful of sexual pleasure, and thus their own bodies, while the outside world introduces them, ceaselessly, to spectacles of exploitative sexuality. Aids on the one hand, Brittany Spears on the other. Is it any wonder that one-fourth of our teens have STDs?

Capitalist schooling imbues kids with the idea that it is natural to have to sell yourself, your labor, and then, through high-stakes exams for example, teaches kids the thousand forms of selfishness that make class rule possible (Schneider 1975, 22). As Wilhelm Reich said, the inner cop is the Trojan Horse of any society rooted in domination (Reich 1970). And Marx was clear that capitalism reduces love and passion to cash—Elliot Spitzer, Randy Cunningham, etc. But money is not an early childhood wish. Human connection is. However, this connection is broken in a broken world.

It is illegal in US capitalist schools to teach the central issues of life: Labor (involving the communist movement), rational knowledge (opposing the many Imaginary Friends that people think are in charge), love (tied to pleasure, sensuality, aesthetics, as well as reproduction), and freedom (which does not exist in school life).

With Bob Apter and Susan Harman, I traveled California last fall, meeting with teachers, parents, kids, and community people all over the state, the northern border to the Mexican border. The main thing we learned: Fear is the primary lesson being learned by everyone connected to schools. Lessons learned in fear teach, for the most part, abuse and more fear. We know the abused commonly turn around and abuse. Empathy linked to passion may transform that, or not.

The idea that we are responsible for our own histories, if not our birthrights (inheritance seen as natural), is banned in most capitalist schooling, as is the viewpoint, true, that we can comprehend and change the world. To the contrary, children are taught lies (nationalism for example) using methods so obscure that kids learn to not like to learn, a dubious achievement of capitalist schooling.

We know the education-by-commands-and-fear NCLB's child victims can be restored to life to some extent by good, persevering, teaching, but it is a terrible burden to overcome. For the most part, NCLB works toward teaching obedience, servility, and nationalism, eradicating history to the point that Chalmers Johnson claims people in the United States, "have no framework to link cause and effect." (Johnson 1982, 2)

The NCLB sets up the three processes driving school today: (1) the regimentation of the curricula and methods of instruction, (2) surveillance through racist, antiworking class exams using a pretense of science to sort children, and (3) militarism, a veritable invasion of the schools in poor and working class areas while all are taught the normalcy of endless warfare.

In this context, how do we connect reason to passion? I think we do that, in part, by addressing the fact that freedom is insight into unfreedom, that we must sacrifice our narrower interests in order to participate collectively, but beyond that we must build passion, friendship, caring, empathy, aesthetics, and as much freedom as possible into a resistance group addressing the whole of the problems of the system of capital.

That does not mean we need to take on Abstract Democracy. It means we must find ways to make collective decisions about serious actions for the common good. It does not mean lowest common denominator consensus building, nor the isolation of voting. It means a resistance group based on reason, friendship, and figuring out how to make the best decisions possible.

Opportunists have no principles, ethics, and have lots of friends who know nearly nothing important.

Sectarians have rigid principles and no friends; generals without armies. Marxists have lots of friends yet keep their principles, ethics, intact, and seek to teach others—combining ethics, action, and empathy for those who must live in fear—as many educators do.

We need to find ways to allow people to be as fully human, celebratory, as possible, connected, each demonstrating their creativity and connectedness with unfreedom as a commonly understood problem to be solved, because we are lambs among wolves.

It is this condition that can allow us to connect passion to the willingness to sacrifice that fundamental change, or any important social change now, will require to create and sustain. This is not going to be easy. This path beyond reason demands that people sacrifice treasure, sleep, sometimes jobs, certainly time and promotions, maybe jail or life, for the common good. Without that sacrifice, which can be achieved with collective joy, nothing.

We must not promise ourselves a future of material abundance. That will not happen. The ruling classes will destroy their own factories, hospitals, and even the water supply. What can transport us to a world where people can share is the idea that we might have to share misery for awhile because, per Marx, ideas can be a material force—and have always been.

This brings us to *organization, power and action*. Surely we can see that justice demands organization. The Rouge Forum changed the discussion in the education reform movement. Our insistence on the role of capital, on class struggle is best illustrated by Wayne Ross's immortal comment interrupting a particularly boring executive committee meeting of the National Council for the Social Studies: "Hey, this is a lot of nonsense. We Need To Read Marx and Make Class War!"

We have had a dramatic impact on academic historians, whole language specialists, the critical pedagogy crowd, and the k12 world as well. The conversation always has to, at worst, worry about us saying, "now wait a minute." We ruptured the habits of daily academic life that only reproduces the system of capital, diminishing all it touches.

The Rouge Forum brought together people throughout the United States, Canada, Mexico, South Africa, Great Britain, and India within an organization that has grasped, for eleven years, that it is possible to have an organization, be friends, and be both critical and self-critical. We united parents, kids, school workers, and community organizers.

We predicted both these wars, what became the NCLB as early as 1997, the economic collapse, and published much of the initial research on the real impact of NCLB in academic and popular journals. We were among the first to plan ways to fight it. We traveled the United States and other nations pointing out the centripetal power of educators in deindustrialized nations, among the last workers who have health benefits or predictable wages.

We organized and led direct actions in workplaces and communities like the high-stakes test boycotts in Michigan, Florida, New York, and California. We did not just breach discourse and habits, we disrupted the unjust social relations in schools, shutting them down and, in very limited ways, offered youth freedom schooling. We marched on Mayday before the massive immigrant Mayday marches of 2006, and happily joined those huge outpourings of the working class when they took place. Now, with Calcare and others, we participate in a mass opt-out campaign, hoping to lead test boycotts to cut the school to war pipelines. We are building a base of thinking activists inside and outside the unions to reject the coming demands for school worker concessions, teaching people how to strike in solidarity—and to supply the Freedom Schools that can show how the future might be.

We reminded everyone that the key to understanding the twentieth century is understanding revolution.

We have operated loosely. It worked for about ten years, with about 4,600 people steady on our email lists, our yearly conferences, our publications, our joint work with Substance News, Calcare, the Whole Language Umbrella, and Susan Ohanian.

What we do counts now more than ever. Events move even more quickly than my comment at the Rouge Forum conference in 2008 that the sky is falling. We need to take that purposefully and plan the resistance with care.

We are lambs among wolves. Kindness, reason, organization, must prepare to meet those willing to spill—rivers of blood.

We can win.

To quote the classic labor song, Solidarity Forever:

"In our hands is placed a power greater than their hoarded gold;
Greater than the might of armies, magnified a thousand-fold.
We can bring to birth a new world from the ashes of the old."

Down the banks and Up the rebels! And don't forget to smash the state.

References

Babeuf, G. 1794. Acte Insurrecteur (Act of Insurrection). Accessed on February 12, 2009 at http://www.marxists.org/archive/bax/1911/babeuf/ch06.htm.

Breisach, E. 2003. *The Future of History, The Postmodern Challenge and its Aftermath*. Chicago: University of Chicago Press.

Fischer, E. 2005. *How to Read Karl Marx*. New York: South End Press. 163.

Gibson, R. 2006. "The Torment and Demise of the United Autoworkers' Union." *Cultural Logic*. Accessed on January 12, 2011 at http://clogic.eserver.org/2006/gibson.html.

Gibson, R. 2000. "What is fascism?" Accessed on February 10, 2010 at http://www.thirdworldtraveler.com/Fascism/What_Is_Fascism_Gibson.html.

Horkheimer, M. and T. W. Adorno. 2002. *Dialectic of the Enlightenment*. Stanford: Stanford University Press.

Jaszi, O. and John Lewis. 1957. *Against the Tyrant*. Glencoe, IL: Free Press.

Johnson, Chalmers. 2006. *Nemesis, the Last Days of the American Republic*. New York: Metropolitan Books.

Johnson, Chalmers. 1982. *Revolutionary Change (second edition)*. Stanford: Stanford University Press.

La Boetie, E. 1997. *The Politics of Obedience, The Discourse of Voluntary Servitude*. New York: Black Rose Books.

Marx, K. 1995. *The German Ideology*. New York: International Publishers.

Marx, K. and Frederick Engels. 2008. *The Communist Manifesto*. New York: Oxford University Press.

Moore, S. 1957. *Critique of Capitalist Democracy*. New York: Paine-Whiteman.

Reich, W. 1970. *The Mass Psychology of Fascism*. New York: Simon and Schuster.

Salinger, J. D. 1976. *The Catcher in the Rye*. New York: Bantam Books. Chapter 6.

Schnieder, M. 1975. *Neurosis and Civilization*. New York: Seabury Press.

Sun Tzu. 1910. *The Art of War*. Accessed on February 20, 2009 at http://www.chinapage.com/sunzi-e.html

Szymanski, Al. 1978. *The Capitalist State and the Politics of Class*. Cambridge, MA: Winthrop Publishers.

Chapter 4

Class, Neoliberal Capitalism in Crisis, and the Resistant and Transformative Role of Education and Knowledge Workers

Dave Hill

Introduction: The Aims of This Chapter

This chapter calls for transformative activism by education and other cultural workers—teachers, lecturers, journalists—in order to develop an economically just economy, polity, and society.

This chapter sets out key characteristics of neoliberal global capitalism (and, importantly, its accompanying neoconservatism) and its major effects on society and education. It highlights the obscene and widening economic, social, and educational inequalities both within states and, globally, between states; the detheorization of education and the regulating of critical thought and activists through the ideological and repressive state apparatuses; and the limitation and regulation of democracy and democratic accountability at national and local educational levels.

The chapter analyses three components of the "Capitalist Agenda for/in Education" within the current neoliberal/neoconservative globalizing project of capital, and calls for critical engagement with challenging the Radical Right in its neoliberal, Conservative, neoconservative, traditionalist, religious, and its social democratic (sometimes revised as "Third way") manifestations.

The chapter also calls for engagement with ideological and cultural fashions and with fashionable "knowledge workers" within the media and the academy—fashions such as postmodernism, which, together with social democracy / left revisionism, ultimately serve the function of "naturalising" neoliberal Capital as the dominating "common sense." They do this partly by virtue of their ignoring, or deriding Marxist derived/ related concepts of social class, class conflict, and socialism. Such academic fashions as postmodernism and left revisionism debilitate and displace viable solidaristic socialist counterhegemonic struggles.

What role can we, as critical transformative and revolutionary socialist educators and cultural/media workers play in ensuring that the Capitalism, with its dystopian class-based apartheid, is replaced by an economic and social system more economically and socially just and environmentally sustainable than national/international capitalist, state capitalist, social democratic, and (secular or religious) traditionalist alternatives?

SECTION 1

NEOLIBERAL GLOBAL CAPITAL AND THE CURRENT CRISIS OF CAPITALISM

In the current juncture of the crisis of capitalism, as in the repeated crises of capital and overproduction and speculation predicted by Marx, capitalists have a big problem. Their profits, the value of the shares and part control of companies by chief executive officers and other capitalist executives (late twentieth century/early twenty-first century capitalists), so carefully and successfully wrested back from the social and economic gains made by workers during the 1940, 50s and 60s (Harvey 2005; Dumenil and Levy 2004), are plummeting. The rate of profit is falling, has fallen.[1]

The political response to "the credit crunch," the current crisis of capital, in particular finance capital, by parties funded by capital, such as the Democrats and Republicans in the United States, and Labour, Liberal Democrat, and Conservative Parties in the UK, and conservative and social democrat parties globally, is not to blame the capitalist system. Not even to blame the neoliberal form of capitalism (new brutalist public managerialism/management methods, privatization, businessification of education, health, welfare, and social care provision, for example, increasing gaps between rich and poor, between schools in well-off areas and schools in poor areas).

They have criticized only two aspects of neoliberalism: what they now (and only now!) see as the overextent of deregulation, and the (obscene) levels of pay and reward taken by "the big bankers," by a few Chief Executive Officers (CEOs). There has been almost no criticism of the capitalist system itself, despite a few late 2008 press items "was Marx right"? And, in the Murdochized television and newpaper coverage of the crisis in the capitalist world, there is now, in 2009–2011, the mantra once again that "there is no alternative," that public sector and public service cuts are necessary to clear national debt. Dissenting voices are rarely heard on television, rarely appear in mainstream newspapers, although some *vox populi* views from the streets, for example the general strikes and demonstrations in Syntagma Square, Athens in, June and July 2011 against the cuts / austerity programmes in Greece, do creep into news broadcasts and burst out of Facebook and other social networking sites (Hill 2011b).

What Is Neoliberal Capitalism?

For neoliberals, "profit is God," not the public good. Capitalism is not kind. Plutocrats are not essentially, or even commonly, philanthropic. In capitalism, it is the insatiable demand for profit that is the motor for policy, not public, or social, or common weal, or good. With great power comes great irresponsibility. Thus privatized utilities, such as the railway system, health and education services (schools, trade/ vocational education, universities), free and clean water supply, gas and electricity supply, are run, just as much as factories and finance houses, to maximize owners' and shareholders' profits and rewards, rather than to provide a public service.

The current and recently (since the 1970s and 80s) globally dominant form of Capitalism, neoliberalism, requires that the state establishes and extends the following policies:

1. The control of inflation by interest rates, preferably by an independent central bank.
2. The balancing of budgets, which should not be used to influence demand—or at any rate to stimulate it (in the current credit crisis this policy has been put on hold/reversed).
3. The privatization / private ownership of the means of production, distribution, and exchange.
4. The provision of a market in goods and services—including private sector involvement in welfare, social, educational, and other state services (such as schools, health services, savings banks, air traffic control, pensions, postal deliveries, prisons, policing, railways).
5. Within education, the creation and exacerbation, through selection, of "opportunity" to acquire the means of education (though not necessarily education itself) and additional "cultural capital."

6. The relatively untrammeled selling and buying of labor power, for a "flexible," poorly regulated labor market, deregulation of the labor market—for labor flexibility (with consequences for education in providing an increasingly hierarchicalized schooling and university system).
7. The restructuring of the management of the welfare state on the basis of a corporate managerialist model imported from the world of business, known as new public managerialism (NPM).
8. The deriding, suppression, and compression of oppositional counterhegemonic critical thought, spaces, and thinkers/activists within the media and education.
9. Within a regime of denigration and humbling of publicly provided services. (With the temporary and limited readoption of Keynesian public works measures—the state stepping in, and state investment—this is, at times, somewhat mitigated).
10. Within a regime of cuts in the postwar welfare state, the withdrawal of state subsidies and support, and low public expenditure—except in the current credit crunch, for the trillions of dollars capitalist states are now spending on bailing out the banks and some companies/corporations.
11. Accompanied by tax cuts for the richest (see, for example, Hearse 2009; Packer and Leplat 2011; Pizzigati 2011).

Internationally, neoliberalism requires that

1. Barriers to international trade and capitalist enterprise should be removed.
2. There should be a "level playing field' for companies of any nationality within all sectors of national economies.
3. Trade rules and regulations, such as the General Agreement on Trade in Services (the GATS), are necessary to underpin "free" trade, with a system for penalizing "unfair" trade policies.

One increasingly important proviso, in the face of growing Chinese and Indian economic muscle and exports, is that

4. Rich and powerful countries reserve the right to exempt themselves from these rules, to slap on quotas, and to continue subsidizing their own agricultural industry, for example the subsidies afforded to agricultural production in the United States and the European Union.

What Are the Results of Neoliberalism? Widening Inequalities

Impacts of Neoliberal Capitalism

In its current neoliberal form in particular, Capitalism leads to human degradation and inhumanity and increased (gendered and "raced"/ racialized) social class inequalities within states and globally.
Neoliberal policies globally have resulted in

1. a loss of equity, economic and social justice for citizens and for workers at work
2. a loss of democracy and democratic control and democratic accountability
3. a loss of critical thought and space.

The Growth of National and Global Inequalities

Inequalities, both between states and within states, have increased dramatically during the era of global neoliberalism. Global capital, in its current neoliberal form in particular, leads to human degradation and inhumanity and increased social class inequalities within states and globally. These effects are increasing (racialized and gendered) social class inequality within states, increasing (racialized and gendered) social class inequality between states. The degradation and capitalization of humanity, including the environmental degradation, impact primarily in a social class related manner. Those who can afford to buy clean water don't die of thirst or diarrhoea. In many states across the globe, those who cannot afford school or university fees, where charges are made, end up without formal education or in grossly inferior provision.

Hearse (2009) points out that

> The golden age for the salaried worker across all the OECD countries was between 1945 and 1973, when ordinary working people gained their highest percentage share of GDP. Since then the real wages of the middle and working class have stagnated or fallen, while income for the rich has rocketed and that of the super-rich has hit the stratosphere.[2]

Our cities and towns are in crisis. Grotesque and widening inequalities between rich and poor, the chasm of despair amongst the dispossessed, the underclass, the weak, the unfortunate, the alienated, the deterioration of public and welfare provision and services have despoiled large parts of capitalist cities. Jonathan Kozol in the United States (1995, 2001, 2006), Polly Toynbee in Britain (2003), John Pilger (2003), Naomi Klein (2008a, b) worldwide—and writers across the globe—thrust shattering and shocking detail of the world of the poor, of the "raced" social class apartheid in our cities, of the spiral of dismay and desperation of the black and white and minority working classes and unemployed, their desperado counterassertiveness or their apathy, belabored by a neoliberal capitalist system that gorges on inequality, proclaims its necessity, and ratchets up its effects.

Dorling (2010a) points out that in the UK, "The 1,000 richest people in Britain became 30 percent richer in the last year. That's a £77 billion rise in wealth—enough to wipe out around half the government's budget deficit" (see also, Dorling 2010b, c).

Dorling's book, about inequality in Britain, (Dorling 2010b; see also Ramesh 2010) notes that London's richest people are worth 273 times more than the poorest, that society has the widest divide since the days of slavery.

Ramesh (2010) summarizes:

> London is most unequal city in the developed world, with the richest tenth of the population amassing 273 times the wealth owned by the bottom tenth—which creates a "means chasm" not seen since the days of a "slave owning society", according to a new book…
>
> In *Injustice: Why Social Inequality Persists…*, Danny Dorling says the government's latest figures show that in the capital the top 10% of society had on average a wealth of £933,563 compared to the meagre £3,420 of the poorest 10%—a wealth multiple of 273.

In neoliberalized countries across the globe the rich get richer—much richer—the poor get poorer, publicly funded community, social services and welfare services are replaced by costly private provision, the glorification of private consumption and profit, and middle-income and low-income workers work ever harder simply to keep the same standard of living. They suffer pay cuts, union curbs, and a slashed social wage—a sundered social support and survival network of services, provision, and benefits. In contrast, billionaires live in "Richistan" (Frank 2007; TimesOnline 2007) where a particular anxiety appears to be that there is a five year wait for luxury Rolls Royce cars. Millions of workers' main anxiety is the weekly or monthly wait for the next pay cheque to buy the family groceries. Millions in advanced capitalist countries, billions globally, live in "Pooristan." In Britain, "Britain is moving back towards levels of inequality in wealth and poverty last seen more than 40 years ago," as "Both poor and wealthy households have become more and more geographically segregated from the rest of society" (Joseph Rowntree Foundation 2007, reporting on Dorling et al. 2007). In the United States, "Inequality in the United States is on the rise, whether measured in terms of wages, family incomes, or wealth and is much higher than that of other advanced countries" (Economic Policy Institute 2006). And, millions in the United States are outraged by a level of class inequality that has taken on obscene proportions not seen since the 1920s, where today 130,000 people have as much wealth as the poorest third of the country. Millions are appalled by rampant corruption, war profiteering, and drastic cuts in desperately needed social services while billions are being spent each week to destroy Iraq. (*International Socialist Review* 2007).

And, as Yates reminds us, in the United States,

> Over the years 1950 to 1970, for each additional dollar made by those in the bottom 90 percent of income earners, those in the top 0.01 percent received an additional $162. In contrast, from 1990 to 2002, for every added dollar made by those in the bottom 90 percent, those in the uppermost 0.01 percent (today around 14,000 households) made an additional $18,000. (Yates 2006)

Writing in August 2011, Myers points out that executive pay at 200 big US companies last year went up by an average 23 percent over 2009. The median executive salary was US$10.8 million. By contrast, "The average American worker was taking home $752 a week in late 2010, up a mere 0.5 percent from a year earlier. After inflation, workers were actually making less." Again with respect to the United States, Pizzigati (2011) notes:

> If corporations and households taking in $1 million or more in income each year were now paying taxes at the same annual rates as they did back in 1961, the IPS researchers found, the federal treasury would be collecting an additional $716 billion a year.
> In other words, if the federal government started taxing the wealthy and their corporations at the same rates in effect a half-century ago, the federal debt to investors would almost totally vanish over the next decade.

In education,

> despite the glowing reports from the White House and the Education Department, the most recent iteration of the National Assessment of Educational Progress, the test of fourth- and eighth-grade students commonly referred to as the nation's report card, is not reassuring. In 2002, when No Child Left Behind went into effect, 13 percent of the nation's black eighth-grade students were "proficient" in reading, the assessment's standard measure of grade-level competence. By 2005 (the latest data) that number had dropped to 12 percent. (Reading proficiency among white eighth-grade students dropped to 39 percent, from 41 percent.) The gap between economic classes isn't disappearing, either: in 2002, 17 percent of poor eighth-grade students (measured by eligibility for free or reduced-price school lunches) were proficient in reading; in 2005, that number fell to 15 percent. (Tough 2006)

And, globally, the poor die…and die young, and children through the developing world wish wistfully for an entry through the school gates, denied them by the new school fees demanded by the international clubs of the capitalist class—the International Monetary Fund, the World Trade Organization—with their Structural Adjustment Programmes (SAPs) and their demands that public services are no longer free but have to paid for (Hill and Kumar 2009; Hill and Rosskam 2009).

The current form of globalization is widening rather than narrowing the international poverty trap. Living standards in the least developed countries are now lower than thirty years ago. Inequalities within states have widened partly because of the generalized attack on workers' rights and trade unions, with restrictive laws passed hamstringing trade union actions (Rosskam 2006. See also Hill 2006a, 2009a, b; Hill and Kumar 2009; Hill and Rosskam 2009). And it is workers now being asked to pay for the crisis. Under capitalism, it usually is. It is workers and their trade unions voluntarily, or under pressure, accepting cuts in pay and conditions. It is workers and their families in the advanced capitalist world, whose children will pay back the state for the billions of dollars handed to industrial and finance capital.

The Growth of Education Quasi-Markets and Markets and the Growth of Educational Inequality

There is considerable data globally on how, within marketized or quasi-marketized education systems, poor schools have, by and large, got poorer (in terms of relative education results and in terms of total income) and how rich schools (in the same terms) have got richer.[3]

Whitty, Power, and Halpin (1998) examined the effects of the introduction of quasi-markets into education systems in United States, Sweden, England and Wales, Australia and New Zealand. Their conclusion is that one of the results of marketizing education is that increasing "parental choice" of schools, and/or setting up new types of schools, in effect increases school choice of parents and their children and thereby sets up or exacerbates racialized school hierarchies (Gillborn and Youdell 2000; Hill 2006a; Lewis, Hill, and Fawcett 2009).

Hirtt comments on the apparently contradictory education policies of Capital, "to adapt education to the needs of business and at the same time reduce state expenditure on education". He suggests that, for neoliberal Capital, "it is now possible and even highly recommendable to have a more polarized education system.... education should not try to transmit a broad common culture to the majority of future workers, but instead it should teach them some basic, general skills" (Hirtt 2004, 446. See also Hirtt 2009).

The Growth of Undemocratic (Un)accountability

Within education and other public services, business values and interests are increasingly substituted for democratic accountability and the collective voice. This applies at the local level, where, in Britain, the United States, Pakistan, and many other countries, for example, private companies—national or transnational—variously build, own, run, and govern state schools and other sections of local government educational services. There is an important democratic question here. Is it right to allow private providers of educational services, whether based inside a country or outside, for example, of India, or Brazil, or Britain. Where is the local democratic accountability? In the event of abuse or corruption or simply pulling out and closing down operations, where and how would those guilty be held to account?

This antidemocratization applies at national levels too. GATS locks countries into a system of regulations making it virtually impossible for governments to change policy, or, indeed, for voters to choose a new government with different policies (Grieshaber-Otto and Sanger 2002; Rikowski 2001a, 2003; Hill and Kumar 2009; Verger and Bonal 2009; Devidal 2009).

Detheorized Education and the Loss of Critical Thought

The increasing subordination and commodification of education, including university education have been well-documented (Levidow

2002; Giroux 2002, 2003). In my own work, I have examined how the British government has, in effect, expelled most potentially critical aspects of education, such as sociological and political examination of schooling and education, and questions of social class, "race" and gender, from the national curriculum for what is now, in England and Wales, termed "teacher training" (Hill 2001, 2005b, 2007). It was formerly called "teacher education." The change in name is important, both symbolically and in terms of actual accurate description of the new, "safe," sanitized, and detheorized education and training of new teachers.

"How to" has replaced "why to" in a technicist curriculum based on "delivery" of a quietist and overwhelmingly conservative set of "standards" for student teachers. Teachers are now, by and large, trained in skills rather than educated to examine the "whys" and the "why nots," and the contexts of curriculum, pedagogy, educational purposes, and structures and the effects these have on reproducing capitalist economy, society, and politics (Hill 2005a, 2010a; Hill and Boxley 2007).

SECTION 2
SOCIAL CLASS EXPLOITATION

The development of ("raced" and gendered) social-class-based "labour-power" and the subsequent extraction of 'surplus value" is the fundamental characteristic of capitalism. It is the primary explanation for economic, political, cultural, and ideological change. Social class is the essential form of capitalist exploitation and oppression and it is also the dominant form of capitalist exploitation and oppression.

What Is the Project of Global Capitalism at This Current Time of Capitalist Crisis?

The fundamental principle of capitalism is the sanctification of private (or corporate) profit based on the extraction of surplus labor (unpaid labor-time) as surplus value from the labor-power of workers. This is a creed of competition, not cooperation, between humans. It is a creed and practice of (racialized and gendered) class exploitation, exploitation by the capitalist class, the bourgeoisie. "By bourgeoisie is meant the class of modern capitalists, owners of the means of social production and employers of wage labor" (Engels 1888), of those who provide the profits through their labor, the working class, the appropriation of surplus value from the labor of the proletariat, "the class of modern wage laborers who, having no means of production of their own, are reduced to selling their labor power in order to live" (Engels 1888).

The State and Education: Labor Power, Surplus Value, Profit

In Britain and elsewhere, both Conservative and New Labour governments have attempted to "conform" both the *existing* teacher workforce and the *future* teacher workforce (i.e. student teachers) and *their* teachers, the reproducers of teachers—the teacher educators. Why conform the teachers and the teacher educators at all? Like poets, teachers are potentially dangerous. But poets are fewer and reading poetry is voluntary. Schooling is not. Teachers' work is *the production and reproduction of knowledge, attitudes and ideology.*

Glenn Rikowski (2001) develops a Marxist analysis based on an analysis of "labour power"—the capacity to labor. With respect to education, he suggests that teachers are the most dangerous of workers because they have a special role in shaping, developing and forcing *the single commodity on which the whole capitalist system rests: labor-power*. In the capitalist labor process, labor-power is transformed into value-creating *labor*, and, at a certain point, *surplus value*—value over-and-above that represented in the worker's wage—is created. *Surplus-value* is the first form of the existence of capital. It is the *lifeblood of capital*. Most importantly for the capitalist, is that part of the surplus-value forms his or her *profit*—and it is this that drives the capitalist on a personal basis.

In particular, it becomes clear, on this analysis, that the capitalist state will seek to destroy any forms of pedagogy that attempt to educate students regarding their real predicament—to create an awareness of themselves as future labor-powers and to underpin this awareness with critical insight that seeks to undermine the smooth running of the social production of labor-power. This fear entails strict control of teacher education, of the curriculum, of educational research.

The Salience and Essential Nature of Social Class Exploitation within Capitalism

Social class is the inevitable and defining feature of capitalist exploitation, whereas the various other forms of oppression are not *essential* to its nature and continuation, however much they are commonly functional to this—and however obviously racialized and gendered capitalist oppression is, in most countries. The face of poverty staring out from post-Katrina New Orleans was overwhelmingly black. It was overwhelmingly black working class. But it was also poor white working class. Richer black and white car owners drove away.

Within the educational curricula and pedagogy, and within the media (and, indeed, wherever resistant teachers and other cultural workers can find spaces), the existence of various and multiple forms of oppression and the similarity of their effects on individuals and communities should not disguise or weaken class analysis that recognizes the structural centrality of social class exploitation and conflict (Cole and Hill 2002; McLaren and Scatamburlo-D'Annibale 2004; Kelsh and Hill 2006a; Greaves, Hill, and Maisuria 2007; Hill 2008a). In capitalist society this has consequences for political and social strategy, for mobilization and for action.

As McLaren notes, "the key here is not to privilege class oppression over other forms of oppression but to see how Capitalist relations of production provide the ground from which other forms of oppression are produced" (McLaren 2001, 31; see also, Ebert and Zavarzadeh 2008).

McLaren and Farahmandpur note that "recognizing the 'class character' of education in Capitalist schooling, and advocating a socialist re-organization of Capitalist society (Krupskaya 1973) are two fundamental principles of a revolutionary critical pedagogy" (McLaren and Farahmandpur 2001, 299; see also McLaren and Farahmandpur 2005; Kelsh, Hill, and Macrine 2010).

Marxist and Postmodernist Analyses of Social Class

Outside the Marxist tradition, it is clear that many critics of class analysis confound class-consciousness with the fact of class—and tend to deduce the nonexistence of the latter from the "absence" of the former, or, if not "the absence," then the decline in salience in class consciousness in advanced capitalist countries. The collapse of many traditional signifiers of "working-classness" has led many to pronounce the demise of class, yet "Class inequality exists beyond its theoretical representation" (Skeggs 1997, 6).

Marx took great pains to stress that social class is distinct from economic class and necessarily includes a political dimension which, in the broadest sense, is "culturally" rather than "economically" determined. Class-consciousness, a "cultural phenomenon," does not follow automatically or inevitably from the fact of (economic) class position. In *The Poverty of Philosophy* (1847) Marx distinguishes a "class-in-itself" (class position) and a "class-for itself" (class consciousness) and, in *The Communist Manifesto* (Marx and Engels 1848), explicitly identified the "formation of the proletariat into a class" as *the* key political task facing the communists. In *The Eighteenth Brumaire of Louis Napoleon* (1852), Marx observes:

> In so far as millions of families live under economic conditions of existence that divide their mode of life, their interests and their cultural formation from those of the other classes and bring them into conflict with those classes, they form a class. In so far as these small peasant proprietors are merely connected on a local basis, and the identity of their interests fails to produce a feeling of community, national links, or a political organisation, they do not form a class. (Marx 1852 in Tucker 1974, 239)

The recognition by Marx that class consciousness is not necessarily or directly produced from the material and objective fact of class position, enables Marxists to acknowledge the wide range of contemporary influences that may (or may not) inform the subjective consciousness of identity—but in doing so, retain the crucial reference to the basic economic determinant of social experience.

The notion of an essential, unitary self was rejected, over a century and a half ago, by Marx in his *Sixth Thesis on Feuerbach*, where he stated

> But the human essence is no abstraction inherent in each single individual. In its reality it is the ensemble of the social relations. (Marx 1845 in Tucker 1978, 45)

The absence of class in postmodern theory actively contributes to the ideological disarmament of the working-class movement (Cole et al. 2001; Hill et al. 2002; Cole 2004; 2008; Rikowski et al. 1997; Kelsh, Hill, and Macrine 2010; Callinicos 1989; Eagleton 1996).

The fundamental significance of economic production for Marxist theory integrates a range of analytic concepts, which include the metanarrative of social development and therefore the proposal of viable transformatory educational and political projects. In contrast, the local, specific, and partial analyses that mark the limitations of postmodernism are accompanied by either a lack of, or opposition to, social-class-based policy.

SECTION 3
THE EDUCATION AND MEDIA: IDEOLOGICAL STATE APPARATUSES

Education and the media are the dominant ideological state apparatuses, though from the United States to Iran and elsewhere, organized religion is also assuming a more salient role. Each ideological state apparatus contains disciplinary repressive moments and effects.

One of its greatest achievements is that capital presents itself as natural, free, and democratic and that any attack on free-market neoliberal capitalism is damned as antidemocratic. Any attack on capitalism becomes characterized as an attack on world freedom and democracy itself. As does any attack on the "freedom of the Press," with its "mass production of ignorance" (Davies 2009).

The most powerful, restraint on capital (and the political parties funded and influenced by capitalists in their bountiful donations) is that capital needs to persuade the people that neoliberalism—competition, privatization, poorer standards of public services, greater inequalities between rich and poor, indeed, in the current period, workers paying for the bankers' crisis—are legitimate. If not, there is a delegitimation crisis, government and the existing system are seen through as grossly unfair and inhumane. It may also be seen as in the pocket of the international and/or national ruling classes and their local and national state weaponry. Certainly, mass anger currently (2011) in Greece is focussed against "The Troika" of the International Monetary Fund (IMF), the European Bank (EB) and the European Commission (EC).

To minimize this delegitimation, to ensure that the majority of the population considers the government and the economic system of private monopoly ownership legitimate, the state uses the ideological state apparatuses such as schools and colleges and the Media to "naturalise" capitalism—to make the existing status quo seem "only natural" (Hill 2009). Of course, if and when this doesn't work, the repressive state apparatuses kick in—sometimes literally, with steel-capped military boots, water cannons, draconian legislation and *coups d'etat*. Throughout Europe, the role of the police, especially the riot police, has become more pronounced, more evident, and more critiqued in social networking in particular, throughout the various mass demonstrations of 2008–2011 in, for example, Britain and Greece. In the demonstrations in Syntagma Square, Athens of the general strike of June 15, and of June 28–29 , 2011, the police used very brutal brutal tactics (Hill 2011a; Laskaridis 2011). On the first two-day general strike in recent Greek history, 28–29 June, police fired stun grenades, 3,000 canisters of tear gas, including into the metro station, and 500 demonstrators were hospitalized.

The term "State Apparatus" does not refer solely to apparatuses such as ministries and various levels of government. It applies to those societal apparatuses, institutions, and agencies that operate on behalf of, and maintain the existing economic and social relations of production. In other words, the apparatuses that sustain capital, capitalism and capitalists.

Educators and cultural workers are implicated in the process of economic, cultural, and ideological reproduction. (Kelsh and Hill 2006).

Ideological and Repressive State Apparatuses

Althusser argues that the ideological dominance of the ruling class is, like its political dominance, secured in and through definite institutional forms and practices: the ideological apparatuses of the state. As Althusser suggests, *every Ideological State Apparatus is also in part a Repressive State Apparatus*, (Althusser 1971; Hill 1989, 2001a, 2004, 2005b, 2009) punishing those who dissent:

> There is no such thing as a purely ideological apparatus... Schools and Churches use suitable methods of punishment, expulsion, selection etc., to "discipline" not only their shepherds, but also their flocks. (Althusser 1971, 138)

Ideological State Apparatuses have internal "coercive" practices (e.g., the forms of punishment, nonpromotion, displacement, being "out-of-favour" experienced by socialists and trade union activists / militants historically and currently across numerous countries). Similarly, *Repressive State Apparatuses* attempt to secure significant internal unity and wider social authority through ideology (e.g., through their ideologies of patriotism and national integrity). Every *Repressive State Apparatus* therefore has an ideological moment, propagating a version of common sense and attempting to legitimate it under threat of sanction.

Governments, and the ruling classes in whose interests they act, prefer to use the second form of state apparatuses—the Ideological State Apparatuses (ISAs). Changing the school and initial teacher education curriculum, abandoning "general studies" and "liberal studies" and horizon-broadening in the UK for working class "trade" and skilled worker students / apprentices in "Further Education" (vocational) colleges, is less messy than sending the troops onto the streets or visored baton-wielding police into strike-bound mining villages, or against peasant demonstrations or protests by the landless.

SECTION 4
CAPITALIST AGENDAS AND EDUCATION

Global Neoliberal capital and its international and national apparatuses have an antihuman and anticritical business agenda for education and the media.

The Contexts of Educational Change and the Neoliberal Project

The restructuring of the schooling and education systems across the world needs to be placed within the ideological and policy context of the links between capital, neoliberalism (with its combination of privatization, competitive markets in education characterized by selection and exclusion) and the rampant growth of the national and international inequalities.

The current crisis of capital accumulation—the declining rate of profit, has given an added urgency to the neoliberal project for education globally.

Cutting Public Expenditure

Not only have education and the media the function of creating and reproducing a labor force fit for capitalism, but capital also requires (in "normal times," not necessarily all the time) cutting public spending, cutting the social wage (the cost and value of the state pensions, health and education services) (Hill 2001a, b, 2003, 2004), reducing the "tax-take" as a proportion of gross domestic product. These are all subject to the variegations of short-term policy and local political considerations such as upcoming elections or mass demonstrations, the balance of class forces—the objective and subjective current labor-capital relation (relationship between the capitalist class and the working class and their relative cohesiveness, organization, leadership and will).

Capital and the Business of Education

The capitalist state has a capitalist agenda *for* education and a business plan *in* education (Hatcher 2001; Hill 2001c, 2004a, b). It also has a capitalist agenda *for education business*. The capitalist agenda *for* education centers on socially producing labor-power (people's capacity to labor) for capitalist enterprises. The capitalist agenda *in* education focuses on setting business "free" in education for profit-making.

The first aim is to ensure that schooling and education engage in ideological and economic reproduction. National state education and training policies in the capitalist agenda *for* education are of increasing importance for national capital. In an era of global capital, this is one of the few remaining areas for national state intervention—it is the site, suggests Hatcher (2001), where a state can make a difference. Thus, capital, first, requires education fit for business—to make schooling and further and higher education geared to producing the personality, ideological and economic requirements of capital.

Second, capital wants to make profits from education and other privatized public services such as water supply and healthcare. The second aim—the capitalist agenda *in* education—is for private enterprise, private capitalists, to make money out of it, to make private profit out of it, to control it, whether by outright control through private chains of schools/universities, by selling services to state funded schools and education systems, or by voucher systems through which taxpayers subsidize the owners of private schools.

Thus, business, first, makes education fit for business—to make schooling and further and higher education subordinate to the personality, ideological and economic requirements of capital, to make sure schools produce compliant, ideologically indoctrinated, procapitalist, effective workers.

The third education business plan for capital, the capitalist *for education business*, is to "bring the bucks back home," for governments in globally dominant economic positions (e.g., the UK, the United States), or in locally dominant economic positions (e.g., Australia, New Zealand, Brazil) to support locally based corporations (or, much more commonly, locally based transnational corporations) in profit taking from the privatization and neoliberalization of education services globally (Hill 2004, 2005a; Hill and Kumar 2009; Schugurensky and Davidson-Harden 2003, 2009).

Capitalist Responses to the Current Crisis: Not an End to Capitalism or Even to Neoliberal Capitalism

Talk of an end to neoliberalism is premature, so is talk of an end to capitalism (Hill 2008b). Criticism in the mainstream capitalist media and mainstream capitalist political parties is only of the excesses of capitalism, indeed, only the excesses of that form of capitalism—neoliberal capitalism—that has been dominant since the 1970s, the Thatcher-Reagan years—dominant in countries across the globe, and within the international capitalist organizations such as the World Bank, the International Finance Corporation, the World Trade Organization.

Premature, too, is talk of a return to a new Keynesianism, a new era of public sector public works, together with (in revulsion at neoliberalism's—in fact—capitalism's—excesses) a new Puritanism in private affairs / private industry.

The current intervention by governments across the globe to "save banks" can be seen as "socialism for the rich," a spreading of the pain and costs amongst all citizens/taxpayers to bail out the banks and bankers. Side by side with this bailing out of the banks (while retaining them as private—not nationalized institutions!) is the privatization, and individualization, of pain—the pain that will be felt in wallets and homes and workplaces throughout the capitalist countries, both rich and poor. Across Western Europe, neoliberal parties (whether Conservative and Liberal Democrat government in Britain, or Conservative governments in Ireland and Germany, or, social democratic governments in Spain and Greece, are "making savings" in order to pay for the bankers' crisis, the crisis of finance capital of 2009–2011. Governments across the capitalist world are cutting pensions, wages/salaries, local and nationally administered public and welfare services, and dismissing hundreds of thousands of public sector workers, and making them work longer before receiving a state pension. In Britain the only major difference between the Con-Dem (Conservative and Liberal Democrat) government policies on the fiscal crisis and the policies of the Labour party are on the speed of the cuts, and on Labour preferring to raise more of the costs of the crisis from taxation as opposed to spending cuts. But there isn't much difference.

Capitalist governments throughout the world will, unless successfully contested by class war and action from below, make the workers and their/our public services, pay for the crisis.

Capital and the parties it funds will seek to ensure that capital is resurgent, and that after what they see as this temporary "blip" in capitalist profitability, it will once again confidently bestride the world, though with less of an obvious smirk on its face, and with less obvious flashing of riches. At least for the time being.

In times such as these, of economic crisis and of the inevitable retrenchment, it will be the poor that the capitalist class tries to make pay for the crisis, in fact, not just the poor, but the middle and lower strata of the working class.

Controlling the Workers

And who better to "control" the workers, the workforce, to sell a deal—cuts in the actual wage (relative to inflation) and the social wage (cuts in the real value of benefits and of public welfare and social services)—but the former workers' parties such as the Labour party, or, in the United States, the party with (as with Labour in Britain) links to the trade union movement—the Democrats. (See *Against the Current* 2011). So US capital swung massively behind Obama in the US presidential election, and large sections of British capital have swing behind Gordon Brown and what is still regarded by many as a workers' party, or at least, the more social democratic of the major parties on offer. Better to control the workers when the cuts do come. And to return to a slightly less flashy form of capitalism— more regulated, but still the privatizing, neoliberal, managerializing, commodifying, neocolonial, and imperialistic capitalism in ideological conjunction with neoconservative state force.

SECTION 5

MARXISM AND RESISTANCE TO NEOLIBERAL CAPITAL

Forms and ideologies of resistance to neoliberal capital should be critiqued from a democratic, structuralist neo-Marxist political and ideological perspective.

The Right and Revised Social Democracy

Social democratic advances of "the thirty glorious years" of the 1940s to the 70s (the postwar boom in advanced capitalist economies) did succeed in some redistribution of life chances across a number of booming industrialized states. And what there was, was important— welfare states, pensions, state provided social housing, minimum wages, trade union recognition and rights, rights for workers at work, equal opportunities legislation on grounds of "race," gender, sexuality, disability. These are not to be sneered at. They have improved the lives of hundreds of millions.

But so much more could have been done![4] And needs to be done. And, since the 1970s in particular, with crises of capital accumulation, these hard-won rights, the "social wage," state comprehensive provision of services such as education, health, pensions, transport—have been widely degraded, privatized, and/or sold off to capital. This really is class war (Chomsky 1996; Harvey 2005), or more precisely, as Harvey exclaims, "class war from above." This class war from above has been successful, other than where street resistance has numbered millions, stalling government neoliberalizing plans.

Radical right and centrist ideology on education serves a society aiming only for the hegemony of the few and the entrenchment of privilege, whether elitist or supposedly meritocratic—not the promotion of economic and social justice with more equal educational and economic outcomes.

Structuralist Neo-Marxism, Agency and the State

The autonomy and agency available to individual teachers, teacher educators, schools and departments of education, journalists and other cultural workers is particularly circumscribed when faced with the structures of capital and its current neoliberal project for education—and its velvet glove, or not so velvet glove covering the mailed fist of suppression and repression.

The differences between the structuralist neo-Marxist theory (within a classical Marxist analysis) I am putting forward here, and culturalist neo-Marxism are that culturalist neo-Marxists, such as Michael Apple, in their analyses, overemphasize autonomy and agency in a number of ways. First, they overemphasize the importance of ideology, of the cultural domain. Second, and connectedly, they rate too highly the importance of discourse. Third, they lay too much store on the relative autonomy of individuals, on how effective human agency is likely to be when faced with the force of the state, without overall, major change and transformation of the economy, and society. Fourth, they overemphasize the relative autonomy of state apparatuses such as education, or particular schools. Fifth, they overestimate the relative autonomy of the political region of the state from the economic—the autonomy of government from capital (see Cole et al. 2001; Hill 2001a, 2005b). In Apple's case (e.g. Apple 2004, 2005, 2006) they also underplay the salience of social class—racialized and gendered and layered though it is, as the primary and the essential form of exploitation in capitalist society (Kelsh 2001; Kelsh and Hill 2006)[5].

To use concepts derived from Louis Althusser, the autonomy of the education policy / political region of the state from the economic has been straightjacketed. There are, in many states, greater and greater restrictions on the ability of cultural workers and teachers to use their pedagogical spaces for emancipatory purposes.

Spaces do exist for counterhegemonic struggle, whatever space does exist should be exploited. Whatever we can do, we must do, however fertile or unfertile the soil at any given moment in any particular place. But schools and colleges, and newsrooms and studios are not the only place for resistance and transformation. In the current crisis of capital, the streets are, too. And the workplace, the social group, the social and community organization, the trade union.

SECTION 6

CRITICAL EDUCATION FOR ECONOMIC AND SOCIAL JUSTICE

Critical education for economic and social justice can play a role in resisting the depredations and the "common-sense" of global neoliberal capital and play a role in developing class-consciousness and an egalitarian sustainable future.

Critical education for economic and social justice is where teachers and other cultural workers act as critical transformative and public intellectuals within and outside of sites of economic, ideological, and cultural reproduction. Such activity is both deconstructive and reconstructive, offering a Utopian politics of anger, analysis and hope based on a materialized socialist, or revolutionary, critical pedagogy that recognizes, yet challenges, the strength of the structures and apparatuses of capital.

Such activity encompasses activity within different arenas of resistant and revolutionary activity. These arenas encompass

- Activism within the cultural sites of schooling/education and the media within the workforce, within the curriculum / knowledge validation systems, and within pedagogy/social relations.
- Activism locally outside of these sites, exposing the capitalist reproductive nature of those sites both per se, and activism locally, linked to other sites of economic, ideological and cultural contestation, mobilizations and struggle.
- Activism within mass movements, United Fronts, and within democratic Marxist/Socialist groupings, factions and organizations.

The Role of Intellectuals and the Politics of Educational Transformation

What role can intellectuals such as educators and other cultural workers play in the struggle for economic and social justice?

1. Support the current system?
2. Ignore it?
3. Play with the postmodernists in irony and pastiche, body performativity and transgression, textual and semiotic deconstruction, shorn of any solidaristic reconstructive urge or capacity (however enjoyable and individually liberating they can be)?
4. Or should education and other cultural workers organize in opposition to "the excesses" of capital, seeking its modification, seeking to "reform" it? Or should resistant counterhegemonic educators and cultural workers seek its replacement, its transformation. But its transformation into what - a religious state, a theocracy, Christian, or Zionist, or Islamic, or Hindu or whatever? Or its replacement by democratic socialism?

These are four alternatives for intellectuals and educators—and, indeed by all workers who are aware of such choices.

Within classrooms, critical transformative intellectuals seek to enable student teachers and teachers (and school students) to critically evaluate a range of salient perspectives and ideologies—including critical reflection itself—while showing a commitment to egalitarianism. Critical pedagogy must remain self-critical, and critique its own presumed role as the metatruth of educational criticism. This does not imply forced acceptance or silencing of contrary perspectives. But it *does* involve a privileging of egalitarian and emancipatory perspectives. But the aim is not egalitarian indoctrination.

Revolutionary Critical Pedagogy

McLaren and Farahmandpur (2005) ask, "how do we organize teachers and students against domestic trends [e.g. the deepening inequalities and exploitation under Capital]...and also enable them to link these trends to global capitalism and the new imperialism? What pedagogical discourses and approaches can we use?" They cite the five pillars of popular education articulated by Deborah Brandt (1991):

> First, critical pedagogy must be a collective process that involves utilizing a dialogical (i.e., Freirean) learning approach.

Second, critical pedagogy has to be critical; that is, it must locate the underlying causes of class exploitation and economic oppression within the social, political, and economic arrangements of capitalist social relations of production.

Third...it reconstructs and makes the social world intelligible by transforming and translating theory into concrete social and political activity.

Fourth, critical pedagogy should be participatory. It involves building coalitions among community members, grassroots movements, church organizations and labor unions.

Finally, critical pedagogy needs to be a creative process by integrating elements of popular culture (i.e., drama, music, oral history, narratives) as educational tools that can successfully raise the level of political consciousness of students and teachers. (McLaren and Farahmandpur 2005, 9)[6]

Radical Left Principles for Education Systems

It is important to develop schools and education systems with the following characteristics (Hill 2002b, 2010a; Hillcole Group 1991, 1997; Hill and Boxley 2007):

- to level up education workers' pay, rights, and securities rather than level down to a lowest common denominator. This applies both within countries and globally.
- to widen access to good quality education (by increasing its availability within countries and globally. Widening access to underrepresented and underachieving groups, can, with positive action and support, play a part in reducing educational inequalities between groups).
- to secure vastly increased equality of educational outcomes.
- to organize comprehensive provision (i.e., comprehensive, nonselective schooling with no private or selective or religiously exclusive provision of schooling).
- to retain and enhance local and national democratic control over schooling and education democratic community control over education.
- to use the local and national state to achieve an economically just (defined as egalitarian), antidiscriminatory society, rather than simply an inegalitarian meritocratic focus on equal opportunities to get to very unequal outcomes.
- to recognize and seek to improve education systems that are dedicated to education for wider individual and social purposes than the

production of hierarchicalized, ideologically quiescent and compliant workers and consumers in a neliberal/liberalized world.

SECTION 7
ARENAS FOR RESISTANCE

What education, and changes to the education systems of the capitalist world can do to ameliorate or to challenge the currently intensified "class war from above" is both important and limited. This is, as ever, subject to resistance and the balance of class forces (itself related to developing levels of class consciousness, political consciousness, and political organization and leadership). Resistance is possible, and is erupting in raw anger, general strikes, mass mobilizations, televized pictures of demonstrating students, workers and trade unions from the mass mobilizations from France, to Britain, to Portugal, to Greece, to Ireland, and who knows where next. Demonstrations, strikes, anger, outrage at cuts, will increase, perhaps dramatically, in the coming period. To repeat, to be successful instead of inchoate, such anger and political activism needs to be focussed, and organized. In such circumstances, the forces of the Marxist Left in countries across the globe, need to put aside decades old enmities, doctrinal, organization and strategic disputes. As Hearse (2009) notes,

> The left cannot adopt a spontaneist, wait and see attitude, hoping for a working class upsurge and the appearance by some magical process of a broad left alternative. Class politics, of the kind provided by Respect, aids the development of class consciousness and trade union struggle.

Of course, regroupment by itself just organizes current activists and supporters. Regroupment needs to be followed by, and accompanied by, recruitment. At this particular moment in the crisis of capital accumulation and the actual and potential for loosening the chains of ideology / false consciousness promulgated by knowledge workers in the (witting or unwitting) service of capital. And now it's not just the potential that socialist activists have been talking about and promoting for decades...it's happening.

The signs of struggle, the scale of anticapitalist struggle, the raised hopes and understandings of new generations of school children, students, public sector workers, and also private sector workers.

In Britain, students are revolting! And quite rightly too. From the 52,000 strong demonstration in Westminster, London, on

November 10, 2010 (which went via an occupation of the Millbank Tory party HQ—not your average day at the office!) to disciplined and organized student occupations, sit-ins and teach-ins at Leeds, Manchester, Sussex, Middlesex and other Universities, through subsequent days of action, to student protests across Europe—Paris, Lisbon, Athens, Dublin. Saying, chanting, acting, demanding, "No to Education Cuts", "No to (increased) Charges for Education", "Education should be Free!" The November 10, 2010 demonstration, organized by the National Union of Students and the college lecturers union, UCU, was the biggest student demonstration in a generation.

The next round was on Wednesday, November 24, 2010, "Day X." 130,000 students at universities, further education colleges, sixth forms and secondary schools walked out, and demonstrating against cuts and tuition fees, in a national day of action. Some marched on their local Tory party offices, just as 300 students and trade unionists in Barnet marched earlier on the local Conservative party HQ in Finchley!

The next "Day X" was the day of the vote in parliament on December 9, 2010, over the fees increase. There'll be another massive demonstration. The Facebook group "Tuition Fee Vote: March on Parliament" had 2,300 "attending" within 45 minutes of being set up! Students and workers realize this is a common struggle—Day X was supported by the three main anticuts umbrella organizations, The NSSN (National Shop Stewards Network), the RtW (Right to Work campaign) and the CoR (Campaign of Resistance) whose November 27 London rally brought together organizations, socialist/Marxist parties and groups, national organizations, local anticuts groups, students, and school students.

One of the most remarkable and inspiring speeches, by 15 year old Barnaby, on Youtube at http://www.youtube.com/watch?v=Crg zpPvJxmQ&feature=player_embedded#! explicitly linked the student struggle to wider struggles and workers struggles.

This time round, students are saying much more than "No Fees." Saying and chanting "Students and Workers Unite and Fight", "We are Part of a Wider Struggle!" A recognition that our struggle is a common struggle for a better, a fairer, not a diminished and crueller, society. Facebook sites such as "School and FE students Against the Cuts" have brilliant, basic, bold slogans—"Education for the masses not just for the ruling classes!"

Another powerful speech at the CoR rally was by John McDonnell, one of the very few remaining socialist MPs left in the Labour party (available online at http://www.youtube.com/watch?v=nl0PMdUMOPw&feature=player_embedded).

> This generation was meant to be apathetic, only interested in careers.... They've taught my generation, that we have been too long on our knees. And it's time to stand up and fight. You students (who were arrested during Millbank and the kettling) You are not the criminals...The real criminals are the ones attacking our education system...say this to the TUC, it is time to play your role! We want co-ordinated industrial action, co-ordinated strike action across the country. It is time for generalized strike action. We are posing an alternative.... When Parliament refuses to represent. When politicians lie. When governments seek to ignore us...We have no other alternative but to take to the streets. And direct action to bring them down. Take to the streets.

Student demonstrations, far exceeding in size the expectations of their organizers, stimulated, provoked, national trade union action against the cuts, for example against cuts in pension entitlement. The March 26, 2011 national demonstration in London was the largest trade union march/demonstration since the Second World War, between 250,000 and 500,000 marchers (BBC 2011; Curtis 2011; *Socialist Party* 2011; *Socialist Worker* 2011), the largest in Britain since the antiwar in Iraq demonstration in 2003.

It was followed by "J30", the June 30, which was even larger and was significant not just because of its huge size, but because it was a coordinated national action by a number of different public sector trade unions involving, for example, teachers, lecturers, civil servants, local government workers . Around three quarters of a million were on the streets of London, and around 100,000 in cities and towns across Britain (Counterfire 2011).

Local anticuts movements, occupations, sit-ins, demonstrations, and national coalitions such as the Coalition of Resistance, and (smaller national coordinating organizations such as the National Shop Stewards Network, bring together workers, trade unionists, different socialist groups, students, teachers, Old Age Pensioners—the people!—black, white, men, women, people of all religions and sexualities—in a common fight for equality.

What the bankers' crisis, the current crisis of neoliberal capitalism, "making the workers pay for the crisis," the millionaire Con-Dem millionaire government is doing, is stoking raw anger. Not just among mainly middle-class university students, but among working-class students at further education colleges and sixth form colleges.

As *Counterfire* (a split-off from the Socialist Workers' party in Britain) analyses,

> The unions are central to the struggle, and they are likely to grow as the struggle rises. But they are not, and cannot be, the whole of the struggle
> The anti-cuts movement is not a movement of the unions. It is a movement in which the unions are central, but it extends far beyond them to the working class as a whole.... What really matters about J30 is the dynamic fusion of the mass strike and the mass demonstration. And it was the demos that energised the strike. From Cairo, to Athens, to London, the mass strike and the mass demonstration have become political twins.
> A new kind of mass movement is rising. It is a movement of working class resistance to unprecedented austerity and privatisation. The unions are therefore central, but because the unions have been much weakened, the movement is far broader... The movement draws on the union tradition, but also on the tradition of the anti-capitalist movement and the street protests. These two traditions are now cross-*fertilising*. The result is a new birth of mass class-based resistance.

But resistance needs organization and leadership—mass, inchoate, angry, unfocussed action with limited demands such as civil rights, removal of a leader (as in Egypt, Tunisia, Libya, Syria) has its weaknesses. While reforms, minimum demands, are hugely necessary, how far should a revolution go? Should it be a political revolution (e.g., a bourgeois democratic revolution, focusing on political demands such as political and civil rights)? Or should it be a social and economic revolution? (with a redistribution of power, wealth, and income, following from a socialist replacement of capitalist economic and social relations, of capitalism? This is a distinction shown vividly in the Ken Loach film on the Irish Independence Struggle, *The Wind That Shakes the Barley*).

My own interpretation of Marxism is Trotskyist, in particular the democratic and pluralist version subscribed to by the Fourth International, sometimes known as the USFI (Unified Secretariat of the Fourth International) and by its British organization, Socialist Resistance.

Trotskyist educators, cultural workers, activists argue (Trotsky 1922, 1938; Bensaid 2009) for

1. A commitment to permanent revolution, that is to extend beyond political rights / human rights / social justice (political revolution)

(historically the bourgeois/capitalist revolution) to social and economic revolution (nationalizations, workers control, workers' assemblies, accountability of elected officials);
2. Through "the /a party" with party organization and leadership;
3. Through pluralist democratic internal party organization, which welcomes different "factions" / organized views / dissent / tolerance and welcoming of alternative views;
4. With a commitment to anti bureaucratization of the state and party/opposition to the party-class, and party-state, in favor of mass workers' democracy;
5. With a democratic Marxist organization of work and the state;
6. Within an understanding of the necessity for and a commitment to internationalism;
7. Making, within the current capitalist system, demands that are a "Transitional Programme" (Trotsky 1938) (combining "reformist" minimum demands with maximum demands (e.g., jobs for all), demands that capitalism/capitalists would deny and that they would regard as impossible.

> There is no such thing as a "spontaneous" upsurge. The potential for mass resistance can be realized only through the work of thousands of activists. And effective work depends on understanding the mass movement, the state of the working class, and the character and probable trajectory of the struggle. (Counterfire 2011)

Through well organized and focused nonsectarian campaigns organized around class and anticapitalist issues,[7] those committed to economic and social equality and justice and environmental sustainability can work towards local, national, and international campaigns, towards an understanding that we are part of a massive force—the force of the international- and growing- (see Harman 2002; Hill 2003; Hearse 2009; Counterfire 2011)[8] working class—with a shared understanding that, at the current time, it is the global neoliberal form of capitalism—indeed, capitalism itself—that shatters the lives, bodies, and dreams of billions. And that it can be replaced.

Notes

1. Many, though not all, Marxist economists and analysts agree with Dave Packer and Fred Leplat that the current crisis is "a deep structural crisis of capital accumulation". Wade notes that "the rate of profit of non-financial corporations fell steeply between 1950–73 and 2000–06—in the US, by roughly a quarter. In response firms 'invested' increasingly in financial speculation (Packer and Leplat 2008: 11)." The "falling

rate of profit thesis" is contested, for example, by Dumenil and Levy (2011) who cite more complex explanations. Michael Roberts is a proponent of the "falling rate of profit thesis," in both, his book The Great Recession, (2011a) and in his discussion of competing theories of the current crisis of capitalism, (2011b).
2. Hearse (2009) continues, "The facts are astounding. Contrary to the delusions of the free-market fundamentalists, the Thatcher/Reagan revolution has come at a great cost to the working and middle classes. In the US, the top one per cent have seen a 78 per cent increase in their share of national income since 1979 with the bottom 80 per cent of the population experiencing a 15 per cent fall."
3. See Gillborn and Mirza 2000; Hill 2008a, 2009e, f, 2011 on (racialized and gendered) social class inequalities in income, wealth, and educational attainment in England and Wales—and how much inequality has increased in Britain since 1979. For a discussion on competing theoretical analyses—and programmatic implications—between "class theorists" such as myself and Mike Cole on the one hand, and "race" based theorists—critical race theorists—such as Davis Gillborn- see Cole 2009b, c, 2011; Gillborn 2008; Hill 2008a, 2009e, f, 2011a. See Harris 2007, for a critique of the super-rich, 'Richistan' in the USA.
4. For Left critiques of New Labour education policy in Britain, see Hill 2006b, 2007; Jones 2003; Tomlinson 2004, Green 2011.
5. This must not be seen as an *ad hominem/* personal attack on Michael W. Apple, the most influential of all radical left USA educational critics, in his analysis of the relationship between capitalism and education. See, for example, Apple 2004. His attacks on classical Marxists, and revolutionary Marxism, are contained, for example, in Apple 2005, 2006. But he *is* a left reformist. For critiques of his work, see Farahmandpur 2004; Kelsh and Hill 2006; Rikowski 2006.
6. In *Capitalists and Conquerors: A Critical pedagogy Against Empire* (2005), McLaren develops this. See, also, McLaren 2001, 2005; McLaren and Farahmandpur 2001, 2005; Hill 2009c; Macrine, McLaren and Hill 2009. Recent UK books on a social justice curriculum for primary/elementary schools are Cole 2009a; Hill and Robertson 2009.
7. Harman (2002) suggests that "what matters now is for this (new) generation (of activists) to connect with the great mass of ordinary workers who as well as suffering under the system have the collective strength to fight it" (p. 40) Moody (2002) concurs—"By itself, and despite its ability to breach police lines, this 'movement of movements' lacks the social weight to carry out the very task it has set itself—the dismantling of the mechanisms of capitalist globalisation" (p. 293). See Hill 2008b for a brief discussion of resistance, and 2010b for detail on student resistance in Britain in late 2010.

8. As Hearse (2009) notes, "Socialism is not inevitable but only the working class can develop the consciousness and organisation to bring it about. That certainty remains at the heart of socialist strategy and tactics."

References

Against the Current. 2011. "Budget Woes, Class Wars." *International Viewpoint*, 36. Accessed on July 20, 2011 at http://www.internationalviewpoint.org/spip.php?article2140.

Althusser, Louis. 1971. "Ideology and State Apparatuses" in *Lenin and Philosophy and Other Essays*. London: New Left Books.

Apple, M.W. 2004. *Ideology and Curriculum, 25th Anniversary 3rd Edition*. New York: Routledge.

———. 2005. "Audit Cultures, Commodification, and Class and Race Strategies in Education." *Policy Futures in Education* 3(4): 379–399.

———. "Review Essay: Rhetoric and Reality in Critical Educational Studies in the United States." *British Journal of Sociology of Education* 27(5) (2006): 679–687.

BBC News. 2011. "Anti-Cuts March: Tens of Thousands at London Protest." Accessed on March 26, 2011 at http://www.bbc.co.uk/news/uk-12864353

Bensaid, D. 2009. *Strategies of Resistance and "Who are the Trotskyists?"* London: Resistance Books.

Bensaid, D. et al. 2009. "From the LCR to the NPA." *International Viewpoint*, 408. Accessed on May 2009 at http://www.internationalviewpoint.org/spip.php?article1585.

Brandt, D. 1991. *To Change This House: Popular Education under the Sandinistas*. Toronto: Between the Lines.

Callinicos, A. 1989. *Against Postmodernism: A Marxist Critique*. Cambridge, UK: Polity.

Chomsky, N. 1996. *Class War—the Attack on Working People*. London: Pluto Press.

Cole, M. 2008. *Marxism and Educational Theory: Origins and Issues*. London: Routledge.

Cole, M., 2009a. ed. *Equality in the Secondary School: Promoting Good Practice Across the Curriculum*. London: Continuum.

Cole, M. 2009b. *Critical Race Theory and Education: A Marxist Response*. London: Palgrave Macmillan.

Cole, M. 2009c. "On 'White Supremacy' and Caricaturing, Misrepresenting and Dismissing Marx and Marxism: A Response to David Gillborn's 'Who's Afraid of Critical Race Theory in Education.'" *Journal for Critical Education Policy Studies* 7(1). Accessed on February 22, 2010 at http://www.jceps.com/index.php?pageID=article&articleID=143.

Cole, M. 2011. *Racism and Education in the UK and the US: Towards a Socialist Alternative*. New York and London: Palgrave Macmillan. Forthcoming.

Cole, M et al. 2011. "Red Chalk: On Schooling, Capitalism and Politics." Brighton: Institute for Education Policy Studies. Accessed on June 13, 2011 at http://www.ieps.org.uk/redchalk.php.

Chossudovsky, M. 2005. *"The Globalisation of Poverty and the New World Order"* second edition. Montreal, Canada: Centre for Research on Globalization. Accessed on September 12, 2011 at http://globalresearch.ca/globaloutlook/GofP.html.

Counterfire. 2011. "J30: The Rise of a New Kind of Mass Movement?" *Counterfire*. Accessed on August 13, 2011 at http://www.counterfire.org/index.php/articles/51-analysis/12800-j30-the-rise-of-a-new-kind-of-mass-movement

Curtis, B. 2011. "Massive Demonstration in London Against Government Cuts." *International Viewpoint Online*. March 28. Accessed on April 15, 2011 at http://socialistresistance.org/1870/massive-demonstration-in-london-against-government-cuts.

Davies, N. 2009. *Flat Earth News*. London: Vintage Books.

Devidal, P. 2009. "Trading Away Human Rights? The GATS and the Right to Education: A Legal Perspective" in *Global Neoliberalism and Education and its Consequences* edited by D. Hill and R. Kumar. New York: Routledge.

Dorling, D. 2010a. "Divided Britain's Growing Inequality." *Socialist Worker*, 2203. Accessed on June 15, 2011 at http://www.socialistworker.co.uk/art.php?id=21308.

———. 2010b. *Injustice: Why Social Inequality Persists*. Bristol: Policy Press.

———. 2010c. "Why Social Inequality Exists." Video on Youtube. Accessed on June 20, 2011 at http://www.youtube.com/watch?v=MBzYYeAolAA.

Dorling, D., J. Rigby, B. Wheeler, D. Ballas, B. Thomas, E. Fahmy, D. Gordon and R. Lupton. 2007. *Poverty, Wealth and Place in Britain 1968 to 2005*. Bristol: The Policy Press on behalf of the Joseph Rowntree Foundation.

Dumenil, G. and D. Levy. 2004. *Capital Resurgent: Roots of the Neoliberal Revolution*. London: Harvard University Press.

Dumenil, G. and D. Levy. 2011. *The Crisis of Neoliberalism*. Cambridge, MA: Harvard University Press.

Eagleton, T. 1996. *The Illusions of Postmodernism*. London: Wiley-Blackwell.

Economic Policy Institute. 2006. "Wealth Inequality is Vast and Growing." August 23. Accessed on May 13, 2011 at http://www.epi.org/content.cfm/webfeatures_snapshots_20060823.

Engels, F. 1888. Note to *The Communist Manifesto 1888*. English edition. Accessed on April 20, 2011 at http://www.anu.edu.au/polsci/marx/marx.html.

Farahmandpur, R. 2004. "Essay Review: A Marxist Critique of Michael Apple's Neo-Marxist Approach to Education Reform." *Journal of Critical Education Policy Studies* 2(1). Accessed on November 10, 2010 at http://www.jceps.com/index.php?pageID=article&articleID=24.

Frank, R. 2007. *Richistan: A Journey Through the American Wealth Boom and the Lives of the New Rich*. New York: Crown Publishers.

Gillborn, D. and H. Mirza. 2000. *Educational Inequality: Mapping Race, Class and Gender*. London: Ofsted.

Gillborn, D and D. Youdell. *Rationing Education: Policy, Practice, Reform and Equity*. Buckingham, UK: Open University Press.

Giroux, H. 2002. "The Corporate War Against Higher Education." *Workplace: A Journal of Academic Labour* 5(1). Accessed on September 20, 2010 at http://www.louisville.edu/journal/workplace/issue5p1/giroux.html

———. 2003. "Selling out Higher Education." *Policy Futures in Education* 1(1): 17–200. Accessed on March 11, 2010 at http://dx.doi.org/10.2304/pfie.2003.1.1.6

Greaves, N., D. Hill, and A. Maisuria. 2007. "Embourgeoisment, Immiseration, Commodification—Marxism Revisited: A Critique of Education in Capitalist Systems." *Journal for Critical Education Policy Studies* 5(1). Accessed on May 12, 2010 at http://www.jceps.com/index.php?pageID=article&articleID=83

Green, A. 2011. *Blair's Legacy: Thirteen Years of New Labour*. London: Palgrave MacMillan.

Grieshaber-Otto, J. and M. Sanger. 2002. *Perilous Lessons: The Impact of the WTO Service Agreement (GATS) on Canadian Public Education*. Ottowa, ON, Canada: Canadian Center for Policy Alternatives.

Harman, C. 2002. "The Workers of the World." *International Socialism*, 96(Autumn): 3–45. Accessed on March 6, 2009 at http://pubs.socialistreviewindex.org.uk/isj96/harman.htm

Harris, R. 2007. "Welcome to Richistan, USA." *The Observer*. Accessed on June 20, 2011 at http://observer.guardian.co.uk/world/story/0,,2131974,00.html

Harvey, D. 2005. *A Brief History of Neoliberalism*. Oxford, UK: Oxford University Press.

Hatcher, R. 2001. "Getting Down to the Business: Schooling in the Globalised Economy." *Education and Social Justice* 3(2): 45–59.

Hearse, P. 2009. "Has Working Class Consciousness Collapsed?" *International Viewpoint*. Accessed on August 23, 2011 at http://www.internationalviewpoint.org/spip.php?article1516

Hill, D. 2001a. "State Theory and the Neoliberal Reconstruction of Teacher Education: A Structuralist Neo-Marxist Critique of Postmodernist, Quasi-Postmodernist, and Culturalist Neo-Marxist Theory." *British Journal of Sociology of Education* 22(1): 137–57.

———. 2001b. "*The Third Way in Britain: New Labour's Neoliberal Education Policy*." Paper presented at the Conference Marx 111, Universite de Sorbonne/ Nanterre, Paris, September. Accessed on May 7, 2011 at http://www.ieps.org.uk

———. 2002a. "Globalisation, Education and Critical Action." *EDUcate: A Quarterly on Education and Development* (The Sindh Education Foundation, Pakistan) 2(1): 42–45.

———. 2002b. "The Radical Left and Education Policy: Education for Economic and Social Justice." *Education and Social Justice* 4(3): 41–51.

———. 2003. "Global Neoliberalism, the Deformation of Education and Resistance." *Journal for Critical Education Policy Studies* 1(1). Accessed on May 12, 2010 at http://www.jceps.com/index.php?pageID=articlean darticleID=7

———. 2004. "Books, Banks and Bullets: Controlling Our Minds—the Global Project of Imperialistic and Militaristic Neoliberalism and its Effect on Education Policy." *Policy Futures* 2(3): 504–522. Accessed on April 17, 2010 at http://www.wwwords.co.uk/pdf/freetoview.asp?j=pfie&vol=2&issue=3&year=2004&article=6_Hill_PFIE_2_3-4_web

———. 2005a. "Critical Education for Economic and Social Justice." In *Teaching Peter McLaren: Paths of Dissent*, edited by M. Pruyn and L. Huerta-Charles, New York: Peter Lang, 146–85.

———. 2005b. "State Theory and the Neoliberal Reconstruction of Schooling and Teacher Education" in *Critical Theories, Radical Pedagogies and Global Conflicts*, edited by G. Fischman, P. McLaren, H. Sünker and C. Lankshear, Lanham, MD: Rowman & Littlefield, 23–51.

———. 2006a. "Education Services Liberalization." In *Winners or Losers? Liberalizing Public Services*, edited by E. Rosskam, Geneva: International Labour Organisation 3–54.

———. 2006b. "New Labour's Education Policy." In *Education Studies: Issues and Critical Perspectives*, edited by D. Kassem, E. Mufti and J. Robinson, Buckingham: Open University Press, 73–86.

———. 2007. "Critical Teacher Education, New Labour in Britain, and the Global Project of Neoliberal Capital." *Policy Futures* 5(2): 204–25. Accessed on May 18, 2010 at http://www.wwwords.co.uk/rss/abstract.asp?j=pfie&aid=2998

———. 2008a. "Caste, Race and Class: A Marxist Critique of Caste Analysis, Critical Race Theory; and Equivalence (or Parallelist) Explanations of Inequality." *Radical Notes* (Delhi, India). Accessed on October 10, 2009 at http://radicalnotes.com/component/option,com_frontpage/Itemid,1/]

———. 2008b. "Crisis, the Bankers' Bailout, and Socialist Analysis/ Strategy." *Radical Notes* (Delhi, India). Accessed on October 12, 2009 at http://radicalnotes.com/journal/2008/11/24/crisis-the-bankers-bailout-and-socialist-analysisstrategy/

———. ed. 2009a. *Contesting Neoliberal Education: Public Resistance and Collective Advance*. London and New York: Routledge.

———. ed. 2009b. *The Rich World and the Impoverishment of Education: Diminishing Democracy, Equity and Workers' Rights*. New York: Routledge.

―――. 2009c. "Theorising Politics and the Curriculum: Understanding and Addressing Inequalities through Critical Pedagogy and Critical Policy Analysis" in *Equality in the Primary School: Promoting Good Practice across the Curriculum*, edited by D. Hill and L. Helavaara Robertson. London: Continuum.

―――. 2009d. "Culturalist and Materialist Explanations of Class and 'Race': Critical Race Theory, Equivalence/ Parallelist Theory and Marxist Theory." *Cultural Logic: An Electronic Journal of Marxist Theory and Practice*. Accessed on November 15, 2010 at http://clogic.eserver.org/2009/2009.html

―――. 2009e. "Race and Class in Britain: a Critique of the Statistical Basis for Critical Race Theory in Britain: And Some Political Implications." *Journal for Critical Education Policy Studies* 7(2). Accessed on October 22, 2010 at http://www.jceps.com/index.php?pageID=article&articleID=159

―――. 2010a. "A Socialist Manifesto for Education." *Socialist Resistance Online*. Accessed on June 10, 2011 at http://socialistresistance.org/?p=905 and http://rikowski.wordpress.com/2010/04/08/statement-and-education-policy-manifesto-by-dave-hill/

―――. 2010b. "Students Are Revolting: Education Cuts and Resistance." Socialist Resistance Online. Accessed on June 20, 2011 at http://socialistresistance.org/1135/students-are-revolting-education-cuts-and-resistance; and http://radicalnotes.com/journal/2010/12/03/students-are-revolting-education-cuts-and-resistance/

―――. 2011a. "Caste, 'Race' and Class Inequality: A Marxist Analysis" in *School Education, Pluralism and Marginality: Comparative Perspectives*, edited by C. Sleeter, S.B. Upadhyay, A.K. Mishra, and S. Kumar. New Delhi, India: Orient Blackswan.

―――. 2011b. Athens General Strike. Accessed on June 12, 2011 at http://hoverepublic.blogspot.com/2011/06/athens-general-strike.html and http://birminghamresist.wordpress.com/2011/06/18/greece-anger-on-the-streets-an-eyewitness-report/

Hill, D. and S. Boxley. 2007. "Critical Teacher Education for Economic, Environmental and Social Justice: An Ecosocialist Manifesto." *Journal for Critical Education Policy Studies* 5(2). Accessed on April 10, 2010 at http://www.jceps.com/index.php?pageID=article&articleID=96

Hill, D. and R. Kumar, eds. 2009. *Global Neoliberalism and Education and Its Consequences*. New York: Routledge.

Hill, D. and Leena H. Robertson, eds. 2009. *Equality in the Primary School: Promoting Good Practice across the Curriculum*. London: Continuum.

Hill, D., P. McLaren, M. Cole, and G. Rikowski, eds. 2002. *Marxism Against Postmodernism in Educational Theory*. Lanham, MD: Lexington Press.

Hill, D. and E. Rosskam, eds. 2009. *The Developing World and State Education: Neoliberal Depredation and Egalitarian Alternatives*. New York: Routledge.

Hillcole Group. 1991. *Changing the Future: Redprint for Education.* London: Tufnell Press.
———. 1991. *Rethinking Education and Democracy: A Socialist Alternative for the Twenty-First Century.* London: Tufnell Press.
Hirtt, N. 2004. "Three Axes of Merchandisation." *European Educational Research Journal* 3(2): 442–453. Accessed on January 12, 2011 at http://www.wwwords.co.uk/eerj/
———. 2009. "Markets and Education in the Era of Globalized Capitalism" in *Global Neoliberalism and Education and its Consequences*, edited by D. Hill and R. Kumar. New York: Routledge.
International Socialist Review. 2007. "Letter from the Editors." *ISR Online.* London: Socialist Workers Party. Accessed on January 16, 2011 at http://www.isreview.org/issues/54/editorletter.shtml
Jones, K. 2003. *Education in Britain: 1944 to the Present.* Cambridge, UK: Polity.
Joseph Rowntree Foundation. 2007. *Poverty and Wealth across Britain, 1968–2005.* York, UK: Joseph Rowntree Foundation. Accessed on April 17, 2011 at http://www.jrf.org.uk/KNOWLEDGE/findings/housing/2077.asp
Kelsh, D. 2001. "(D)evolutionary Socialism and the Containment of Class: For a Red Theory of Class." *The Red Critique: Marxist Theory Critique Pedagogy* 1(1): 9–13.
Kelsh, D. and D. Hill. 2006. "The Culturalization of Class and the Occluding of Class Consciousness: The Knowledge Industry in/of Education." *Journal for Critical Education Policy Studies* 4(1). Accessed on September 12, 2010 at http://www.jceps.com/index.php?pageID=article&articleID=59
Kelsh, D., D. Hill and S. Macrine, eds. 2010. *Class in Education: Knowledge, Pedagogy, Subjectivity.* London: Routledge.
Klein, N. 2008a. *The Shock Doctrine: The Rise of Disaster Capitalism.* London: Penguin.
———. 2008b. *One Year After the Publication of The Shock Doctrine, A Response to the Attacks.* Accessed on September 17, 2009 at http://www.naomiklein.org/articles/2008/09/response-attacks, September 2
Kozol, J. 1991. *Savage Inequalities.* New York: Harper Perennial.
———. 1995. *Amazing Grace: The Lives of Children and the Conscience of a Nation.* New York: Crown Publishers.
———. 2006. *The Shame of the Nation: The Restoration of Apartheid Schooling in America.* New York: Three Rivers Press.
Krupskaya, N. 1985. *On Labour-Oriented Education and Instruction.* Moscow: Progressive Publishers.
Laskaridis, C. 2011. "Greece: After the Storm—What Next?" *Counterfire.* July 11. Accessed on August 5, 2011 at http://www.counterfire.org/index.php/articles/international/12855-greece-after-the-storm-what-next
Lewis, C., D. Hill and B. Fawcett. 2009. "England and Wales: Neoliberalised Education and Its Impacts." In *The Rich World and the Impoverishment*

of Education: Diminishing Democracy, Equity and Workers' Rights, edited by D.Hill, New York: Routledge, 106–135.

Levidow, L. 2002. "Marketizing Higher Education: Neo-Liberal and Counter-Strategies." *Education and Social Justice* 3(2): 12–23. Also available at *The Commoner*, January 3. Accessed on April 18, 2010 at http://www.commoner.org.uk/03levidow.pdf

Macrine, S., P. McLaren and D. Hill. eds. 2010. *Revolutionizing Pedagogy: Education for Social Justice Within and Beyond Global Neo-Liberalism.* London: Palgrave Macmillan.

Marx, K. 1974 [1852]. "The Eighteenth Brumaire of Louis Bonaparte" in *Surveys from Exile.* New York: Vintage Books.

———. 1978 [1845]. "Six Theses on Feuerbach" in *The Marx-Engels Reader*, edited by R. Tucker. New York: W.W. Norton.

———. 1978 [1847]. "The Poverty of Philosophy" in *The Marx-Engels Reader*, edited by R. Tucker. New York: W.W. Norton.

Marx, K. and F. Engels. 1978 [1848]. "The Communist Manifesto" in *The Marx-Engels Reader*, edited by R. Tucker. New York: W.W. Norton.

McLaren, P. 2001. "Marxist Revolutionary Praxis: A Curriculum of Transgression." *Journal of Critical Inquiry into Curriculum and Instruction* 3(3): 27–32.

———. 2005. *Capitalists and Conquerors: A Critical Pedagogy Against Empire.* Lanham, MD.: Rowman and Littlefield.

McLaren, P. and R. Farahmandpur. 2001. "The Globalization of Capitalism and the New Imperialism: Notes Towards a Revolutionary Critical Pedagogy." *The Review of Education, Pedagogy and Cultural Studies* 23(3): 271–315.

———. 2005. *Teaching Against Global Capitalism and the New Imperialism.* Lanham, MD: Rowman & Littlefield.

McLaren, P. and V. Scatamburlo-D'Annibale. 2004. "Class Dismissed? Historical Materialism and the Politics of 'Difference.'" *Educational Philosophy and Theory* 36(2).

Moody, K. 2001. "Unions" in *Anti-Capitalism: A Guide to the Movement*, edited by E. Bircham and J. Charlton . London: Bookmarks.

Myers, A. 2011. "'Recovery' for the Rich, Unemployment and Lower Wages for Workers." *Direct Action for Socialism in the 21st Century.* Accessed on September 16, 2011 at http://directaction.org.au/issue34/recovery_for_the_rich_unemployment_and_lower_wages_for_workers

Packer, D. and F. Leplat. 2011. "From Boom to Bust: The Capitalist Crisis and How to Beat it." *London: Socialist Resistance.* Accessed on June 12, 2011 at http://issuu.com/socialistresistance/docs/boom2bust

Pilger, J. 2003. The New Rulers of the World. London: Verso.

Pizzigati, S. 2011. "Plutocracy: If Corporations and the Rich Paid 1960s-Level Taxes, the Debt Would Vanish." Alternet. Accessed on June 13, 2011 at http://www.alternet.org/economy/151754/plutocracy%3A_if_corporations_and_the_rich_paid_1960s-level_taxes,_the_debt_would_vanish/?page=entire

Ramesh, R. "London's Richest People Worth 273 Times More Than the Poorest." *The Guardian*, April 21, 2010. Accessed on April 17, 2011 at http://www.guardian.co.uk/uk/2010/apr/21/wealth-social-divide-health-inequality

Rikowski, G. 2001a. *The Battle in Seattle*. London: Tufnell Press.

———. 2001b. "Fuel for the Living Fire: Labour-Power!" in *The Labour Debate: An Investigation into the Theory and Reality of Capitalist Work*, edited by A. Dinerstein and M. Neary. Aldershot, UK: Ashgate.

———. 2003. "Schools and the GATS Enigma." *Journal for Critical Education Policy Studies* 1(1). Accessed on May 12, 2011 at http://www.jceps.com/index.php?pageID=article&articleID=8

———. 2006. "In Retro Glide." *Journal for Critical Education Policy Studies* 4(2). Accessed on November 15, 2010 at http://www.jceps.com/index.php?pageID=article&articleID=81

Rikowski, G., M. Cole and D. Hill. "Between Postmodernism and Nowhere: the Predicament of the Postmodernist." *British Journal of Education Studies* 45(2): 187–200.

Roberts, M. 2011a. *The Great Recession: Profit Cycles, Economic Crisis: A Marxist View*. Raleigh, NC: Lulu.Com.

Roberts, M. "The Crisis of Neoliberalism and Gerard Dumenil." *Socialist Bulletin*. May 2011. Accessed on June 12, 2011 at http://www.socialistbulletin.com/economics/thecrisisofneoliberalismandgerarddumenil

Rosskam, E., ed. 2006. *Winners or Losers? Liberalizing Public Services*. Geneva: International Labor Organisation.

Schugurensky, D. and A. Davidson-Harden. 2003. "From Cordoba to Washington: WTO/GATS and Latin American Education." *Globalisation, Societies and Education* 1(3): 321–357.

Schugurensky, D. and A. Davidson-Harden. 2009. "Neoliberalism and Education in Latin America: Entrenched Problems, Emerging Perspectives" in *The Developing World and State Education: Neoliberal Depredation and Egalitarian Alternatives*, edited by D. Hill and E. Rosskam. New York: Routledge.

Skeggs, B. 1991. "Post-Modernism: What Is All the Fuss About?" *British Journal of Sociology of Education* 12(2): 255–267.

Socialist Party. 2011. "TUC Demonstration Biggest in Decades." Accessed on May 10, 2011 at http://www.socialistparty.org.uk/articles/11563/06-06-2011/tuc-demo-26-march-2011

Socialist Worker. 2011. "TUC March Against the Cuts As It Happened." *Socialist Worker*. Accessed on June 13, 2011 at http://www.socialistworker.co.uk/art.php?id=24338

TimesOnline. 2007. "Welcome to Richistan." Accessed on May 15, 2011 at http://entertainment.timesonline.co.uk/tol/arts_and_entertainment/books/book_extracts/article1942088.ece

Tomlinson, S. 2005. *Education in a Post-Welfare Society*. Second edition. Buckingham: Open University Press/McGraw-Hill Education.

Tough, M. "What It Takes To Make a Student." *New York Times Magazine*, November 26, 2006. Accessed on November 16, 2010 at http://www.nytimes.com/2006/11/26/magazine/26tough.html?ex=1322197200&en=365daca642ddcb2f&ei=5088&partner=rssnyt&emc=rss

Toynbee, P. 2003. *Hard work: Life in Low Paid Britain*. London: Bloomsbury.

Trotsky, L. 1938. "The Death Agony of Capitalism and the Tasks of the Fourth International: The Mobilization of the Masses around Transitional Demands to Prepare the Conquest of Power: The Transitional Programme." Accessed on August 19, 2009 at http://www.marxists.org/archive/trotsky/1938/tp/index.htm

———. 1922. "*The First Five Years of the Communist International: On the United Front*." Accessed on November 16, 2010 at http://www.marxists.org/archive/trotsky/1924/ffyci-2/08.htm

Verger, T. and X. Bonal. 2009. "Resistance to the GATS" in *Contesting Neoliberal Education: Public Resistance and Collective Advance*, edited by D. Hill. London: New York: Routledge.

Wade, R. 2008. "Financial Regime Change?" *New Left Review, Second Series*, 53(September/October).

Whitty, G., S. Power and D. Halpin. *Devolution and Choice in Education: The School, the State and the Market*. Buckingham, UK: Open University Press.

Yates, M. 2006. "Preface to the Turkish Edition of Naming the System." *MRZine*, September 9, 2006. Accessed on May 12, 2010 at http://mrzine.monthlyreview.org/yates090906.html

Chapter 5

Rethinking Schools and Society/ Combating Neoliberal Globalization

David Hursh

Over the last several decades, neoliberalism has been presented as a necessary and inevitable outcome of globalization and, therefore, has shaped social, economic, and educational policies. However, neoliberalism or free-market capitalism neither achieves the economic and social benefits claimed for it nor functions as a self-regulating system. Instead, neoliberalism, as the current global recession makes abundantly clear, has devastated global economies and wrecked havoc on the environment. Therefore, I will argue the following:

- Over the last several decades, beginning with Margaret Thatcher in Britain and Ronald Reagan in the United States, politicians, and the corporate and media elite have hijacked the process of globalization (the shrinkage of space and time) to promote neoliberalism as the only way in which the world can be organized. Neoliberalism promises to increase economic growth and reduce poverty and inequality. Consequently, neoliberalism, with its emphasis on privatization, deregulation, competition, and the dismantling of welfare and education programs except in the service of capital, has come to dominate the decision-making process.
- Education, from preschool through the post-secondary level, is increasingly reshaped into competitive markets where students are to be assessed via standardized tests with the goal of creating entrepreneurial individuals who will be economically productive members of society, responsible only for her or him self. Neoliberal societies aim to create instrumentally rational individuals who can compete in the marketplace (Peters 1994)

- However, neoliberalism in practice differs from neoliberals' theoretical assertions. Instead, writes Harvey (2005), neoliberalism is a benevolent mask of wonderful-sounding words like freedom, liberty, choice, and rights, [that] hide the grim realities of the restoration or reconstitution of naked class power, locally as well as transnationally, but more particularly in the main financial centers of global capitalism. (Harvey 2005, 119)

Moreover, by prioritizing profits over other nonmonetary aspects of our lives, neoliberalism has been disastrous for the environment, especially after the election of George W. Bush, who refused to endorse reducing carbon emissions on the grounds that it might hinder economic growth (Bello 2005). In opting out of the Kyoto protocols, Bush claimed: "I will explain as clear as I can, today and every other chance I get, that we will not do anything that harms our economy.... That's my priority. I'm worried about the economy." (McKibben 2006, 18) (Although Bush's real worry seemed not to be the overall economy, including jobs, but corporate profits.)

- Furthermore, neoliberals' faith that markets need not be regulated because markets will regulate themselves, in hindsight may only be true at the cost of everyone's well being. For example, repealing sections of the Glass-Steagall Act prohibiting banks from owning other financial companies and reducing oversight, led to banks becoming involved in insurance and other industries, and making questionable mortgage loans. Consequently, when borrowers were unable to make escalating payments, the mortgage and housing industry collapsed, millions thrown out of work, and we entered a global recession. As Brenner and Theodore (2005) state, "neoliberal political practice has generated pervasive market failures, new forms of social polarization, a dramatic intensification of uneven spatial development at all spatial scales." (Brenner and Theodore 2002, 5)
- The current economic recession has even led some neoliberals, including Alan Greenspan, to acknowledge that if markets are to survive and prosper, they cannot be unregulated. Increasingly, economists and politicians realize that markets need some, albeit minimal, oversight. However, I fear that in the United States, the question is whether Barack Obama will do more than aim to restore market efficiency by instituting some regulations and, instead, subordinate the market to the goal of creating global economic, social, and environmental justice.

- Finally, I will argue that we need a new educational system that does not focus on training individuals to be economically productive but rather aims to answer the essential questions of our time. For example, David Orr (1994, 2002) and Bill McKibben (2007) argue that environmental sustainability requires rethinking the purpose of education and society. Orr begins a recent book by asking,

  > How do we re-imagine and remake the human presence on earth in ways that work over the long haul? Such questions are the heart of what theologian Thomas Berry (1999) calls "the Great Work" of our age. This effort is nothing less than the effort to harmonize the human enterprise with how the world works as a physical system and how it ought to work as a moral system. (Orr 2002, 3)

This great work requires that we situate the question of environmental sustainability within larger issues of ethics/justice, politics, economy, agriculture, design, and science and these become the focus of education.

Hijacking Globalization to Serve Neoliberalism

Thomas Friedman, best selling author of *The World is Flat: A Brief History of the Twenty-First Century*, (2005) is a leading proponent of neoliberalism, whose views are adopted by corporate and governmental leaders around the globe. While Friedman never uses the term neoliberalism, preferring instead free-market capitalism, the policies he advances are the same: competition, markets, deregulation, privatization, and the reduction of the welfare state. Manfred Steger, in *Globalism: Market Ideology Meets Terrorism*, portrays Friedman as providing the "official narrative of globalization" (Steger 2005).

Friedman argues that globalization requires neoliberal policies and that neoliberal policies support the process of globalization. They are essentially two sides of the same coin and we can no more reject free-market capitalism than we can reject globalization. We have, according to Friedman, no choice but to adopt neoliberal policies.

> The driving force behind globalization is free market capitalism—the more you let market forces rule and the more you open your economy to free trade and competition, the more efficient your economy will be. Globalization means the spread of free-market capitalism to virtually every country in the world. Therefore globalization also has its own set of economic rules—rules that revolve around opening, deregulating and privatizing your economy, in order to make it more competitive and attractive to foreign investment (Friedman 1999).

Neoliberals, like Friedman, have promoted their policies sufficiently to dominate the public discourse so that people are increasingly unlikely to challenge their assertions. Neoliberalism has become ingrained as the rationale for social and economic policies and, as such, is rarely challenged, but accepted as necessary and inevitable.

> A whole set of propositions is being imposed as self-evident: it is taken for granted that maximum growth, and therefore productivity and competitiveness, are the ultimate and sole goal of human actions; or that economic forces cannot be resisted (Bourdieu 1998, 30).

Neoliberalism and Education

Neoliberalism transforms education by changing the purpose of education, the nature of the individual, including the relationship between the individual and society, and what is valued. As I will describe below, education from elementary school through the doctorate increasingly focuses on contributing to economic productivity and consumption. Neoliberals argue that education is central to competing in the global economy and, particularly at the university level, have reshaped education to serve corporate interests.

Leitner, Sheppard, Sziarto, and Maringanti describe how neoliberalism replaces the common good and state concern for public welfare with the entrepreneurial individual aiming to succeed within competitive markets. Neoliberal policies favor

> supply-side innovation and competitiveness; decentralization, devolution, and attrition of political governance, deregulation and privatization of industry, land and public services [including schools]; and replacing welfare with "workfarist" social policies.... A neoliberal subjectivity has emerged that normalizes the logic of individualism and entrepreneurialism, equating individual freedom with self-interested choices, making individuals responsible for their own well-being, and redefining citizens as consumers and clients. (Leitner et al. 2007, 1–25)

Because neoliberalism is described as inevitable, neoliberal education reforms are also assumed to be "natural" and inevitable. If we are to compete in the global economy, assert neoliberals, we have no choice, but to adopt education reforms focusing on quantitative measurements, such as standardized exams, and accountability. Furthermore, if we either privatize schools, or make them compete with one another for students, schools will implement the rigorous reforms needed to educate students for the workplace. President Bush's statements supporting the No Child Left Behind act (NCLB) exemplify how neoliberals connect globalization with neoliberal education reforms.

> NCLB is an important way to make sure America remains competitive in the 21st century. We're living in a global world. See, the education system must compete with education systems in China and India. If we fail to give our students the skills necessary to compete in the world in the 21st century, the jobs will go elsewhere. (U.S. Department of Education 2006)

Under NCLB, schools are required to give students in grades three through eight, and once in high school, state-wide standardized exams in English and mathematics. Test scores are then aggregated by race, gender, and ability/disability and if any one of the subgroups fails to reach a minimum passing rate, the entire school fails. The minimum threshold increases each year until 2014, at which time schools must have a one hundred percent passing rate. Each year that a school fails to reach the passing rate results in increasing penalties, including reduced funding, remove of teachers or administrators, and privatization of the school. Some school districts have also increased the high-stakes nature of the exams by requiring students to pass one or more exams for promotion to next grade.

Given the high-stakes nature of the exams, and the potential negative fallout for educational administrators at the state level, many states have made the exams easier over time so that students' passing rates continues to improve. Furthermore, teachers have been explicitly or implicitly pressured to reduce time devoted to teaching subjects that are not tested and to focus on the content areas within math and English, which are likely to be tested. As a result, many students, particularly those in urban areas, who find it most difficult to achieve the minimal test score requirements, are likely to receive a narrowed and simplified instruction (Hursh 2008).

Consequently, contrary to the claims of testing proponents, these reforms have resulted in an increased drop out rate for students of color and students living in poverty, and a slowing in the reduction of the achievement gap between students of color and white students (Hursh 2006, 2007a, 2007b; Orfield 2006).

Similarly, over the last few decades, neoliberal rationalities have been infused into postsecondary education with the university increasingly conceived "as an enterprise," with knowledge as a commodity to be invested in, bought and sold, and academics as entrepreneurs, who are evaluated based on the income they generate.

Accordingly, universities are conceived less as places that generate knowledge that is important in itself or for society in general. Instead, universities look to how they can partner with corporations to create knowledge that has an economic benefit. Moreover, universities themselves have become corporatized, seeking to minimize their costs while maximizing their revenue. Zemsky, Wegner, and Massy (2006) describe American higher education as increasingly market-smart and mission-driven, suggesting the reconciliation of the corporatization of the university with traditional university purposes. Slaughter and Rhoades (2004) and Slaughter and Leslie (1997) describe the emergence of academic capitalism with vivid examples of how fiscal resource tensions and declining state support for higher education have led to a push toward entrepreneurialism, commodification of knowledge and seeing students as consumers whose tuition revenue must be maximized.

The press toward entrepreneurialism is a push to generate a diversification of revenue streams for an institution. New knowledge, existing expertise, and instructional capacity are all commodities to be operationalized to generate revenue and institutional profit. An "academic capitalist knowledge and learning regime" has emerged, replacing an ideology of a "public good knowledge and learning regime" (Slaughter and Leslie 1997; Slaughter and Rhoades 2004). Faculty in the new academic capitalist environment are pressured to develop research that attracts funding, often in the form of corporate sponsorship, and that generates patents that might be utilized by the office of technology transfer to be transformed into profitable lines of business. The danger inherent in the push toward entrepreneurialism in research includes narrowing academic freedom and research to what is fundable and permissible to be published under funding agreements (Mendoza 2007). The knowledge production is distorted to conform to the market.

Similarly, students become valued not as learners and individuals who will become a part of the fabric of society, but as little economic engines whose knowledge will fuel an economy and at the same time whose tuition becomes essential for the economic vitality of institutions of higher education in the United States (Slaughter and Rhoades 2004). The sea change in US policy away from a low tuition and low aid to a high tuition and high aid approach to access and funding of higher education has moved students closer and closer to being pure consumers (Alexander 1998). The high cost of tuition means that institutions work to maximize tuition revenue, through escalating tuition, higher enrollment and decreased costs.

Neoliberalism and the Destruction of the Common Good

Neoliberals desire markets free of regulations, increased corporate profits, minimal governmental expenditure except when it benefits corporations (i.e., military spending), and to measure economic wellbeing in terms of increased consumption, all of which are destructive of the environment and, contrary to its ostensible gains, exacerbate global inequality.

As mentioned above, the United States, under President Bush, opted out of the Kyoto protocols, in part because of how it might negatively affect the economy. In fact, corporations aim to externalize environmental costs, such as their contributions to atmospheric greenhouse gases. Consequently, by privileging markets over the environment, the Bush administration exacerbated global warming to such an extent that implementing carbon emission reductions now may be too late to halt continued melting of ice sheets in Greenland and Antarctica with the related rise in sea levels (Hansen 2006).

While decreasing corporate regulation, neoliberalism requires that "the state create and preserve an institutional framework appropriate to such practices," (Harvey 2005) including international organizations, such as the World Bank and International Monetary Fund, which pressure national governments to eliminate trade barriers and reduce social spending. In the United States, state and federal governments have intervened to create testing and accountability requirements, including regulations privatizing public schools that serve the interests of private corporations. Neoliberals demand that governments reduce corporate regulations while intensifying their intervention into people's lives. Under neoliberalism, governments exist to promote corporate profit rather than public welfare.

Moreover, recent research has revealed how neoliberalism contributes to increasing economic (Davis 2005; Leitner et al., 2007) and educational (Anyon 2005; Lipman 2004) inequality within cities. Mike Davis, in *Planet of Slums* (2005), details the negative consequences that neoliberalism has for most of the world. Many countries, especially in the global South, currently create few, if any, formal jobs. Davis cites one UN projection that only 10 percent of Africa's new workers will find formal jobs, and, therefore, few will have jobs in which they earn more than a meager insecure income. Contrary to Friedman's cheerful description of India's high tech boom, it is, according to a "leading Western economic consultant...a drop in the bucket in a sea of poverty" (Davis 2005, 173).

In addition, neoliberal governments play a minimalist role in providing services. Davis cites a Nairobi slum-dweller: "The state does nothing here. It provides no water, no schools, no sanitation, no roads, no hospitals" (Davis 2005, 62). Because of the lack of housing and services, the urban slum population continues to grow exponentially, with Black Africa estimated to have 332 million slum-dwellers by 2015. Illnesses related to inadequate water supply, waste disposal, and garbage currently kill 30,000 people daily. In 46 countries, people are poorer today than in 1990. Many of the world's cities and much of the world's populations are growing poorer and the world is becoming more, not less, unequal (Jomo and Baudot 2007, xvii–xxvii).

The rise of neoliberalism, then, has resulted in the further destruction of the environment, the commons that we all share and which supports us, and increased inequality within and between cities.

Beyond Neoliberal Economic and Education Policies

Neoliberalism, then, is a failed policy that has increased economic and social disparity, has led to our current global recession, and has subverted education's goals in the service of the commodification of knowledge. However, activists, scholars, students have long resisted the subversion of education for the purpose of economic growth and the current financial and environmental crises have further revealed the dangers and contradictions of neoliberal policies.

Consequently, we need to rethink both our economic and our educational systems so that our educational institutions can become resources for developing a sustainable and just world. We need to reveal how neoliberalism, capitalism unconstrained by the state, results in an environmentally, socially just world. We need to ask, as I stated above, how we can reimagine the remaking of the human presence on the earth in ways that work over the long haul? (Orr 2002)

We need, therefore, to understand the consequences neoliberalism has for the environment and education and reduce the role capitalist rationales have in our political and personal decision making. For example, Bill McKibben, whose early books were on the environment, most recently, in *Deep Economy: The Wealth of Communities and the Durable Future*, (McKibben 2007) advocates that we rethink our economic principles so that rather than focusing on growth and increasing the Gross Domestic Product, we focus on improving the quality of our lives and our local communities. How do we measure people's quality of life and how do we develop economies that work towards improving the well being of everyone?

Figuring out how do develop such a world requires that we develop an interdisciplinary understanding of the world that incorporates global politics and local initiatives, science and ethics, history and technology. A good example of the interrelatedness of seemingly disparate issues is Michael Pollan's (the author of *The Omnivore's Dilemma* (2006) and *In Defense of Food* (2008a)) argument that if we, in the United States, are to decrease the amount of energy we use, improve people's health, reduce our reliance on fossil fuels, and combat global warming, we need to rethink what we eat. A month before the election, Pollan's (2008b) open letter to the incoming "Farmer in Chief" outlined his proposal for a new food policy to the incoming president. In the article, he argued that because our current agriculture policies subsidize growing corn, soy, wheat, and rice (most of the corn is turned into corn syrup for our soft drinks or feed for livestock), the subsidies make fast food burgers and soft drinks cheap but vegetables and fruit expensive. Consequently, people are more likely to be obese and suffer from illnesses, such as adult onset diabetes. In fact "four of the top killers in America today are chronic diseases linked to diet: heart disease, stroke, Type 2 diabetes, and cancer." Therefore, while our fast food may be cheap, we pay for it with our health and rising medical costs. In addition, the amount of energy necessary to plant, fertilize, harvest, and ship these crops so that they can be made into foods is significant. In the United States, the food industry uses more energy than used by people to commute to and from work. Moreover, by subsidizing crops that are grown not for human consumption but for cattle, and are shipped long distances, contributes significantly to global warming. In writing about food policy, Pollan interweaves what he has learned about agricultural policies and practices, nutrition, diseases, health care, energy use, and global warming and concludes that we must change our food policies if we are to reduce energy use, slow global warming, and improve nutrition and people's health. In fact, he argues that we cannot solve the problem of global warming and our worsening health without confronting our abysmal agricultural policies and developing a new food (rather than agricultural) policy.

Answering this essential question requires that we take an interdisciplinary approach to examining a wide range of complicated questions that will require our best scientific, philosophical, political, and economic thinking. For example, we need to ask: How do we develop a global system in which countries that are at various stages of development agree on issues of energy production and use? How do we rethink the production and consumption of food so as to place less of a burden on the environment?

Rather than places that focus on producing productive workers, consumers, and profits, schools and universities can be places in which students and teachers work to reshape society. For example, I am beginning to work with a school in Uganda to develop and implement curriculum and pedagogy that would enable students to examine the interconnections between health, the environment, and economics, with the aim of students conducting participatory action research and becoming leaders in their community. Also, over the last several years I have worked with secondary students in the United States to examine the presence and consequences of toxins in their environment and what they can do both personally and politically to reduce their health risks (Hursh, Martina, Fantauzzo 2009).

It is crucial that those who are actively working for more humane and equitable educational alternatives in cities across the globe develop specific proposals that would eliminate the neoliberal presence in education policy and, instead, reconnect the agenda of human welfare and the protection of basic human rights. In particular, we need to develop theoretical and practical proposals for how both formal and informal education can be central to rethinking what kinds of cities and society we want to live in. As David Harvey writes, "The question of what kind of city we want cannot be divorced from that of what kind of social ties, relationship to nature, lifestyles, technologies and aesthetic values we desire. The right to the city is far more than the individual liberty to access urban resources: it is the right to change ourselves by changing the city.... The freedom to make and remake our cities and ourselves is, I want to argue, one of the most precious yet more neglected of our human rights" (Harvey 2008).

How we make ourselves, what kinds of environments we want to live in, what kinds of relationships we want to have, and how to reform our economic system so that it supports the welfare of all living things can and should be central to our education.

References

Alexander, F. King. 1998. "Private Institutions and Public Dollars: An Analysis of the Effects of Federal Direct Student Aid on Public and Private Institutions of Higher Education." *Journal of Educational Finance* 23(3): 390–416.

Anyon, Jean. 2005. *Radical Possibilities: Public Policy, Urban Education, and a New Social Movement.* New York: Routledge.

Bello, Walden. 2005. *Dilemmas of Domination: The Unmaking of the American Empire.* New York: Metropolitan Books.

Berry, Thomas. 1999. *The Great Work*. New York: Bell Tower.
Bourdieu, Pierre. 1998. *Act of Resistance: Against the Tyranny of the Market*. New York: The New Press
Brenner, Neil and Nicholas Theodore. 2000. "Cities and the Geographies of 'Actually Existing Neoliberalism.'" In *Spaces of Neoliberalism: Urban Restructuring in North America and Western Europe*, edited by Neil Brenner and Nicholas Theodore. Oxford: Blackwell, 2–32.
Davis, Mike. 2005. *Planet of Slums*. New York: Verso.
Friedman, Thomas. 1999. *The Lexus and the Olive Tree*. New York: Farrar, Straus & Giroux.
——— (2005). *The World is Flat: A Brief History of the Twenty-First Century*. New York: Farrar, Straus, & Giroux.
Hansen, James. 2006. *New York Review of Books*, 53(1) (January 12): 19.
Harvey, David. 2005. *A Brief History of Neoliberalism*. Oxford: Oxford University.
——— (2008). "The Right to the City." *New Left Review* 53 (September/October): 23–40.
Hursh, David, 2007a. "Exacerbating Inequality: The Failed Promise of the No Child LeftBehind Act," *Race, Ethnicity and Education* 10(3), 295–308.
——— (2007b). "Assessing No Child Left Behind and the Rise of Neoliberal Policies." *American Educational Research Journal* 44(3) (September): 493–518.
——— (2008). *High-Stakes Testing and the Decline of Teaching and Learning: The Real Crisis in Education*. Latham, MD: Rowman and Littlefield.
Hursh, David, Camille A. Martina, and Michael Fantauzzo. 2009. "Toxins in Our Environment: Health and Civic Responsibility" in *Social Studies and Diversity Teacher Education: What We Do and Why We Do It*, edited by E. Heilman. New York: Routledge.
Jomo. K.S. and Jacques Baudot. 2007. Preface in *Flat World, Big Gaps: Economic Liberalization, Globalization, Poverty, and Inequality*, edited by Jomo K.S. and Jacques Baudot, New York: Zed Books, xvii–xxvii.
Krugman, Paul. 2009. *The Return of Depression Economics and the Crisis of 2008*. New York: W. W. Norton & Co.
Leitner, Hilga, Eric S. Sheppard, Kristin Sziarto and Anant Maringanti. 2007. "Contesting Urban Futures: Decentering Neoliberalism" in *Contesting Neoliberalism: Urban Frontiers* edited by H. Leitner; E. S. Sheppard and J. Peck. New York: Guilford Press.
Lipman, P. 2004. *High Stakes Education: Inequality, Globalization, and Urban School Reform*. New York: Routledge.
McKibben, Bill. 2006. "The Coming Meltdown." *New York Review of Books* 53(1) (January 12):16–18.
——— (2007). *Deep Economy: The Wealth of Communities and the Durable Tuture*. New York: Times Books.
Mendoza, Pila. 2007. "Academic Capitalism and Doctoral Student Socialization: A Case Study." *The Review of Higher Education*, 78(1): 71–96.

Nichols, S. L., and D.C. Berliner. 2005. "The Inevitable Corruption of Indicators and Educators Through High-Stakes Testing." *Education Policy Studies Laboratory.* Accessed on April 23, 2009 at http://greatlakescenter.org/docs/early_research/g_l_new_doc/EPSL-0503-101-EPRU.pdf.

Orfield, Gary. 2006. *Forward.* Tracking Achievement Gaps and Assessing the Impact of NCLB on the Gaps: An In-Depth Look into National and State Reading and Math Outcome Trends. Boston, MA: The Civil Rights Project of Harvard University.

Orr, David.1994. *Earth in Mind.* Washington: Island Press.

Orr, David. 2002. *The Nature of Design: Ecology, Culture and Human Intention.* Oxford: Oxford University Press.

Peters, Michael. 1994. "Individualism and Community: Education and the Politics of Difference." *Discourse: Studies in the Cultural Politics of Education.* 14(2) (June): 65–78.

Pollan, M. 2006. *The Omnivore's Dilemma: A Natural History of Four Meals.* New York: Penguin.

——— 2008a. *In Defense of Food: An Eater's Manifesto.* New York: Penguin.

——— 2008b. "An Open Letter to the Farmer in Chief." *New York Times Magazine.* (October 12): MM62.

Slaughter, Sheila and Larry Leslie. 1997. *Academic Capitalism: Politics, Policies, and the Entrepreneurial University.* Baltimore, MD: The John Hopkins University Press.

Slaughter, Sheila and Gary Rhoades. 2004. *Academic Capitalism and the New Economy: Politics, Markets, State and Higher Education.* Baltimore, MD: The John Hopkins University Press.

Steger, Manfred. 2005. *Globalism: Market Ideology Meets Terrorism.* Lanham, MD: Rowman & Littlefield.

US Department of Education. 2006. *Overview: NCLB is Working.* Washington, DC. Accessed on March 3, 2009 at http://www2.ed.gov/nclb/overview/importance/nclbworking.html

Zemsky, Robert; Gregory R. Wegner and William F. Massy. 2006. *Remaking the American University: Market-Smart and Mission-Centered.* New Brunswick, NJ: Rutgers University Press.

Chapter 6

Education Toward War

Faith Agostinone-Wilson

Currently, the United States is experiencing economic stagnation, to put it mildly. Foreclosures are a common sight, with entire streets featuring homes for sale. Home equity is the lowest it has been since 1945 and the nation's savings rate is zero. Household debt levels mirror the national debt, with many people putting doctors' visits and college tuition on multiple credit cards, maxed to their limits. Food costs are rising at the fastest rates of inflation in 15 years, far outpacing the amount of food stamps allotments. Charity-based food pantry levels—arguably the real measure of economic health—are low. In 2010, we have double digit unemployment with unofficial levels estimating 19 percent of the US workforce without a job.

The American economy is linked like a ball and chain to the cash- and soul-sucking Iraq invasion, along with bloated military budgets sustaining a global, imperial presence, mostly used to protect business interests. *Substance News* documents a record number of school closings in Chicago, paving the way for more "acceptable" whites and upper middle class families to "reclaim" neighborhoods. These schools, if they are reopened, are made over into selective public or private charter schools that set admissions standards and continually deny services to the poor and families who have children with special learning needs. The "success" of the Chicago model has been put into play in New Orleans (Quigley 2007).

An economy on the edge of instability creates the perfect conditions for militarism as the solution to societal problems. This is reflected in soaring incarceration rates, with 2008 estimates being— one out of every 100 adults behind bars (Liptak 2008). The situation for African American adults is even worse in 2008 with one out of 15 being imprisoned. At the root of militarism is the belief that humans are inherently bad and in need of authoritarian controls—specifically, controls for those perceived more unruly, such as the poor and minorities. Artificially created scarcity is the only spark needed to ignite the chain of events the war-makers desire.

Education plays a key role in the justification of militarism and the naturalization of war as "the only solution," accompanying the dogma "there is no alternative to capitalism." Biological determinism resurrects itself through evolutionary biologists like Steven Pinker arguing that humankind is built for war and the free-market (Gasper 2004). War is a common feature for analysis in K-12 history and social study content standards for the 50 states. History is taught with war being the primary force of meaning and the locus of social change, while at the same time strongly discouraging the rights of oppressed groups to resist through force or extralegal methods. When people do not perceive themselves as having agency in history, they absorb the prevailing ideology, which, according to Marx, is always the ideology of the ruling class.

Overview

The first of two parts examining the school-to-military pipeline, this chapter is not an overarching exploration of state sponsored militarism or armed forces advertising in the mass media, as beautifully presented in *Education as Enforcement* (Saltman and Goodman 2008). Though corporate connections are always behind militarism, this chapter instead looks closely at the problems facing those interested in resisting militarism at its choke point—recruiting. It also examines the school-to-war pipeline's targeting of young people aged 13–29, including college students. While assuming that right-wing resistance toward antimilitarism is rampant and ubiquitous, scholar-activists cannot ignore the influence of centrist-liberal support for military presence within the schools, contributing to its veneer of acceptability.

The two ideologies that make resisting military recruiting the most difficult include (1) the presentation of the "all volunteer" army and (2) the military being perceived as a jobs training program and college financial aid institution. This chapter will examine these ideologies, along with counterarguments that teacher educators and other war resistors can use to deconstruct them. Until these two ideologies can be effectively challenged, building a compelling—and lasting—case for resisting military recruiting in postdraft era schools will not happen.

Though not intending to contribute to a climate of despair, it is very important for those interested in resisting recruiting to understand the scope of what we are up against. In this vein, a presentation of laws and policies will be the opening, followed by a discussion of the volunteer army and military-as-jobs ideologies. Counterarguments will be presented in the form of the economic realities facing young civilians and veterans, often compelling them to enlist. References used are a combination of scholarly as well as mass media sources, along with recruiting manuals. In many cases, alternative media and scholarly journals like *International Socialist Review, Z Magazine, Journal for Critical Education Policy Studies,* and *Substance News* provided the most accurate and contemporary coverage of the school-to-work pipeline rather than traditional academic journals, which seemed reluctant to publish work from a revolutionary or Marxist stance openly opposing military recruiting at both the K-12 and university levels.

Militarism as Public Policy

Overarching the problem of the military's presence in the public schools is the increased dependence on the military—and to a lesser degree the police and prisons—as the foundation of social policy. The US military budget alone makes up over 40 percent of the world's spending on armaments and related industries (Perlo-Freeman, Perdomo, Skons, and Stalenheim 2009). The wars in Afghanistan and Iraq have accounted for sharp increases in this spending, contributing to escalating deficits and a collapsing economy. It is no coincidence in the United States that Wal-Mart is the largest US private employer while the military is the largest public employer. This corporate-military connection is deep and insidious, as explored by Wilcox (2003). Accelerating since the Spanish-American War, US imperialism has been the world's police force as part of creating business-friendly climates in which to advance capitalism. All of this happens against the backdrop of impending environmental degradation as the military desperately attempts to grasp at remaining oil supplies, setting up secret prisons along the way (Johnson 2008).

Abu Ghraib brings home the theme of militarism as a social philosophy and public policy. Giroux (2004) explores the role of empire and power in how the Abu Ghraib scandal was portrayed in the media. He also examines the psychological dynamics of dependency upon militarism as a force for organizing:

> Under certain modes of domination with all of its stress-inducing consequences, those who exercise a wanton and dehumanizing power

often feel that everything is permissible because all of the rules appear to have broken down. The stress soldiers experience under such circumstances is often satisfied through the raw feel and exercise of power. Abu Ghraib remains, tragically, a terrible site of violence, a site in which an ethics of non-violence seems almost incomprehensible given the tension, anxiety, and daily violence that framed both what happened in the prison and in daily life in Iraq. Under these conditions, neither education nor an ethics of peace may be enough. (Giroux 2004, 18)

With a crumbling infrastructure, real insecurity about a falling economy is channeled into the faux safety of hypermasculinity and celebrated violence, by both military personnel and the public at large.

The Military Presence in the Schools

At a November 2007 Chicago board of education meeting, 14 active-duty military personnel were in attendance. Schmidt (2007, 1) recounts the unusual events:

> In order to get in the door, you had to say "excuse me" to a uniformed soldier. Inside, a squad of Marines was standing, all in uniform, along the walls at the side and back of the meeting room. One soldier in desert combat fatigues and desert boots was standing in the group of Marines. There were uniformed soldiers or Marines at both entrances.

Schmidt was later told by Marine officials that the soldiers had been asked to attend the meeting as a show of support for allowing recruiter access for the Chicago Public Schools (CPS). After an antiwar Iraq veteran in support of limited recruiter access testified about her experiences with the Junior Reserve Officer Training Corps (JROTC) and their misrepresentations—including paying her $100 per day to wear her uniform as a high school student to entice others to enlist—the uniformed soldiers had departed the meeting.

Recruiters have open access to schools, at both K-12 and postsecondary institutions. This has been accomplished through a combination of legislation and relentless cultivation of friendly relationships between the schools and the military through various programs targeting students and faculty. Asserting that the military should have the same access to colleges as other employment firms, the Solomon Amendment (1996) not only allows access to college campuses, but it can also authorize the government to take action against postsecondary institutions that prevent recruiting, including denying certain federal funds. Noncompliance with the policy is reported by recruiters, who present documentation of potential offenses to the Recruiting Battalion Education Services (School Recruiting Program Handbook 2004).

An extension of the Solomon Amendment, the Hutchinson Amendment (2002) allows recruiter access to secondary schools. Educational agencies have to report directory information to the department of defense, specifically regarding colleges and universities (School Recruiting Program Handbook 2004, 9). Mirroring the process of being sent to the principal's office, schools that do not comply are reported by the secretary of defense "to the specified congressional committee, Senators of the State in which the school is located, and the member of the House of Representatives who represents the school district."

Closely related to the Hutchinson Amendment, The Armed Forces Recruiter Access to Students and Student Recruiting Information, Section 9528 of the No Child Left Behind act (2001), ties federal funding to the release of secondary student directory information to military recruiters. While providing the chance for parents and students to opt out, individuals have to make the request in writing, adding an extra step in the paperwork trail that parents are inundated with already. Most revealingly, the Recruiting Operations Manual (2006, 21) states that while military officials can "remind" schools that they have to comply, "recruiters and their leaders cannot rely on public law to gain access to schools and students. Real success can come only with a well planned and well executed school recruiting plan."

Taking the threat of withholding funding to the extreme and in an act of "red meat revenge," Senators Jim DeMint (famous for his recommendation that gay people or single mothers who live with their partners not teach in public schools) and Jim Inhofe (who believes climate change is a hoax and that the Weather Channel is in on it) introduced H.R.5222 otherwise known as the "Sempre Fi Act." Ignoring the concept of "local control" often favored by conservatives when it comes to excluding minorities, the act was created in response to the recent Berkeley City Council's resolution to limit recruiter access to the city on the basis of (a) the military's discrimination against the LGBTQ community, (b) the tendency of recruiters to renege on promises made to enlistees, and (c) the propensity of the military to engage in illegal invasions of other countries. The Sempre Fi Act would rescind funds that would go to Berkley and transfer those funds to marine recruiting coffers. In mid-February, 2008, an anonymous hold was placed on the bill (Bender 2008).

Within the schools themselves, Section 2302 of No Child Left Behind (2001) authorizes funding for the Troops-to-Teachers program, with a particular emphasis on targeting schools with large percentages of low-income students. Administered by the department of defense, Troops-to-Teachers provides for certification or licensing of veterans to teach in elementary and secondary public schools. As of 2005, more than 6,000 teachers have been placed in school systems via the program to help recruiters establish what they term as "school ownership" (International Action Center, 2005). In some California schools with large minority populations, veterans are given a six-week course and placed immediately in the classroom (Mariscal 2004).

The marine corps have used a program called the Educator Workshop (Mariscal 2004), designed to "win over influencers" (school personnel) by having them attend a week of boot camp (International Action Center 2005). Teachers who take part in the "workshop" every year (40 from each recruiting zone) are flown to San Diego or Parris Island and set up in local hotels. In addition, they are paid $225 (Mariscal, 2004). The idea behind the program is to create a bond with the military and then carry that excitement back to their schools to pass on to "prospective enlistees" (International Action Center 2005, 23). However, Mariscal (2004, 13) points out, "military veterans are considered to be potentially disruptive given their first hand knowledge of military values and practices" and are not allowed to participate in the workshop.

Indeed, the military is highly intent on making as many connections with "influencers" as possible, as indicated in this passage from the School Recruiting Program Handbook (2004, 5):

> Many faculty members are prior service or are current members of the United States Army Reserve. Try to identify these individuals and develop them as centers of influence (COIs). Your goal is to develop as many COIs as possible for the schools. Don't forget the administrative staff since many of them act as policy makers. Establish and maintain rapport and always treat them with respect. Also, have something to give them (pen, calendar, cup, donuts, etc.) and always remember secretary's week with a card or flowers.

The *Handbook* goes on to instruct recruiters to look for student influencers, "...class officers, newspaper and yearbook editors, and athletes" who "can help build interest in the Army among the student body" (2004, 3). "First to contact, first to contract" is the policy outlined, with the warning "if you wait until they're seniors, it is probably too late." Recruiters are expected to actively promote a positive image of the military to students old enough to begin thinking about their career.

The Recruiting Operations Manual (2006, 17) uses a bizarre juxtaposition of military doctrine (in italics) and recommendations (directly below, in regular font) for appealing to students, as in the following two excerpts, begging the question, who is the "enemy"?

Never permit the enemy to acquire an unexpected advantage.
1-26. Recruiters must establish and maintain a visible and active presence in their markets. By so doing, recruiters will promote the Army as the service of choice for the young people they seek to recruit.

Strike the enemy at a time or place or in a manner for which he is unprepared.
1-27. An Army recruiter will likely surprise no one when he or she visits a high school or college campus. However, the recruiter can create surprise—even delight—by demonstrating genuine interest in young people. Some people will expect an Army recruiter to have an interest in nothing more than "filling his quota." The Soldier or civilian employee who counsels and mentors young people and lives the Army values will indeed surprise those people.

The Operations Manual (2006, 29) states that "recruiting quality soldiers to fight the Global War on Terrorism means recruiters and their leaders must be fully engaged with the market" in the schools. Schools are pivotal, because "without a strong schools program, you cannot have an effective grad recruiting program". (2006, 21) Using language like "taking the offensive" (directing the nature of an operation), "market areas of interest" (all educational institutions, public and private), "total market penetration" (schools and the larger community), "target rich environment" (a school with a lot of potential recruits, i.e. poor and minority), the *Operations Manual* is straightforward in its goals, with minimal ambiguity.

School recruiting programs are now targeting Latino/a students, who compose 22 percent of the recruiting market, twice the rate of Latino/as in the general population (roughly 13.5 percent) (Mariscal 2004). "Visit any high school with a large Latino population, and you will find JROTC units, Army-sponsored computer games, and an overabundance of recruiters, often more numerous than career counselors" (2006, 6). An entry point to recruiting minority students is the administration of the Armed Services Vocational Aptitude Battery (ASVAB) during the junior or senior year of high school. The ASVAB is not only an enlistment screening tool, it is a way for recruiters to insert themselves into schools by helpfully casting themselves as career advisors to low-income schools (School Recruiting Program Handbook 2004). As the Handbook (2004, 4) states, it is "reasonable" for school officials to allow recruiters to present help in interpreting ASVAB scores. In addition, each recruiter is supposed to prepare a detailed school folder including the scores, documentation related to teachers' and students' level of interest and opportunities for "career" presentations at school events.

Colleges and universities are not immune from military strategy, either. The Concurrent Admissions Program manual (2002) describes partnerships between postsecondary schools and the army, including assisting veterans in obtaining course credit for time spent in the military (Army/American Council on Education Registry Transcript System). Veterans and active-duty soldiers are encouraged to select a local college from a list of over 1,540 participating schools (The Service members Opportunity Colleges), because the local campus will be easier for the recruiter to "partner" with (2002, 4): "the college will view the recruiter as an excellent source of future students, enabling the recruiter to improve access and high-grad recruiting on that campus". (2002, 3) Colleges are even encouraged to enroll recruiters who are working on degrees: "Help recruiters understand your college so well that they will unhesitatingly refer their enlistees to your college!" (2002, 7).

Militarism as a whole must be resisted and stopping recruiting is a good place to begin. As Mariscal (2004) argues, military values are located at all levels of culture, emanating from the capitalist state. Unchecked and unchallenged, militarism starves the rest of society of necessary resources that would go to meet human needs, not corporate interests. One challenge we face in resisting recruiters is that it is easy to slip into an easy sense of schools being "our" institutions, since many of us attended public schools for 13 years. However, as Gibson, Queen, Ross, and Vinson (2007, 51) warn,

> ...schools embedded within a capitalist nation, especially capital's most favored nation, are capitalist schools, *their* schools, not *ours*, until such time social upheavals or civil strife are at such a stage that schooling is either dramatically upended, or freedom schools operating outside capital's school supersede them.

In a similar vein, it is *their* troops, not "our troops" when it comes to the military. Indeed, the primary purpose of any military, along with the police, is to protect the ruling elite and their property, not the working class. As long as the troops support *their* mission, *they* are not our troops, until they decide to dramatically upend the system by refusing to fight or sabotaging the system from within, keeping in mind that there might be several stages of readiness at play. The fact that they might be working class themselves and buy into the system only makes the situation that much more challenging.

Compulsory Volunteerism

The "volunteer" army is a skillful rhetorical device used to sustain support for military presence in the schools. Alongside volunteerism is rampant privatization, borne out by the figure of 130,000 mercenaries with 145,000 active duty forces serving in Iraq (Scahill 2007). Scahill summarizes the political importance behind the image of the volunteer army on a global level in his book *Blackwater: The Rise of the World's Most Powerful Mercenary Army*:

> What we see here is an insidious system where you want to avoid having a draft in your country; you want to keep it off the table for political reasons. You can't convince the world to participate in your global wars of conquest, and so what you do is you make the whole world your recruiting ground. You use these private companies to go into the poorer countries of the world, countries that have been systematically destabilized by the United States, and you hire up the poor of the developing world, and you deploy them to kill and be killed in Iraq against the poor and suffering of Iraq. (Scahill 2007, 24–25)

While there is no draft in official policy, the poverty draft includes those students being targeted with promises of services that are continually denied them in the larger world, services which are seen as components of basic human rights according to the 1948 *United Nation's Universal Declaration of Human Rights* (International Action Center 2005; Kamenetz 2006; Spring 1999).

People join the military not because they want to, but because they have to (Aleman 2007). Rasmus (2007, 45) describes the historical shift in unions over the past 150 years, ultimately impacting worker/boss power relations among the nonunionized. From the post WWII 1940s to the mid-1970s, there was an expansion of militant collective organizing, with health care, pensions, inflationary raises, and job security being on the list of demands. "...this was the golden age of contract bargaining, and of what might be called 'contract unionism.'"

From the late 1970s onward, a shift occurred as part of a corporate offensive. Massive bargaining agreements were disrupted through legislation and a focus on concessions within existing contracts. According to Rasmus (2007), a form of concessionary unionism emphasized giving in to employer demands in order to maintain the status quo. Now, unions are in the role of partnering with businesses, further eroding hard fought contracts, and shifting health care costs to the employee via high-deductable private insurance plans, and selling off pensions to be managed for profit. "This new condition might be indentified as the era of "corporate unionism" where unions become even more integrated with the strategies, aims, and objectives of global corporate management" (Rasmus 2007, 45).

With traditional avenues of economic security fast disappearing, people are looking at the military as a way to survive (Aleman, 2007). In A Deserter's Tale, Key (2007, 39) outlines in plain talk how his economic situation drove him to enlist with only ten dollars in his pocket the day he stepped into the recruiting office. Key goes on to describe how the recruiter befriended him over the following six weeks, becoming "my coach, my guidance counselor, my adviser, and my personal biographer, as well as the provider of coffee, doughnuts, and submarine sandwiches..." The recruiter visited Key and his wife, promising that life on the military base would be safe and rent free "I learned later that this was not true, that about $700.00 would be docked each month from my paycheck [$1,200 monthly] for the rent" (2007, 42). Knowing that Key wanted to become a welder, the recruiter also promised him access to training while he was posted on the base. Once deployed, Key attempted to talk with an officer to ask about the mismatch between what he was promised and what was actually occurring. The following day, Key was severely reprimanded and punished by his squad and team leaders and never again asked any questions.

War resister and veteran Eugene Cherry noticed that the bulk of the medics he met during his tour were Caucasian, not African American (Ziemba, 2008, 15). Most of the African Americans he encountered tended to serve infantry ranks, which were predominantly black. He saw a direct connection between the demographics of the infantry units and lowest ranks, and the make-up of the schools and neighborhoods targeted by recruiters: "They're not going into well-to-do areas like Lake Forest and trying to get those kids to join, but I guarantee you if you go to a neighborhood like Englewood, you're going to see a lot of recruiting stations".

The Operations Manual likes to brag about soldiers who "leave behind their comfortable homes and temporarily set aside their personal plans to put on the Army uniform to help protect their country from her enemies" (2006, 133). One of the most high-profile soldiers, Pat Tillman's death (under mysterious circumstances) was exploited to promote the myth of the all volunteer army—that Tillman gave up his high paid professional football career to serve his country (Aleman 2007). The media portrayed this as if it were true for all enlistees—as if everyone had the same number of options yet chose military service out of the goodness of their hearts.

When social class enters the picture, volunteerism takes a hit. Jessica Lynch, from a working class background, was used by the military in a similar manner as Tillman by immediately exaggerating her heroism during the early stages of the Iraq invasion. In both cases, the lies were exposed by Tillman's family and Lynch herself, but not in time to prevent the damage of the mythology of the all volunteer army that still runs strong in the public's mind. And when Lyndie England's famous pictures emerged of her posing with Abu Graib detainees, the media focused on her as being the one responsible, not the higher-ups. Pundits constantly brought up the argument that the soldiers who participated in acts of torture "chose" to join the military and were therefore obligated to face the consequences (the "few bad apples" defense). Then and only then did they invoke the Nuremburg trials and the notion of personal choice, violating their usual "just following orders" logic used to justify their own misdeeds. This is the hard lesson of volunteerism for the rank and file—the construct will be used against them, with the upper ranks avoiding any kind of punishment.

The condition of young people in the United States argues against the concept of a truly volunteer fighting force. According to the International Action Center (2005), almost 40 percent of the homeless population is under age 18. A total of 5.5 million 16–24-year-olds are "officially disconnected"—they are not in school or the military, are unemployed, living with others, or outgrown the age limits for juvenile hall and foster care (Kamenetz 2006). One out of five children in the United States are born into poverty (Sklar 2007) with a larger proportion of people in severe poverty reaching a 32 year high, growing more than 26 percent since 2000 (Aleman 2007). Since the 1970s, the top 1 percent of households has doubled their share of the wealth and white households have seven times as much net worth than households of color (Sklar 2007). Sklar states that one out of six people under age 65 has no health insurance of any kind, with

Aleman (2007) putting the figure at 45 million uninsured for longer than one year, and 55 million partly uninsured the prior year. Nearly 30 percent of 19–29-year-olds have no regular health insurance, which is twice the percentage of the population at large, more than any other age group (Kamenetz 2006).

We have the image of young people as being the best off of any segment of the population on all measures—health, finances, and education. The International Action Center (2005) places the estimates of youth incarcerated in adult jails at 7,600 with 15 states setting the minimum age of the death penalty at eighteen. At the start of 2001, 73 people on death row were there due to crimes they had committed under the age of 18. Youth of color are 34 percent of the juvenile justice system population and 62 percent in custody. In the past 14 years, there has been a 51 percent increase in young people being committed, two-thirds of those being minority youth. One out of every seven black men aged 25–29 are incarcerated. The total number of incarcerated people stands at 2.2 million, with 4.8 million on parole/probation and prison budgets busting at $61 billion (Gasper 2007).

The war on crime mirrors the language of the war on terrorism, with a law-and-order mentality that is essentially veiled racism. Nixon was the first to emphasize tough on crime talk, followed by the Reagan administration's double offensive on "criminals" and "welfare recipients," both coded terms for African Americans (Gasper 2007). This ideology serves to justify militarism aimed at unruly brown citizens, both here and abroad. It also justifies irrational tougher sentencing laws, with many prisoners serving life terms for petty theft or bounced checks, all in the service of the for-profit prison industry. According to Gasper, California spends $35,000 per year on every prisoner and only $7,000 annually per K-12 students and $4,000 for college students. The education-jail connection cannot be more obvious with two-thirds of California's prisoners reading below a ninth grade level and over half being functionally illiterate. Funding for inmate educational programs (shown to be one of the most effective ways of reaching younger inmates) has been slashed, with only 6 percent of prisoners in academic classes or 5 percent in vocational training (Gasper 2007).

Under NCLB, states are allowed to use their own measures for graduation rates, making it impossible to not only obtain national data, but also statewide data. In California, nearly one in three high school students in the class of 2006 did not graduate, the rate dropping to a ten-year low (Aleman 2007). Balfanz and Legsters (2004) estimate that between 900 and 1,000 US high schools have a 50/50 chance of graduating its students. In 2,000 high schools, the freshman class reduces by 40 percent or more by the time the senior year arrives. High dropout rate schools are located in major cities, along with the rural South and West, where large numbers of white students attend. 15 percent of these high schools produce close to 50 percent of the nation's dropouts, causing a media stir when Balfanz and Legters (2006, 2) labeled them "dropout factories."

These high poverty schools are the perfect candidates for the "total market penetration" that the military recruiters seek out. In fact, they have a willing cadre of unelected, self-appointed, bipartisan elites like Bill Gates willing to help in the form of the National Commission on Skills in the Workplace's Tough Choices or Tough Times report. Tough Choices proposes universal exam-based tracking with all tenth graders having to take a regents exam with implications that those who continually failed the exam would cease being allowed to attend school (Miller and Gerson 2008). Miller and Gerson point out that while the report stresses that students can retake the exams and won't fail, it will be up to them to display the motivation to persist in obtaining an education, the objectivists' ultimate dream writ large. In the language of corporate supremacy, that means "i.e. throwing millions of students out into the streets as they turn 16" (Miller and Gerson 2008, 16). One can only guess which remaining public institution will be ready at the helm to welcome in these youngsters.

According to army statistics, recruiters are already finding it necessary to look to enlisting high school dropouts and "lower-achieving" applicants to meet quotas (Schmitt 2005). Even though Army officials insist that they wouldn't "lower standards" to meet quotas, recruiters "... said they were told in February to start accepting more recruits who are ranked in Category 4 on the military's standardized aptitude test—those who scored between the 10th and 30th percentiles on the ASVAB" (Schmitt 2005, 4–6). In 2004, the Army accepted 465 of Category 4 recruits while in 2005 they accepted 800 such recruits (2005, 18). The percentage of new recruits without a high school diploma have reached 10 percent, up from 8 percent in 2004 and 2 percent (the upper limit) of ASVAB low-scorers have been admitted into the Army.

Once in the "all volunteer" military, soldiers are finding that the health benefits they sought to be sorely lacking and highly conditional. As Binh (2007) reports, one veteran and war resister believed that the red tape that people encounter "... is really a smokescreen, because behind the red tape there is next to nothing there. It's just trying to shield people from seeing that the services are not there" (21). VA hospitals, already understaffed, are now seeing active-duty soldiers as patients because the department of defense hospitals are inundated. Continues Binh, "On any given night, there are 195,000 homeless veterans, 9,600 for whom the VA does not have beds. In the last two years, one-third of Afghanistan and Iraq veterans classified as being at risk of homelessness lost their homes...the suicide rate for veterans is double that of the civilian population". (Binh 2007, 52)

The National Coalition of Homeless Veterans estimates that 23 percent of the overall homeless population are veterans, with a bulk of them having served in Vietnam. The department of veterans affairs has located 1,500 young Iraq and Afghanistan veterans who are homeless, out of a total 336,000 veterans homeless during 2006 (McClam 2008). The three main causes of homelessness among veterans are mental illness, financial problems, and difficulty finding affordable housing—conditions that, not coincidentally, led many to enlist in the first place!

Those who do seek treatment find that the same cutbacks and insurance industry trickeries in privatized medical care affecting the civilian population also impact them. In an interview by Ruder (2007), according to Matt Hrutkay, a member of Iraq Veterans Against the War, the VA web site has a section containing a guide for VA medical providers and doctors encouraging them to diagnose veterans with "adjustment disorder," "anxiety disorder," and "personality disorder." "The reason they're doing that is so they can claim there was a pre-existing condition before I joined the army and my issues have nothing to do with being blown up twenty-one times" (2007, 23). Eugene Cherry was a soldier-medic who was given prescriptions instead of treatment for his PTSD. Rather than losing what little bit of sanity remained, he chose to go AWOL in order to get the treatment the military wouldn't give him. Choosing to take on the military, he managed to demonstrate through the legal system that he went AWOL due to the PTSD (Ziemba 2008).

Binh (2007, 52) reports that the VA has a "backlog of more than 600,000 applications and appeals for disability benefits," most of which won't be successful. The case load is projected to grow by 1.6 million over the next two years. Veterans who suffer from severe PTSD often receive low disability ratings. "As of July 2006, 152,669 veterans filed disability claims after fighting in Iraq or Afghanistan, and only 1,502 of them received disability ratings of 100%". (2007, 52)

Binh recounted how one private received a rating of 40 percent and has to support his family on the $700 per month he receives from the government. Unable to work due to the PTSD, he is nearing bankruptcy and has been waiting five months to receive treatment at the VA hospital. A mere 3 percent of veterans going through the medical system have been granted permanent disability status (it used to be 10 percent in 2001). Since 2001, the military has disqualified 22,500 veterans due to "personality disorders" which eliminates them from receiving benefits, "saving the VA $4.5 billion over the course of their lifetimes" (2007, 52).

When confronted with these figures, proponents of volunteerism among the ruling elite point to the fact that soldiers made an "informed choice" and therefore should have understood the consequences before enlisting. The "all volunteer" army is a way to ultimately wash one's hands of the responsibility and discomfort at systematically NOT supporting the troops. The public is catching on. Despite their efforts to own schools, including millions of dollars spent on advertising and padding the ranks of recruiters, enlistments in the army are down by as much as 30 percent (International Action Center 2005). Well-publicized scandals such as last year's Walter Reed debacle creates a space for critically questioning what "support the troops" REALLY means.

No Money/No Jobs

The recent barrage of military advertising uses emotional music and patriotic themes to promise exciting careers to potential recruits. Common images include people operating imposing, high-tech machinery and paratroopers emerging from planes in flight. But, as the International Action Center (2005, 29) points out: "...there aren't many aircraft carriers in Des Moines, Iowa. No one is hiring tank drivers in the Bronx. And civilian airline companies prefer that you keep the doors closed and that nobody jumps out".

One cannot deny the allure of vocational training or money for college. The military has succeeded in the postdraft era by riding the tsunami of public misinformation—who wants to be the hard ass who proposes limiting recruiter's access to the schools when they only want to provide career counseling and financial aid to disadvantaged school districts? The situation facing many young people related to employment isn't exactly upbeat. Unemployment is the highest for young people, with the census listing ten percent compared to three percent for the general population (the rates are most likely higher). One out of every three African American men and women between 16–19 years old are unemployed, as are one out of five between 20–24 (Sklar 2007). In the United States, one out of four workers makes $8.70 or less per hour and the percentage of full-time workers at the poverty level has soared 50 percent. A household with two children would have to work more than three full-time jobs at the prevailing minimum wage to just break even. When it comes to race and labor, African American income is three-fifths that of whites, unemployment twice that of whites and their poverty rate triple that of whites. And youths between the ages of 18 and 24 are the ones most likely to hold low wage jobs and are the first to get laid off, contributing to their 30 percent poverty rate, the highest of any age group (Kamenetz 2006).

When the first baby boomers made their debut in the job market in 1970, the largest employer in the United States was General Motors offering an average hourly wage of $17.50 in today's dollars. Today, the largest employer is Wal-Mart whose average hourly wage is $8.00 (Kamenetz 2006). Kamenetz (2006, 101) describes theses as "crap jobs, positions that are "temporary, part-time, with no benefits, and hourly pay. Included in the crap category are unpaid internships, representing "a $124 million yearly contribution to the welfare of corporate America". These jobs serve not only to enrich the capitalist class, they also intimidate low-wage workers who are always under the threat of dismissal along with serving as a leverage against slightly more privileged salaried employees who fear being replaced by the temps. In this context, "...the value of a college education has grown in the last generation not because college grads make so much more but because high school grads' earning has stagnated" (Kamenetz 2006, 95).

The military capitalizes on the large number of postsecondary school "stopouts," another term for those who fail to re-enroll or drop out from college altogether. According to Kamenetz, (2006, 6) in her book Generation Debt, one in five Americans in his or her 20s was a college dropout. Today, it is one out of three. Not only are young people dropping out of college, they are taking longer to earn their degrees:

> The nationwide high school graduation rate peaked in 1970 at 77%. It was around 67% in 2004...of every 100 young people who begin their freshman year of high school, just 38 eventually enroll in college, and only 18 graduate within 150% of allotted time—six years for a bachelor's degree or three years for an associate's degree. Only

24.4% of the adult population has a B.A., according to the Census. (Kamenetz 2006, 5–6)

The School Recruiting Program Handbook (2004) advises recruiters that "The market is an excellent source of potential Army enlistments due to the high percentage of students who drop out of college, particularly during the first two years...there are certain times during every semester, when, if students are going to drop out, they will do so" (2004, 8–9). The handbook instructs recruiters to compare student rosters from semester to semester in order to identify those who have stopped out.

In a rare fit of honesty, Dick Cheney once remarked that the military isn't about job training or providing financial aid. It exists to wage war. But all of the advertising and presence during sporting events and on MTV emphasizes training and money. Dispelling these myths, the International Action Center (2005) states that on the whole, veterans earn 19 percent less than those with no military experience and that 88 percent of men and 94 percent of women will never utilize their military training in civilian jobs. The enlistment contract itself features a handy clause that allows the military to make any changes to any part of the contract with no notification required, meaning most likely you will not get the job you want, despite all the promises and handshakes.

Often, recruits are told during boot camp that they can choose from an array of military jobs, but once they get out, they are forced into taking less desirable jobs (International Action Center 2005; Ziemba 2008). This happened to Joshua Key, who was promised by a recruiter that he would get to build bridges in the continental United States after finishing boot camp. Instead, he was promptly shipped off to Iraq, and being the lowest ranked in his unit, was the one chosen to dispose of his companies' solid waste, becoming the company's "shit stirrer." Key wasn't assigned this job as punishment—it was considered normal procedure for the lower-ranked enlistees, most of whom were impoverished when they joined the military, to be assigned the worst jobs in the unit.

The same hierarchies that are part of capitalist society are reflected in the ranks and structures of the military. For example, 3 percent of all Latino/as in the Marines are officers—over 80 percent of officers are white (Mariscal 2004). Latinos tend to serve in combat positions. In the JROTC, 54 percent of participants are minority youth; of all JROTC participants, 70 percent end up being in the lower ranks of the military. These programs that reinforce unfair hierarchies cost the high schools in which they are located an average of $50,000 per year (International Action Center 2005).

The other commonly promoted myth about the military are the signing bonuses and money for college, with $70,000 from the G.I. Bill promised. Only 1 in 20 even qualify for the $70,000 to begin with (International Action Center 2005). The most an enlistee can get from the GI Bill is a little over $36,000, barely enough to cover the tuition for four years at a public university. If an enlistee wants the total $70,000, they have to score above the mean on the on the ASVAB and sign up for the military jobs that are the hardest to fill. In fact, the amount of money enlistees will receive in hand after signing the contract is zero. Due to a variety of personal factors, 57–65 percent of GI Bill applicants never receive money for college (International Action Center 2005; Ziemba 2008). To qualify for GI Bill money, you have to be honorably discharged (20 percent aren't), have to be able to attend school (not likely if you have impairments), have to be enrolled in a VA approved program, and have to survive your tour (GI Bill money doesn't go to the survivors) (International Action Center 2005). As Ziemba (2008, 14) explains, "The average person that does receive money from the GI Bill will get a meager $2,151, not the tens of thousands promised in advertisements".

Of all enlistees who finish four years of military service, only 16 percent complete a degree program (International Action Center 2005). Like other victims of "government prioritizing," the GI Bill awards have not kept up with the costs of tuition, which has increased as much as 65 percent between 1995 and 1999 alone, while GI Bill funding has only jumped 16 percent. Making matters worse, the GI Bill and other promised signing bonuses are loans—to apply for the GI Bill a mandatory, non-refundable monthly deduction of $100 is drawn from the enlistee's pay, barely at minimum wage levels to start with. In fact, the military profits from the GI Bill, as people give up applying for the funds, and the non-refundable deposits are placed into Pentagon coffers. If an enlistee doesn't complete her/his required tour, they have to pay back any bonus awarded.

Rampant tuition inflation–public college tuition has gone up four times more than median family income in the 1990s—has not brought on many alternatives for funding a college education (Kamenetz 2006). Like the military, postsecondary institutions have steered students toward loans rather than grants as financial aid. Clinton did not allocate much funding for the Pell Grant during the sixth reauthorization of the Higher Education act in 1992. Instead, student loan maximums were increased and newer unsubsidized loans (where accumulated interest is added to the loan amount) were made available. Making matters worse, Pell Grants and similar aid packages are not tied to inflation costs but are adjusted during each reauthorization. "In 1976, the maximum Pell covered 72% of costs at the average four-year public school; in 2004 it paid just 36%" (Kamenetz 2006, 26).

Reflecting the privatization trend in social services, college education costs are being shifted to students and their families, even as enrollments soar. In the early 1980s, most federal financial aid came in the form of grants. Now, most of the funding comes in the form of loans—almost 60 percent with nearly two-thirds of students borrowing to pay tuition. As a result, the student loan industry is itself has become a profit-making entity. According to Kamenetz (2006, 29), in 2005, Sallie Mae made the Fortune 500 as the "second most profitable company in returns on revenue..." Eighty-five billion dollars in new loans were the result. Now, two-thirds of four year students graduate with an average of up to $23,000 in loan debt, an average unpaid credit card balance of $2,169, and one fourth of these students putting their tuition on their credit cards. (Kamenetz 2006, 5) Predictably, rates of default on student loans began to rise in the late 80s, reaching 22 percent in 1992.

Kamenetz (2006, 33) explains that even when students drop out of school, they have to repay the loans and considering that freshman attrition rests at one-third, further possibility for the debt-and-default cycle begins when one is young: "If student loans go into default, the government can garnishee 15% of your wages without taking you to court. Under a 1996 law, the feds can seize your Social Security, tax refunds, or even emergency and disaster relief payments to pay off old student loans." Even declaring Chapter 7 bankruptcy won't help—student loans are exempt from forgiveness. Kamenetz presents economists' data on "manageable" debt burdens, where payments should be no more than 8 percent of monthly income. By these measures, 39 percent of student borrowers now graduate with unmanageable debt, including 55 percent of African American and 58 percent of Hispanic graduates.

The trend is also moving toward college savings plans / IRAs, with government support being thrown behind benefits that are more likely to enrich those with the money to set aside for these kinds of plans, rather than direct assistance to poor and working class families. This mirrors what Kamenetz (2006) notes about recent "merit-based" grants and scholarships, which she argues, are helping the very families who can already afford full tuition in the first place. Indeed, university awards to families making $100,000+ annually have grown by 145 percent, while families making less than $20,000 annually grew by only 17 percent! In addition, "the lowest achieving rich kids attend college at about the same rate (77%) as the smartest poor kids (78%)" (Kamenetz 2006, 42).

As Kamenetz (2006) points out, today's college students, compared to students in the 1970s, are older, require child care assistance, need increased financial aid to offset lower-paying jobs while in school, have more gaps in attendance between high school and college (and between semesters once in college), and require weekend and evening class offerings along with intense advising to ensure graduating. When our institutions of higher education push these students aside, many will turn to the military for its perceived benefits. And when the military reflects the same hierarchies and lack of financial aid seen at the colleges and universities, this feeds the cycle of debt and drop-outs that benefits capitalism the most.

Conclusion

In order to resist recruiting, we have to take a hard assessment of the situation, which is fast deteriorating for all segments of the population. This includes respecting the reasons why many young people are interested in the military and comprehending the combination of debt and desperation facing not only high school students, but also those attending colleges. Continuing the military metaphor, the government has been in full retreat from funding social services and infrastructure since the mid 1970s. Politicians have been the ones to "cut and run" in the face of an incredibly patient populace. In this climate, military service looks like the only option until young people join only to discover that it's the same government denying them health care and education!

References

Aleman III, George. 2007. "Manufacturing Conscription." *Z Magazine* 20(7/8): 12–13.
Balfanz, Robert & Nettie Legters. 2004. "Locating the Dropout Crisis." Report 70, Center for Research on the Education of Students Placed at Risk. Typescript.
———. 2006. "Closing 'Dropout Factories': The Graduation-Rate Crisis We Know, and What Can Be Done about It." *Education Week* 25(42): 42–43.
Bender, Kristin. 2008. "Lawmakers Won't Back Down Following Berkeley Council's Vote Retracting Statement to U.S. Marine Recruiters."

The Mercury News, February 14. Accessed on July 16, 2009 at http://www.mercurynews.com/breakingnews/ci_8260944?nclick_check=1.
Binh, Pham. 2007. "Disposable Heroes." *International Socialist Review* 55: 48–53.
Concurrent Admissions Program. 2002. Washington, DC: *United States Army Recruiting Command, USAREC Regulation 621–2*: 1–11.
Gasper, Phil. 2004. "Is Biology Destiny? Genes, Evolution, and Human Nature." *International Socialist Review* 38. Accessed on July 18, 2009 at http://64.233.167.104/search?q=cache:JsgKEYLBXqwJ:www.isreview.org/issues/38/genes.shtml+is+biology+destiny+gasper&hl=en&ct=clnk&cd=2&gl=us&client=firefox-a.
———. 2007. "Prisoners of Ideology." *International Socialist Review* 52: 18–19.
Gibson, Rich, Greg Queen, E. Wayne Ross, and Kevin Vinson. 2007. "I Participate, You Participate, We Participate…They Profit. Notes on Revolutionary Educational Activism to Transcend Capital: The Rouge Forum." *Journal for Critical Education Policy Studies* 5. Accessed on February 23, 2009 at http://www.jceps.com/index.php?pageID=article&articleID=97.
Giroux, Henry. 2004. "What Might Education Mean After Abu Ghraib: Revisiting Adorno's Politics of Education." *Comparative Studies of South Asia, Africa, and the Middle East* 24: 3–22.
International Action Center. 2005. *We Won't Go: The Truth on Military Recruiters and the Draft, A Guide to Resistance.* New York: International Action Center.
Johnson, Chalmers. 2008. *Nemesis: The Last Days of the American Republic.* New York: Holt Paperbacks.
Kamenetz, Anya. 2006. *Generation Debt: Why Now Is a Terrible Time to Be Young.* New York: Riverhead Books.
Key, Joshua. 2007. *The Deserter's Tale: The Story of an Ordinary Soldier Who Walked Away from the War in Iraq.* New York: Grove Press.
Liptak, Adam. 2008. "1 in 100 Adults Behind Bars, U.S. Study Says." *New York Times*, February 28. Accessed on May 29, 2009 at http://www.nytimes.com/2008/02/28/us/28cnd-prison.html?hp.
Mariscal, Jorge. 2004. "No Where Else To Go: Latino Youth and the Poverty Draft." *Political Affairs Magazine.* Accessed on April 3, 2009 at http://cutjrotc.pbworks.com/w/page/8187976/Latino%20Youth%20and%20the%20Poverty%20Draft%20-%20Jorge%20Mariscal.
McClam, Erin. 2008. "Why Does Johnny Come Marching Homeless?" *YahooNews.* Accessed on June 12, 2009 at http://abcnews.go.com/US/wireStory?id=4159240.
Miller, Steven and Jack Gerson. 2008. "The Corporate Surge against Public Schools." *Substance News*, 33: 10–16.
No Child Left Behind Act of 2001. 2001. Accessed on February 2, 2008 at 2009http://www.ed.gov/policy/elsec/leg/esea02/107–110.pdf.

Perlo-Freeman, Sam, Catalina Perdomo, Elisabeth Skons, and Petter Stalenheim. 2009. *Military Expenditure*. Stockholm International Peace Research Institute. Accessed on June 3, 2010 at http://www.sipri.org/yearbook/2009/files/SIPRIYB0905.pdf.

Quigley, Bill. 2007. "Fighting for the Right to Learn in New Orleans, Part II." *Substance News*. Accessed on June 7, 2009 at http://64.233.167.104/search?q=cache:kUQePByBWuAJ:www.substancenews.net/issues/2007/october2007/sections/october2007_afterthoughts.html+new+orleans+charter+schools+2007+substance&hl=en&ct=clnk&cd=1&gl=us&client=firefox-a.

Rasmus, Jack. 2007. "VEBAs in the Auto Industry: How Companies Dump Union Negotiated Health Plans." *Z Magazine* 20: 42–45.

Recruiting Operations. 2006. Washington, DC: *United States Army Recruiting Command*. Accessed on September 9, 2009 at http://www.usarec.army.mil/im/formpub/rec_pubs/man3_0.pdf.

Ruder, Eric. 2007. "Iraq Veterans Speak Out." *International Socialist Review* 53: 20–23.

Saltman, Kenneth and David Gabbard, eds. 2003. *Education as Enforcement: The Militarization and Corporatization of Schools*. New York: Routledge.

Schahill, Jeremy. 2007. "Blackwater's Heart of Darkness." *International Socialist Review* 56: 23–31.

Schmidt, George. 2007. "U.S. Marines Occupy Chicago Board of Education Meeting." *Substance News* 33: 1–10.

Schmitt, Eric. 2005. "Army Recruiting More High School Dropouts to Meet Goals." *The New York Times*, June 11. Accessed on September 7, 2009 at http://www.nytimes.com/2005/06/11/politics/11recruit.html.

School Recruiting Program Handbook. 2004. Washington, DC: *United States Army Recruiting Command, USAREC Pamphlet*, 350–413. July 4, 2009 at http://www.nodraftnoway.org/public_html/USAREC%20Pam%20350-13%2020040901.pdf.

Sempre Fi Act (H.R.5222). 2008. Accessed on May 5, 2009 at http://www.indybay.org/uploads/2008/02/13/semper_fi.pdf.

Sklar, Holly. 2007. "Imagine a Country." *Z Magazine* 20: 26–31.

Spring, Joel. 1999. *Wheels in the Head: Educational Philosophies of Authority, Freedom, and Culture from Socrates to Human Rights*. New York: McGraw Hill.

Wilcox, Richard. 2003. "United States Militarism, Global Instability, and Environmental Destruction." Typescript. Accessed on May 7, 2009 at http://www9.ocn.ne.jp/~aslan/rwilcox.htm. 7

Ziemba, Rynn. 2008. "Iraq War Veteran." *Z Magazine* 21: 14–16.

Chapter 7

Neoliberal Politics Impacting Education: Imagining Possibilities of Resistance

Ravi Kumar

Understanding the Educational Processes

One would often wonder, looking at the dominant discourse within Indian educational discourse, if education signifies merely the acts and activities that happen within the four walls of a classroom or if it would have a wider recognition of pedagogical spheres. No doubt that there has been a tradition of looking at education from a completely different perspective in India—Rabindranath Tagore would have looked at education as a liberating instrument that overcomes fear and repression and that moves beyond the narrowness of fragmented realities, while Gandhi looked at the relationship of education with work (which has been vulgarized into vocational education by postindependent India's ruling class). Gandhi meant much more than literal "manual labour" when he was talking of connecting education with work. He was looking at education beyond the classroom—he considered the diverse aspects of one's individual as well as collective life as a medium of education. Nonetheless, there has been virtually no Marxist reflection/analysis in the educational debates in the country, except for some that have emerged as critiques of state policies from the left political formations. Today, Indian educational debate has travelled a long distance along with the trajectory of capital. While Indian education system has become more unequal and the idea of knowledge more fragmented, there are also different types of "alternatives" that have emerged. However, these alternatives do not question state or posit education within the labor-capital framework.

What we have developed in form of a educational discourse in the country is largely a response to the bourgeois state's policy making and the "progressive" school has largely fallen in the trap of a Keynsian framework, wherein the preneoliberal phase seemed more promising in terms of promises of equality in terms of access and "critical" nature of education. Today the discourse, even the most "progressive" one, (which, obviously, is quite distant to Marxism), presents a limited and disjuncted view of the world, which not only hides the systemic contradictions but also allows a process of regimentation to become possible. The fact that the Brahmins (the priestly caste) and the Kshatriyas (the warrior caste), or the entrenched hegemonic class interests of a particular social order, needed to segment the processes of education so that it sustained the segmentation of the social order, could never be understood as such unless one overcame the myopia of understanding how processes of knowledge production are linked to the production processes in a society. It is this myopia, which allows us to still celebrate an undemocratic idiom of explaining the teacher-taught relationship by equating the teacher with God. It is the intrinsic uncritical appraisal of such an idiom, which leads us even today to say that the teacher reveals the path to the kingdom of God. And it is this belief in the existence of a particular kind of system that celebrates the existence of gods and consequently the caste system and supremacy of Brahmins. Such a belief bases itself on uncriticality and opposition to dissent, which has been one of the functions of supernatural entities. It is the same belief, which by natural corollary, fails to understand the Dronacharya—Eklavya[1] relationship as embedded in the class-caste relations as expressing how segmentation of education was ultimately about segmentation of society along classes. And this was not only ancient India, the same continues to happen even today wherein a vision of understanding the processes of education as going beyond classroom and institutionalized structures is seldom encouraged. Even if it is done, the connections between mode of production and educational systems is rarely explored.

This, in effect, means an analysis emerges which fails to understand the neoliberal impact on education and its implications for the working class. There appear serious problems in analysis which can be summed up through the following issues:

1. There exists a *dehistoricized* understanding, that is, denying conjuncturality of different stages of development of capital and the nature of education discourse and conditions on the ground
2. There exists a *disjunctural* understanding of education and structures / social relations

3. Education is *discounted* as a site of class struggle and therefore a battlefield where the everyday class struggles are reflected
4. There is a serious *absence* of reflection on the issue by the Indian left.
5. Because of the above-mentioned factors, education is largely identitied with what happens within the institutionalized structures, shorn of class politics and outside the ambit of labor-capital conflict.
6. Consequently, education acquires a kind of *autonomy* and an agency of its own, which leads us to imagine social transformations as effected by educational reforms; it does not recognize how educational reforms (especially when the framework is largely about state run policies and institutions) are themselves products of a dynamics, which does not only involve state but may also be effected by social movements.

A comprehensive understanding of the developments taking place today with respect to education and knowledge formation at large can emerge only if the above-mentioned factors are taken care of. It is only then can one understand that neoliberalism does not only affect the institutions, moulding them to its own end but also alters radically the way even welfarist, social-democratic forces understood education. For instance, it does tell us in very clear ways that the classical idea of a classroom must be altered—it should not only be replaced with schools without teachers/instructors where teaching-learning happens *online* but it can also happen through mobile phones or through satellite television. In other words, when the state offers alternatives of online education as the new method or when private enterprises tell us through their advertisements that it does not matter if you miss classes because there is a virtual classroom or when Abhishek Bachchan (a film actor) graphically shows how classrooms can happen anywhere (which would even mean, at the cost of exaggerating it, that child labor can go hand in hand with education) with education being imparted through mobile phones or when the new symbol of humane, concerned, and conscientious India—Aamir Khan (another film actor)—tells you that education is possible even through satellite channels, there is an underlying commonality in their visions.

They are telling that equality of access to education is possible even within neoliberal capitalism; they are suggesting that access need not always be seen in direct person-to-person or person-to-institution contact, it can be impersonalized as well; they are suggesting why do we always need to locate the question of equality within a framework of class relations or consider state as the provider of educational means and facilities; they are telling that profiteering or mindless urge to accumulate surplus can go hand in hand with the principle of equality and justice. In a nutshell, it is a denial of conjunturality of capital-labor contradiction with the issue of knowledge formation and dissemination. This denial appears, in a not so stark and unabashed manner, when the progressive voices and forces uncritically get into the nostalgia of reinstating welfarism. In other words, when they, knowingly or unknowingly, take an approach of ensuring *equality* or *justice* outside the ambit of class struggle because it then does not problematize the intentionality of capital at different moments in history.

Neoliberalism is the New Name of Politics of Capital

The Indian political scenario can be defined by one characteristic, despite so much of upheaval in it, that it has wide consensus among different political formations towards falling in line with neoliberal capitalism. Hence, when neoliberalism arrived, except for some token resistance, there has not been much of organized resistance to it. The traditional left has been on a constant decline and divided due to, primarily, sectarian politics and failure to develop a critically introspective politics. On other hand, the newer voices of discontent, represented primarily through identitarian politics of caste or gender, failed to develop a sharp critique of neoliberalism, primarily because of absence of a critique of capital in general. Due to such a situation, neoliberalism has flourished and even in times of recession it did not confront the difficulties that it did elsewhere in world. This made it confidant and unabashedly shrewd, callous, and calculating. It uses the instruments of consensus as well as coercion with utmost dexterity, becomes part of our individuality and has all possible designs to alienate us from our collective working class consciousness in such a way that for sometime the battlefield becomes hazy with the mirage of all kinds of possibilities. Within the given system, we work hard and give our lives to it. This is the age of neoliberal capitalism, which represents the tyranny of capital in the most organized and atrocious manner and India's economic and political scenario for last one-and-a-half decades represent this tyranny. It is a stage or a moment in capital accumulation, which plays with rhetoric of justice and equality but is extremely undemocratic.

In this phase of capitalism, it is also difficult times for those who believe in resisting the rule of capital, despite the fact that the Indian state has become shamelessly neoliberal as it uses the instruments of coercion as well as consensus to achieve its goals. In fact, there has been a neoliberal consensus evolving across diverse political formations and amply clear in the situation post-2009 general elections (Kumar 2010). The rhetoric of social justice, demands for equity built on a premise of identitarian politics as well as the hollowness of the justice and equity driven market has been exposed. What, then, remains as the subject of concern for all of us is: (1) to comprehend the logic and strategy of capital at the current conjuncture; (2) enquire into the way this is manifested in the arena of education; and (3) evolve ways of resisting this onslaught of capital. Toward achieving these tasks, this chapter tries to understand the idea of neoliberalism and what it does.

While it would be a repetition to say that there has been a continuing decline in the expenditure on "social sector" by the Indian state, it would be erroneous to reiterate that decline without analyzing it as a consequence of the persistent battle between capital and labor. The mutilations in the education system are no more than embodiments of this conflict in the arena of state, economy, and polity. The state becomes an agent of capital, assisting it in expansion and, whenever/wherever necessary, repression—physical as well as intellectual. In other words, apart from the mere physicality of the neoliberal impact, there are very dangerous and more powerful mental and intellectual instruments working overtime to consolidate the already gained grounds for capital or creating possibilities for newer grounds to be captured. This character of the neoliberal phase of capital accumulation emerges out of the specific historical moment in which it is born. It was the crisis of accumulation in "embedded liberalism" that paved way for this new system to emerge, after the option of deepening "state control and regulation of the economy through corporatist strategies" (Harvey 2007, 12) became problematic because the left, which had forwarded this idea, "failed to go much beyond traditional social democratic and corporatist solutions and these had by the mid-1970s proven inconsistent with the requirements of capital accumulation" (Harvey 2007, 13). Obviously, the increasing influence of left was also becoming problematic for the unhindered expansion of capital. The influence of left unions and mobilizations were strengthening. One finds the vibrant movement of the left flourishing during the era of welfare capitalism even in India. Trade unionism as well as other forms of resistance to the rule of capital (which is otherwise always open to debate) did pose a substantial challenge to the politics of the ruling class. The resistance in these two different phases also becomes a matter of relative comparison as we are confronted with moments of declining resistance to the politics of capital in the neoliberal era. It was this imperative of curtailing the challenges to capital accumulation that compelled neoliberalism to become a political ideology as well.

Hence, we find neoliberalism giving "priority to capital as money rather than capital as production" and, by doing so, it allows "policies to be adopted which clear the decks, removing subsidies and protection, and freeing up capital from fixed positions" intensifying the pace of restructuring. "It allows capital to regain mobility, dissolving the spatial and institutional rigidities in which it had become encased" (Gamble 2001, 131–132). State, which was welfarist and had undertaken campaigns of nationalization and promised to take care of the health and educational concerns of its people, started saying that it was not possible for it to bear the burden of educating every child or taking care of the health needs of its citizens. Consequently, it comes up with an analysis that would suit its market logic. For instance, it argues, in context of secondary schools, that "the doubling of the share of private unaided schools indicates that parents are willing to pay for education that is perceived to be of good quality" (GOI 2008, 15). And extension of this argument results in involving more and more private players in running the education system as a business. Consequently, the government plans to open model schools, which "will be managed and run by involving corporates, philanthropic foundations, endowments, educational trusts, and reputed private providers" (GOI 2008, 17). This tendency to open up new avenues or withdraw from certain roles and responsibilities that the states have been supposed to partake has been intrinsic to the character of the neoliberal state. "The contribution of neo-liberalism to the restructuring of capitalism was therefore to provide a means by which capital could begin to disengage from many of the positions and commitments which had been taken up during the Keynesian era" (Gamble 2001, 132).

Rhetoric of Dignity, Freedom, Autonomy and Well-Being—The Neoliberal Politics

Neoliberalism functions on the premise that the "human well-being can best be advanced by liberating individual entrepreneurial freedoms and skills within an institutional framework characterized by strong private property rights, free markets, and free trade" (Harvey 2007, 2). It uses the principle of *freedom* and *justice* but as concepts that apply to individuals treating them as autonomous beings outside the social relations within which they are embedded. Hence, neoliberalism looks at the role of the state as a body that creates and preserves institutional frameworks that ensure this project of capital. The state has to not only "guarantee, for example, the quality and integrity of money" but also set up structures of coercion "to secure private property rights and to guarantee, by force if need be, the proper functioning of markets" (Harvey 2007, 2). State intervention in management and regulation of market becomes negligible. It has to only facilitate its functioning but not intervene in what it does or wants to do. The quintessential example of this is found in two simultaneous developments in India: (1) the state expenditure on education has been on decline and the share of private sector in it has been on rise because capital thinks that the education "sector" needs to be liberated from the clutches of statist structures and principles; and (2) over 40,000 crores (400,000 millions) of rupees have been spent on organization of a game show (Commonwealth Games), which Indians neither relate to nor did they want, because for them priorities could well have been health and education. It is happening because the postrecession Indian industry needs as many shows as possible like this one. These two developments show how state creates opportunities for the market and for this it withdraws and creates space for private capital in certain areas whereas it subsidizes the expansion of private capital at the cost of it masses. However, it chooses not to spend on education and health to make them accessible to everyone.

It has been argued that liberalism had made life suffocating for people. Mongardini cites Burdeau who argues that it ceased to be "the hope of a whole people" and had rather become "the ideology of a class: the bourgeoisie." The state under bourgeoisie had been transformed into "into a closed power" (Burdeau quoted in Mongardini 1980, 318). In other words, under liberalism, the state, rather than resolving the tension between the individual and the state, had made latter "the natural enemy of liberty" (Mongardini 1980, 318). Neoliberalism is seen as defending the social rights of individuals. It "seems to begin as a civil reaction against the invasion of politics and bureaucratic machinery, of little groups against large groups, the private against the public. It is, however, from another point of view also an attempt to reestablish at ground level that relationship of political representation which has been broken and to recreate consensus on a new ideological platform which restores certainty to individual and social action" (Mongardini 1980, 321). Hence, what one finds is that the ideals of human dignity and individual freedom have become the driving ideology, as the slogan, of neoliberal thought and "in so doing they chose wisely, for these are indeed compelling and seductive ideals. These values, they held, were threatened not only by fascism, dictatorships, and communism, but by all forms of state intervention that substituted collective judgements for those of individuals free to choose" (Harvey 2007, 5). And obviously, the agency to ensure this freedom and dignity has always been the market for neoliberal ideologues and states.

The idea that neoliberalism is dedicated to ensuring the well-being of human beings, through ensuring equity and justice has been instilled into our common sense. It is done through a variety of ways:

(1) There are arguments and theories of development, which never look at the political economic aspects of the development and, therefore, create a well thought out disjunct between, for instance, market, state and development. They tell us how equity and justice is attainable even within neoliberalism without transforming fundamentally the social relations that give rise to these inequities. Herrera, arguing against the development economists, points out how the softer development economists get away as critics of the system, which, in fact, "is a serious misunderstanding, because neither of them recommends rebuilding the welfare state, modifying the ownership structure of capital in favor of the public sector, applying a policy of income redistribution, or promoting public services—much less arguing in favor of state-led planned development. In spite of a few nuances or subtleties, their arguments always imply that the state should fully submit to the dominant forces of global capital and help its capital accumulation" (Herrera 2006). Citing example of Stiglitz, Herrrera argues how during Stiglitz's regime as the chief economist the World Bank published its report on "Knowledge for Development" in 1998–99, which talked about "cooperation" with the private sector "in the fields of information and telecommunications: privatization, dismantlement of public research (even the transformation of research institutes into joint stock companies), and marketization of education (even by helping the poor to pay for their studies)" (Herrera 2006). Amartya Sen, on the other hand, locates, in an occulted manner, the social and political rights within the ambit of market. "Without a liberal-style market," Sen seems to say, "none of the other freedoms can work" (Harvey 2007, 184).
(2) Competition has been made the guiding ethics of everyday life. This ethics is not only based on the farcical idea that everyone has the equal opportunity to participate and perform in the

competition but it also generates a desire among individuals to be part of this system, which, apparently, demonstrates the *possibility of equal probability* to achieve the goal. This sense of competition, which wrongly presumes equal access to required information as well as which ignores the differential material conditions that go into the formation of an individual or group, though being essentially misplaced, generates a sense of constant involvement within the system. This not only complicates, and therefore delays, the task of mobilization along class lines but also gradually fosters a misplaced sense of fidelity towards the system. While the ethics of competition cultivates fantasies, aspirations and generates possibilities to achieve them, it also encourages individuation and therefore diminishes sense of solidarity. This ethics becomes a part of us through the pedagogical experiences of everyday life under the rule of capital.

(3) There is a vast network of ideological apparatuses, which are at work to legitimize the neoliberal system as well as to garner support for it. While a great deal has been written about how media becomes an effective instrument of propaganda, there are misrepresented and fallacious analyses carried out by the intellectuals in favor of the neoliberal order. One very obvious example is the work of James Tooley, who argues, following Oxfam Education Report, that "private schools are emerging for the poor in a range of developing countries" (Tooley 2004, 6). While he quite intentionally ignores the same Oxfam Report when it also says that "while private schools are filling part of the space left as a result of the collapse of State provision, their potential to facilitate more rapid progress towards universal basic education has been exaggerated. They are unable to address the underlying problems facing poor households, not least because their users must be able to pay, which the parents of most children who are out of school often cannot do" (Watkins 2000, 230). Not only this but the whole argument forwarded by likes of Tooley, based on "evidence" from India and elsewhere that "there is considerable evidence available...that suggests that private education is more beneficial to the poor than the government alternative, and hence that parents are making rational decisions by sending their children to private schools" is misplaced and out of context. It not only ignores to analyse the basic and fundamental causation behind the flourishing of substandard (or otherwise) private schools across India but also forwards an argument to encourage privatization of education when it says that "the making of

profits is an important motivation for entrepreneurs to enter the education market, and hence it may have some desirable impact, leading to the provision of schools that poor parents prefer to the government alternative. Without the profit motive, this suggests that there would be fewer private schools available, hence the choices available to poor parents would be severely limited." (Tooley 2004, 16)

They take the notions of competition, performance, and achievement as *apriori* categories and begin their studies on those already given premises (Tooley 2004; Tooley and Dixon 2005). In that sense their whole argument and research is designed to serve the system that is furthering that particular kind of education system, which rejects critical insight as an essential constituent of educational process or which trains students to dream for alternatives. Apart from such intellectuals working overtime to generate sufficient grounds for private capital to expand, the state has also been quite "sensitive" to the needs and demands of private capital. Knowledge Commission, a body of recognized intellectuals, for instance, very clearly points out toward the need to recognize the role played by private educational institutions and suggests that "those providing quality education should be encouraged, especially when they cater to less privileged children." It also suggests that the government bureaucracy should not harass them and "it is necessary to simplify the rules and reduce the multiplicity of clearances required for private schools..." (GOI 2009, 48). These are mechanisms to generate consensus among masses in favor of the restructuration of the economy. And these processes have occurred globally, as Harvey notes,

> So how, then, was sufficient popular consent generated to legitimize the neoliberal turn? The channels through which this was done were diverse. Powerful ideological influences circulated through the corporations, the media, and the numerous institutions that constitute civil society—such as the universities, schools, churches, and professional associations. The "long march" of neoliberal ideas through these institutions that Hayek had envisaged back in 1947, the organization of think-tanks (with corporate backing and funding), the capture of certain segments of the media, and the conversion of many intellectuals to neoliberal ways of thinking, created a climate of opinion in support of neoliberalism as the exclusive guarantor of freedom. These movements were later consolidated through the capture of political parties and, ultimately, state power. (Harvey 2007, 40)

(4) Neoliberalism weaves a world of fantasy around each individual as well as collectivities of achievable possibilities thereby confining their imaginations to function within the operational regime of capital. The delusional mind becomes unaware of the labor-capital dialectic. For it, the possibility of becoming one day what some people around him/her are, or owning what they own has a blinding effect. It never appears to the individual that she herself is located within that labor-capital dialectic. Capitalism, in general, through breaching the possibilities of solidarity among the working class, creates the expansion and sustenance of neoliberalism possible. What adds to this process is simultaneity of all of the above-mentioned socioeconomic and political processes.

Neoliberal Politics of Capital and Education

Neoliberalism, in general, is firmly entrenched today in India and with the tide of resistance getting lower at this moment, its virulent form and tenor is visible in nearly every sector. The education sector is one of the ideal types, which demonstrates how neoliberal assault works. The nature of changes, which have been brought about during last few years and with more vigor during the last one year have shown how neoliberal capital operates. The above-cited four factors that generate consensus and common sense about neoliberalism have been quite obviously active in the Indian context. A host of committees and commissions have been set up to establish how there cannot be any *possible alternative to capitalism* and, therefore, it is better to work within it. In terms of operationalization, the state has been formulating policies that institutionalize discrimination—as different kinds of schools and colleges are established in accordance with the differential purchasing and sociopolitical power of the customers—which draws in more and more private funding in education sector and denies equality of access to educational facilities of similar kind to everyone. The best example of such efforts to create a consensus in favor of neoliberalism can be found in Yashpal Committee, which has sanctioned everything that the neoliberal capital would like to put into place for its expansion. In other words, drastic changes in the form and content of the so-called education are taking place due to the onset of neoliberal stage. Hence, the developments in *policy, content,* and *form* of education need to be seen in conjunction with the changing forms of capital accumulation. Following have been some of the manifestations of this development in the country.

1. Education is more than the formal institutional structures and classroom transactions. It is an arena that reflects the agenda and need of the dominant class interests in a society. Therefore, to understand whatever happens in education, it is important to understand the class politics, or the labor-capital conflict, characterizing a society. But due to this lack, the character of the state is seldom questioned in the Indian education discourse. It, many a times, ends up being a nostalgic, illogical discourse that demands a neoliberal state to become welfarist. (Though I would admit that nostalgia has a potential, here, to generate radical impulse as well).
2. Capital in India never felt the need (during the last 60 years) to spread education (meaning democratize accessibility to education) because (a) the requirements of labor force were being met by an unequal system; (b) it was able to segment the educational levels of people in congruity with the segmented labor market thereby *regulating* the educational apparatus–labor market linkage as well.
3. Even today, the neoliberal capital cannot afford to democratize accessibility to education because it would amount to its decommodification.
4. Quite naturally, neoliberal capital destroys institutions that hamper its progress or appear not to make profits. It also curtails the pedagogic processes that potentially generate a critical perspective against the system—the decline of social sciences and fundamental researches in sciences is an example along with technicization of science and popularization of new "professional" (skill obsessed) courses in social science.
5. Within this scenario, class manifests itself in the following ways in education: (1) there is a particular kind of class formation that the education system foments; (2) the education system becomes an effective Ideological State Apparatus (ISA), evident in the way capital dominates over labor in their conflictual relationship even in the time of such a serious economic recession; and (3) the possibilities of transcending the capitalist mode of production, through creating new imaginations of a world beyond capital, becomes difficult and impossible thereby establishing inevitability of capitalism.
6. Education, if located in the matrix of labor-capital conflict, unfolds as the battleground of competing classes. The constituents of this location—teachers or students remain workers whose realization of their class position is delayed by the character/orientation of this location.

7. While education remains the most vital link for capitalism to sustain, it also remains the location where the link can be broken because it is where the workers (when they realize that they are workers) are also in control of the kind of product that they produce to a great extent (though this freedom is diminishing and is differential across the uneven terrain of educational landscape).

When the Congress party came to power along with a host of regional formations after general elections in 2009, the ministry of human resource development made it amply clear that voices of dissent were not welcomed. Whether it has been the issue of passing bills to further the expansion of capital or the issue of standardizing the functioning of academic institutions such as universities for better control and better manipulation, all decisions are being taken unilaterally and without any attempt of consensus building. One example of how undemocratically decisions to alter the syllabus or examination system, frame new service conditions for faculty members, or completely transform the physical infrastructure have been taken can be found in the University of Delhi where the faculty members as well as the students have been protesting for months. It has been happening in other universities as well but there is hardly any opposition. The tenor of the human resource development minister has been of an outright corporate man. Irrespective of whether the Indian Institute of Technology (IIT) faculty members were justified in demanding more salaries than faculty members of other institutions, the minister, on hearing their demand, remarked, "I am meeting some people from IITs and will ask them for a roadmap for the autonomy. If they tell us how much money from private investors they can get for the next five years, then we will give them more autonomy. They can take more projects and become private" (Business Standard 2009). What gets reflected in this statement is the way terminologies such as autonomy, freedom, and choice are used. It is autonomy in the sense of getting freed from barriers that would impede flow of capital. It is freedom from different kinds of restrictions, ranging from state policies to the ones posed by unionization. "The neoliberal notion of academic freedom arises from viewing knowledge as a commodity... and education as a path to income generation that must be privatized and made profitable in order for it to be maximally effective" (Caffentzis 2005, 600). While elementary education is in dire straits as the state fails to ensure that each child, irrespective of its class, caste, or gender background gets education of similar quality, higher education is moving towards becoming more and more inaccessible.

The neoliberal assault on education in India is different in terms of its trajectory compared to the West—the UK or United States, for instance, as result of struggle by masses as well as because of the needs of capital in those particular moments of history enacted laws and policies that made school education accessible to children. It was the phase of what Harvey calls "embedded liberalism" or what many others call as Keynsianism. The crisis of the Keynsian model of accumulation also reflected in the education when the governments of these nations began the process of withdrawal and started creating space for private capital within the sectors where state control was entrenched. The pattern was not very similar in India because the development of capitalism had a different trajectory. However, the welfare state that came into being postindependence did not create an education system on lines of what Gandhi or others during freedom struggle had conceived. It was a system designed for class biases to perpetuate. The Indian state created distinction in terms of "elite" institutions—the first IITs were born in early 1950s and the Indian Institutes of Management (IIMs) started in early 1960s—and the other institutions of higher education. Similarly, different types of schools were established by the Indian state for different sets of people. Even before these developments, the Indian constitution could not include right to education as a Fundamental Right, which very well reflected the priorities of the state. Though included in the Directive Principles of State Policy, more as a tokenism, expansion of education and ensuring equality of access were not the priorities for the welfare capitalism that was established under Jawaharlal Nehru. The needs of a skilled workforce were limited and the limited number of institutions was meeting those needs. Nothing more was required. The intentions of equality and social justice were being defined in the limited sense of what could have served the needs of capital. It was a notion of equality and justice falling within the mandate provided by that particular stage of capitalism. Hence, it is not only fallacious to get nostalgic about the "great" days of welfare state but it is also myopic in terms of analysis because it falls short of tracing the relationship of capital, in different forms and at different moments, with the education systems.

An extension of this fallacy is manifested in why the arguments for a better educational system or efforts at establishing alternatives that emerge at different points of time always fail. There is an intrinsic relationship between the educational processes and the social processes of reproduction. The two cannot be separated. "Accordingly, a significant reshaping of education is inconceivable without a corresponding transformation of the social framework in which society's educational practices must fulfill their vitally important and historically changing functions" (Mészáros 2009, 216). In other words, it is important to locate oneself in terms of class position before formulating educational analysis or alternatives. One cannot formulate an alternative from the vantage point of capital and claim to fight alongside labor or claim to establish a socially and economically just education system. "The objective interests of the class had to prevail even when the subjectively well-meaning authors of those utopias and critical discourses sharply perceived and pilloried the inhuman manifestations of the dominant material interests" (Mészáros 2009, 217). The reason behind the failure of efforts at changing the educational maladies and institute an alternative has been that they "reconciled with the standpoint of capital" (Mészáros 2009, 217).

Class Struggle as the Only Alternative—Resisting the Politics of Capital

In order to establish an alternative and built a resistance toward it, it is important to recognize that this alternative could happen outside of capitalism only. In this era of neoliberal capitalism, when the offensive of capital has pushed the resistance to backfoot, a counternarrative has to be rewritten. This counternarrative has to be a comprehensive battle plan that would include educational transformation as well.

> Our educational task is therefore simultaneously also the task of a comprehensive social emancipatory transformation. Neither of the two can be put in front of the other. They are inseparable. The required radical social emancipatory transformation is inconceivable without the most active positive contribution of education in its all-embracing sense...And vice-versa: education cannot work suspended in the air. It can and must be properly articulated and constantly reshaped in its dialectical interrelationship with the changing conditions and needs of the ongoing social emancipatory transformation. The two succeed or fail, stand or fall together. (Mészáros 2009, 248)

There are a lot of alternatives being put forth against the so-called neoliberal assault. The most radical of these alternatives find marketization of education, increasing commodification, consumerism, and subservience of education to corporate houses extremely problematic. They also lament about the transformed culture of the new education system that is coming into existence. These concerns appear quite justified and unproblematic. However, the problem begins when (1) the analysis of the situation is undertaken—in terms of why these tendencies emerge and not so much in terms of how they operate; (2) what can be the alternative; and (3) who will be the driving forces of transformation. There is a tendency to enumerate the symptoms without indicating or identifying the socioeconomic processes that give rise to them. Hence, even if such critiques of neoliberalism argue for alternatives, the thrust is on reinstating the welfare stage of capitalism. The location of the problem within labor-capital dialectic always remains absent. Welfare state and its institutions become the possible alternatives as if the idea of exploitation and inequality was absent in such a stage.

A close look at the trajectory of critiques within Indian educational discourse reveals that they have ranged from the ones that would argue for an alternative schooling system (but without acknowledging that such an alternative is restrictive because it neither talks of the social relation that produces the dominant unequal education system nor talk of the need to transcend that social relation by substituting it with another more egalitarian one) to the one which believes that there are possibilities of piecemeal "radical" contributions in state policy making which would have transformative effects. Hence, one finds educationists who would never question the character of the state or get into the question of how inequality in education or the role of state is actually about the politics of capital and system brought into place by capitalism. Consequently, the discourse in education ends up being suggestive of changes in state policies (whose necessity as a short-term reform to sharpen contradiction of capitalism cannot be denied) or results in setting up of schooling experiments, which ultimately fail in their agenda.

Such critiques are compelled to remain silent witnesses at moments when the neoliberal state adopts a welfarist stance on some of the issues. This happens because there is a distinct failure to unravel how and why certain institutions or policies come into being at particular moments in history and how those moments have also not been exclusive of the class antagonism. Therefore, scholars and activists alike begin imagining that a particular state institution within capitalism can have the potential of being revolutionary and antistate (read anticapitalist). Such an understanding destroys the possibility of systemic transformation without which an education system, which is liberating, is impossible to achieve. What can be more naïve than to think that capitalism would allow its education systems to produce critical, self-reflexive and radical beings who would question the basic premises of the system founded on the principles of private property, exploitation, and mindless race for accumulating wealth. Unless this naivety of the "radical-progressive" agenda of back-to-welfarism is taken care of, which discounts class struggle as the only possible alternative for transforming iniquitous education or health "sector," the battle cannot become sharp enough to threaten the neoliberal capital.

The path of resistance to capitalist education in general and neoliberal capital's agenda in education in particular lies in imagining an education system (1) that moves beyond classroom activities as pedagogical sources; (2) where teachers become transformative agents with a political agenda to rupture the politics of capital; (3) that looks at education process as emerging out of the social context, which is characterized by exploitation, abuse, and oppression of different kinds; and (4) which brings into the teaching-learning process the reality of the lives of students and teachers as people located within the dynamics of labor-capital conflict.

Note

1. Dronacharya and Eklavya were characters in the epic Mahabharata. Dronacharya was the teacher of the princes of the kingdom who refused to teach Eklavya because he was from a lower caste. Eklavya then decided to practice archery on his own in front of the statue of Dronacharya. He had the potential to become a better archer than one of the princes, namely Arjun, who was considered the best archer, and was also the pet student of Dronacharya. Dronacharya went to meet Eklavya, where he saw his statue being worshipped as a teacher. Because he was assumed to be the teacher the student was duty bound to pay him back with whatever the teacher asked him. Dronacharya asked for Eklavya's right thumb as the fee (because without the right thumb he could not hold the arrows and therefore could not be better than Arjun). Eklavya cut his right thumb and gave it to him.

References

Business Standard. September 26, 2009. "*Kapil Sibal Rules Out Salary Hike for IIT Faculty.*" Accessed on January 12, 2010 at http://www.business-standard.com/india/news/kapil-sibal-rules-out-salary-hike-for-iit-faculty/371345/.

Caffentzis, George. 2005. "Academic Freedom & the Crisis of Neoliberalism: Some Cautions." *Review of African Political Economy* 32(106): 599–608.

Gamble, Andrew. Autumn 2001. "Neoliberalism." *Capital and Class* 75 (Autumn): 127–134.

Government of India. 2009. *Knowledge Commission: Report to the Nation 2006–2009*, New Delhi: Knowledge Commission.
Harvey, David. 2007. *A Brief History of Neoliberalism*. Oxford: Oxford University Press.
Herrera, Rémy. 2006. "The Neoliberal 'Rebirth' of Development Economics." *Monthly Review* 58(1). Accessed on August 10, 2010 at http://www.monthlyreview.org/0506herrera.htm.
Kumar, Ravi. Winter 2010. "India: General Elections 2009 and the Neoliberal Consensus." *New Politics* XII (4, Whole Number 48): 107–111.
Mészáros, István. 2009. *The Challenge and Burden of Historical Time: Socialism in the Twenty-First Century*. Delhi: Aakar Books.
Mongardini, C. 1980. "Ideological Change and Neoliberalism." *International Political Science Review* 1(3): 309–322.
Planning Commission, Government of India. 2008. *Eleventh Five Year Plan (2007–2012), Volume II*. New Delhi: Oxford University Press.
Tooley, James. 2004. *Could the Globalisation of Education Benefit the Poor?* Occasional Paper No.3, Potsdam: The Liberal Institute of the Frierdrich Nauman Foundation.
Tooley, Jame and Pauline Dixon. 2005. *Private Schools Serving the Poor*. Working Paper: A Study from Delhi. Accessed on May 12, 2010 at http://www.ccs.in/ccsindia/pdf/Delhi-Report-Tooley-new.pdf.
Watkins, Kevin. 2000. *The Oxfam Education Report*. Oxford: Oxfam GB.

Chapter 8

The Struggle and Its Generalization: The Case of the University

Paresh Chandra

Preliminaries

Minor Issues

I feel duty-bound to warn the reader right at the beginning, of certain inadequacies this chapter suffers from. Its subject is such, and I discovered this while working on the chapter, that the chapter was always already destined to be part of a larger work. A number of assertions and assumptions are insufficiently supported here, and have been explored better in other pieces. Hopefully, qualifications and short notes will allow the reader to make her/his way through. The organization of the chapter was also a bit of a struggle because the other essays are not immediately available to the reader. To make reading what could otherwise have turned out to be a fragmentary piece easy, I have given it a form that is somewhat unconventional in the social sciences. The division into titled parts and subparts, in my view, makes the chapter a lot easier to comprehend as a whole.

To help readers hold parts of the argument together in their heads as they read, I have used titles that, I think, will facilitate this. The first, a prefatory section, and the second, which describes an incident that forms the context of these deliberations, are easy enough to categorize. The third and the fourth are called "The Structure" and the "The Subject." These are terms often used to signify the systemic totality and the agent who lives/struggles inside it respectively. Some of the subdivisions follow a similar schematic logic. As was said earlier, these are to help the reader hold on to separate pieces of the puzzle till they begin to fall in place.

Students and the Commonwealth Games

It is one thing to have a theory, another to have information of concrete situations, and quite another to be able to ground the theory in these concrete situations, after having taken into account the layers that mediate the abstract and the concrete. As this chapter unfolds, a concrete situation will be explored, and eventually a theoretical understanding will appear, without our entering the realm of theory as such.[1] But to be able to represent this unfolding of the internal logic of the concrete, I need to specify certain experiences, which helped me in formulating this dialectical attempt at bringing together the abstract and the concrete.

In 2010, when the "nation" was preparing to host the Commonwealth Games, the students of the University of Delhi were having a rather hard time. Evidently, the hostels that housed many students were needed for the guests supposed to arrive to watch the Games. So, the students were duly thrown out. There was already a dearth of hostels and many students lived in areas surrounding the university. With hostels being emptied the demand for places close to the university increased, and so did rents. A group of students, and some students' organizations, called meetings during the summer break to see if something could be done about the situation. I have offered a detailed analysis of the proceedings elsewhere.[2] Something else is of relevance here.

The "University Community for Democracy" (UCD), the umbrella group formed to organize protests, was not a homogenous body—it consisted of many individuals and organizations that did not agree on a variety of issues. Internal conflict arose on the question of where the "movement" was headed, or should be headed (not altogether a useless event, as we shall see). One particular disagreement led to what is in my view, if not in that of the two main participants, a useful debate. One group (the New Socialist Initiative, referred to as the NSI in the rest of this chapter), the dominant one numerically, among other things, seemed to want to the keep the movement limited to students. Their logic was that before the movement is generalized it should consolidate its base among students. The other (the Krantikari Yuva Sangathan, henceforth referred to as KYS), although not disagreeing with NSI on the need to consolidate the base among students, thought that generalizing the movement, among workers for instance, should be an immediate step.

Leaving aside the KYS's somewhat mechanical[3] labeling of students as "petty bourgeois," the manner in which they envisaged the generalization of the movement is instructive. According to the KYS, simply opposing the eviction of students from hostels was insufficient because it left out the vast majority of students who were not allotted hostel rooms in the first place. Looking at this as a sort of segmentation within the student body they argued that the movement should also, without delay, ask for more hostel rooms for those who did not get them earlier. However, not stopping here, they followed the logic of their argument to its culmination. The "housing question,"[4] they argued, was by no means limited to students. It affected the whole of the working class (in this case identified as a sociological entity). So if the movement was to also raise the demand of "rent regulation" by the state, it could spread to many others segments of the population.

Because of the various issues, some theoretical, others personal, the group eventually fell apart. The UCD, now made up mainly of NSI members and their sympathizers, continued the campaign, which did not go beyond a few token demonstrations. The KYS tried to continue in the direction they had so theorized, but they too failed to go much further, possibly due to lack of hands and adverse objective circumstances. The significant thing that comes out of this whole process, as far as the purposes of this chapter go, is a useful model of "generalization": the spreading of the internal logic of a movement to other sectors of the working class.[5]

A New Event

Writers, at least these days, need an event before they start writing, and readers need an event before they read. Sadly, leftists too need an event before they act. For these reasons, let me begin with an event.

Despite strong resistance from teachers, the University of Delhi adopted the "Semester System" in May 2011. Ever since talk of changing from the annual mode of examination to the semester mode began, the university administration had steamrolled a countless of number of opposing voices. Initially the official teachers' body, the Delhi University Teachers' Association (DUTA) took the case. Later on, concerned teachers realized that the DUTA had been compromised right from the beginning. The DUTA allowed the university administration to pass the semester system, managing to keep the teachers off by telling them that this concession was necessary; apparently, by accepting the semester system, the DUTA was keeping out new service regulations that would make life very difficult. It became increasingly clear that the service regulations were more or less a red herring being used to divert attention from the actual issue.

For some reason the semester system was very important, to the university administration, and even more to people much higher up, like the minister in charge of education, Kapil Sibal.

Subsequently, some militant teachers formed an independent body, called the Joint Action Body (JAB).[6] They took, and are still taking, independent action against this move of the university. After the court, in a ruling, disallowed teachers from striking work[7] (in the process infringing a fundamental right), the JAB tried other measures, including legal ones. Almost all they tried came to nothing. The administration was able to threaten some teachers out of the movement.[8] Still others got discouraged after nothing but negative signs and some pretty unjustifiable rulings came from the courts. At some points various student organizations and independent students tried to work with the JAB, but this too came to nothing.

Whether because a big part of those who comprised the JAB was made of teachers inexperienced in agitational politics, or because of lack of perspective on part of the leftists, at some point the JAB got completely lost in legal recourses. They kept hoping that something would stop the semester system, and, like frogs in a well, seemed unable to grasp the big picture. For some reason they even now seem to hope that the court will intervene, if not the High Court then the Supreme Court; a sort of liberal democratic naivety keeps them going. The cost of this naivety, however, may turn out to be big.

Movements often begin when the state takes a step that makes the situation worse than it is to begin with. The people affected respond by trying to stop that move. Sometimes they succeed, in which case the status quo is maintained. Sometimes they do not. In this case two things can be done: either they can accept their fate and try to make the best of it (teachers can accept the semester system and make the best of it by at least having a say in the drafting of new syllabi), or they can continue their struggle. If they choose the latter, a further question arises: if the unfavorable move cannot be stopped, the choice of what sort of action is one left with? The answer lies in looking around—the bigger picture. We are all clever enough to know that these changes in education policy are connected to larger issues like privatization, commercialization, foreign policy, the Bologna Agreement,[9] and so on, but somehow, many a times, all this information is received by a lot of concerned people in a sort of ideological vacuum; it remains ungrounded in a coherent understanding of the system. What lies beyond all of these facts and incidents? There is a reason why the court rules against us all the time. There is a reason why we have no control over the space in which we spend most of our time and almost all of our energy. Capitalism needs our labor power, and needs to use it in the way that suits it best. To go by our terms and conditions is to undermine its own logic, and the logic of capitalism dictates something very clear-cut at this moment.

The Structure

Theoretical Interlude

Those familiar with the history of Marxist theorizations of capitalism will know that ambivalence pervades the ones who try to understand it diachronically. With time, capitalism has gone through a number of internal mutations (presuming that even though these mutations, each an expansion, are responses to intensification of class struggle, they are still part of the contradictory inner logic of capitalism). With each mutation, one has to ask the question: has the structure changed qualitatively? Or is this change an aspect of the unfolding of the same essential logic that has remain unchanged? Marxism is essentially an engagement with materiality, based on "concrete analyses of concrete situations," and if such an engagement requires us to throw aside principles that may have become truth producing functions to us, then we must do so. So, in a way, each mutation of capitalism asks for a regrounding of Marxism's representation of capitalism. At no point can a universal be allowed to feel safe in the assumption that each new particular is only more of the same.

In his book *Representing Capital*, Fredric Jameson writes about why we need to return to Marx's *Capital*:

> The reason lies in the identity and difference between the stages of capitalism, each one remaining true to the latter's essence and structure (the profit motive, accumulation, expansion, exploitation of wage labor) at the same time that it marks a mutation in culture and everyday life, in social institutions and human relationships. (Jameson 2011, 9)

So, we must speak of both the said identity and the said difference. What is new about the structure today, and what has always defined the structure. With that we move on to our representation of the "structure".

Difference: What is New Today?

Labor and Law

It is not news to Marxist historians in India, and Indian Marxists in general, that the reason behind state ownership in the social and industrial infrastructure after independence, was not (at least not only) the influence of socialist powers within and without the national boundaries. "In 1944–45 when prominent capitalists sat down to ponder the possibilities facing an Independent India, and divined the Bombay Plan, they knew that they were going to have a very big say in the path the country takes. As a result of underdeveloped infrastructure, it seemed convenient to Tata, Birla and Co. to lay out an arrangement which required the state to make all necessary large investments, before they take over. To overstate for rhetorical effect, the next thirty years fulfilled the wishes of the Indian capitalist class. Of course, the Bombay Plan was never actually followed, but the 'development' that ensued in these years was more or less in concert with it. In the 80s, as construction of infrastructure reached its culmination, and internal contradictions of the so-called 'mixed economy' began to seem, or were made to seem unbearable, the judiciary's earlier attempts to strengthen labor laws and expand the purview of Constitutional provisions like the 'Right to Life' took a down turn." (Chandra 2010b). The era of Krishna Iyer[10] and those like him had ended.

It is also not news to us that it is very hard to change labor laws in India by going through the legislative bodies; which is to say, it is very difficult to actually *change* these laws at all. Many constitutional safeguards, and on top of that the reasonable strength of the left in the parliament in last few decades have ascertained this. Repeatedly, as a result, the judiciary, with its antilabor *interpretations* of laws, has been the way out for the worker-bashing schemes that privatization brought under the neoliberal regime. Right from the 1980s, the judiciary has never intervened, at least not in a big way, to defend the rights of the working people against profit interests (see, for instance, the direction that courts have recently taken in cases involving mining companies like Vedanta and POSCO, despite the odd "pro-people" ruling), and has in fact acted as an antiworker institution. It is the same thing that we witness in these spectacularly undemocratic and antilabor rulings of the court, made against teachers.

Selling the University

Though it is often termed a conspiracy theory, what actually seems a reasonably consistent and sensible theory is doing the rounds in the university. It is well known that there is no internal necessity to change from the annual mode to the semester mode in the University of Delhi. Even administrators cite reasons like, "the semester system is used all over the world," and so on. Given below are some reasons why the semester system is undesirable (most of them have been picked up directly from a pamphlet brought out by the "Campaign for Democracy", a students' group formed in the context of the anti-semester system mobilizations in the University of Delhi, of which the writer is also a part):

1. Because of the huge size of the university (it includes over 70 colleges, not to mention the various faculties and departments and centers), a centralized system (of examination, for instance) is already a lot of work. But it is still manageable in the annual mode. In the semester mode it would prove absolutely unfeasible. For instance there will be no time for revaluation of a students' marks in case s/he is not satisfied with them; and mistakes in evaluation are aplenty in a system as large as this one. The burden on the administrative staff will also be huge. Because of all these reasons the centralized system will not be able to exist in the semester mode.
2. Admissions for students belonging to reserved categories (Scheduled Caste / Tribe or Other Backward Classes) go on till very late in the year. These students will have very little time left to prepare for the first semester examinations.
3. Outstation students, for whom the university will already be inaccessible to an extent because of unavailability of accommodation, will not have any time to orient themselves to a completely new system and environment.
4. Extracurricular activities will be reduced greatly, once again because of the lack of time between semesters.
5. The workload on students will increase without really profiting them. Sheer quantity of assignments and tests will hardly help. Related to this is the watering down of many courses of study that cannot be taught in their current form in the semester mode.

At the macro level, we have seen in the last few years that the government is trying to reduce spending on education, health etc. To this we add, at the micro level (University of Delhi), the increasing problems of handling a centralized system in the semester mode. And into this mix we throw in the well-known fact that many prominent colleges of the University of Delhi (such as St. Stephens, Lady Sriram College etc.) are already pushing for autonomy. (Autonomization means giving college trusts greater power and effectively opening the gates for privatization.) Does it seem unlikely that the next step would be to sell off all university-owned colleges to private bidders? The usual response, experience will tell us, to alleged inefficiency in the public sector, is to privatize. If this theory holds any water, and it would seem so to all reasonably aware minds, we can rest assured that the judiciary is not going to be of any help, no matter how undemocratic the university administration gets in order to bring in the semester system. With what was said about privatization earlier, if we take into consideration recent changes in the nation's educational policies, this theory will indeed seem much more believable.

Transforming Education

Over the last five years, most leftist students' organizations that run awareness campaigns in universities in India invariably ended up speaking about privatization in education. Most of the time, to people who heard them, they seemed to be talking about nonexistent bogeys—the Foreign Educational Institutions (FEI) bill, FDI in education, the Model Act, and so on. But the funny thing is that no matter how unconvincing these campaigners sounded, what they were talking about was as true as death.

For instance, the Model act spoke of privatizing and commercializing education, and was held off only after a lot of resistance from teachers and students. Vijender Sharma, in a short piece titled "Yashpal Committee Report: Prescriptions not for Renovation and Rejuvenation of Higher Education," points out that even the apparently "progressive" *Yashpal Committee Report*, is not far from the Model act on this matter and recommends that "imaginative ways will have to be devised to find complementary sources of funds. Universities and other academic institutions should be able to hire professional fund raisers and professional investors to attract funding from non-government sources." (Sharma 2010a, 11)

In another essay called "FEI Bill Jeopardizes Our Higher Education System, Vijender Sharma says:

> Kapil Sibal, the new minister for Human Resource Development, immediately after assuming office on May 29, 2009 declared that bringing in the pending Foreign Education Institutions (FEI) Bill would be his top priority. The prime minister's office has been backing the bill. The Foreign Educational Institutions (regulation of entry and operation, maintenance of quality and prevention of commercialization) Bill, 2007 was planned to be introduced in the parliament (Rajya Sabha), in the first week of May 2007. But due to the opposition of the CPI(M), it was withdrawn at the last moment. (Sharma 2010b, 54)

I need not go into all the details about the FEI Bill[11] and foreign direct investment in education. At least the fact that they are connected to privatization of education can be assumed. The point of all this was to prove that disinvestment and privatization are actually taking place in Indian education. The Yashpal Committee Report mentioned earlier is internally contradictory. In the same breath as it seems to talk of these "imaginative ways" of finding funds, and making education market-oriented, it also expresses concern over the mushrooming of "deemed university." It mentions the problems that the emergence of unregulated private (and hence autonomous) educational institutions brings with it. In any case, the problem is severe enough for semiofficial bodies like the Yashpal Committee to take cognizance of it, despite their larger neoliberal thrust.

For all its problems, and for all the problems of the involvement of communist organizations in parliamentary politics, it cannot be denied that till the Communist Party of India (Marxist), or the CPI(M), had some hold over the United Progressive Alliance (UPA), it managed a few "achievements." In addition to the role they played in the implementation of the National Rural Employment Guarantee Act (NREGA), the CPI(M) also managed to keep out such proprivatization bills concerning education. Now, with the decline in their parliamentary hold and influence, these bills are being and will be passed thick and fast. This is what forms the background of the events unfolding in the University of Delhi.

But how does knowing all this help? What can the university community do to resist this? As was seen in the semester system case just mentioned, dissent seems to come to nothing. Why is it that concerned teachers or students can do nothing about their concerns? And what can be done to rectify this situation? To be able to address these questions better, it would be useful to take a look at how the university makes its decisions and how the organizational structure of the university affects its functioning.

Identity: The Structure of the University

Besides the vice-chancellor, in the normal workings of the university, the Executive Council (EC) and the Academic Council (AC) are supposed to be responsible for most administrative decisions taken. The presence of these bodies gives these decisions the weight of having being made democratically. Assertions to this effect are made so often and with such assurance that we begin to take them for granted. At most, struggling teachers or students will question the constitution of this or that EC or AC; the charge being that they were not made according to rules. No one ever questions the rules themselves. Let us spare a glance for what these rules are.

Statutes 5 and 7 of the "Act of the University" deal with the constitution of the EC and the AC respectively. Briefly, I will lay down the basic facts.

1. The Executive Council contains seven ex officio members: the vice-chancellor, the pro-vice-chancellor, the dean of colleges, the director of South Campus, the director of the Campus for Open Learning, the treasurer, and the proctor. It includes three deans of faculties, principals of three colleges, four members elected by the university court, two people nominated by the Visitor, and one person nominated by the vice-chancellor. This means that the EC is made up of 22 members, out of whom two are elected, and twenty are nominated or selected by the administration.[12]
2. The Academic Council consists of the vice-chancellor, the pro-vice-chancellor, the dean of colleges, the director of South Campus, the director of the Campus for Open Learning, the librarian, deans of faculties (the university has sixteen faculties listed on its official website), heads of departments (there are 88 departments listed on the website), eight professors (more or less in order of seniority), principals of fifteen colleges, the dean of students' welfare, five students, two external experts and twenty-six elected members. According to the list put down above, the AC is made up of 168 members, out of which 26 are elected. The five students' representatives (usually excluded from meetings), who are supposed to be part of the AC, are also not elected directly by the student community.

No matter how much teachers, or, for that matter, students, or members of the office staff *(karamcharis)* agitate, no matter how much opinion they generate, it all comes to nothing because the final decisions are made by the Executive and the Academic Councils. As has been shown above, these bodies are made up, predominantly, of nominated members, not of elected ones. Which is to say that all major decisions about the university, which, even when they are said to be made democratically, are made by nonelected bodies. If this is the case, then to have greater control over the conditions in which teachers/students/*karamcharis* work, the first thing to be brought onto the table should be the issue of democratization of these bodies. Those concerned need to bring into question the laws according to which these bodies are constituted.

As we saw earlier, the Joint Action Body (JAB), or at least that part of it that decides, is still bent on legal action. Petitions within the university and petitions to the court, trying to hold the university to its own laws—the claim is that the law has infringed itself. They try to prove that the particular Executive Council or the particular Academic Council that made these particular decisions was invalid, because all members who were supposed to be there were not present. Desiring to work within the law, they are still a far way off from questioning the law itself. Even if all the members had been there, decisions, very legitimately and legally made, would have still gone against them. The problem is not the infringement of these rules; the problem is the rules themselves.

When a group of students (who later formed the "Campaign for Democracy") proposed this approach to the JAB, they were only mildly interested. Evidently, their main objection was that this demand was too impractical and would never be fulfilled. They seemed to, at that point, lose sight of the fact (otherwise very clear to all of them) that even the fight they were in (to roll back the semester system, on grounds of its undemocratic introduction), was only going to end with their defeat. More importantly, there was a problem with the perspective from which they were viewing the entire matter.

The Subject

Generalizing the Struggle

There are ways and there are ways of raising the same questions. Let us look at the question of the semester system. A big part of the teaching community (especially those from the humanities and social sciences), and some students, take this as an attack on the space for "free thought", which it undoubtedly is. So, when they speak out against this move, it sounds like a defense of a privilege that they have had for very long, and are now about to lose. "The humanities are under attack! The humanities are a good thing that must be defended. They allow the people who are a part of this space and time to think, and think freely."

There are two criticisms of such a stand. The first is on politico-ethical grounds: why should they have the right to a privilege in a world in which we know that privileges for some inevitably mean greater pain and exploitation for others. Of course, "free thinking" does not hurt anybody, but it could be argued that asking for a state funded space to do this, might. The second criticism is on politico-pragmatic grounds: the university community, or that part of it which is concerned about the problem being discussed, is proving too weak to win, and they need help from elsewhere. Which essentially means that they need solidarity from other struggling people. If they continue to raise their demands in this form, as a defense of privilege that most never had, solidarity would be hard to come by. They must find a way of including others into their demands.

Elsewhere,[13] while explaining the tendency among students and intellectuals to identify easily with struggles of peasants fighting for their lands, I had made a few observations that can come in useful here. The struggles of peasants are defensive; they fight to defend privileges that they had and are losing. As we saw above, intellectuals fighting against possible proletarianization[14] (in this case through mechanization, commercialization, privatization of education) also fight to defend their privilege. What has been said for peasants/farmers so often in the history of various communist movements applies to intellectuals/teachers/students as well. They must go beyond defending past privileges, because only then will they be able to mingle with the vast majority who have no privileges to defend.

The space to think freely must be defended at all costs. But the way to do it is not to try and save what space is already there, because it excludes too many, but to try and expand it. In other words, the demand needs to be made in terms that make its "generalization" possible. The basis of generalization has to be what is common to all who are not privileged, to the proletariat—the lack of control over their own lives and labor. Keeping this in mind, let us return to the problem of perspective mentioned at the end of the previous section.

A group fighting to defend its privileges looks at only its local interests. It will question this or that particular move of the state but will remain unwilling to question the status quo as a whole. As was pointed out earlier, this is a problem because on the one hand such individuals fail to problematize their situation and are not self-reflexive enough to see the cost of their privileges. On the other, they do not seem to realize that local demands will not be met, because dissent is simply not strong enough to move the state. If they were aware of these problems they would take up the next important question—how to generalize? How to raise a demand that will facilitate generalization? What will this demand be?

The university community has little say in the decisions that affect their lives. Evidently, a big reason for this powerlessness is that they do not have control over the official bodies that make these decisions. While the national parliament may be elected, unelected bureaucrats control the work process (in public sector enterprises; there is absolutely no pretense in privately owned companies). This is exactly what must be changed. If the university community asks for the complete democratization of the Executive Council and the Academic Council, it effectively means that it is asking the state to withdraw from the university's functioning; it implies complete self-management. This demand questions the very core of the system—the alienation of man from his labor, loss of control over one's labor, and so on. Furthermore, it is also a demand that applies to all work places.

Before going on, it is absolutely essential to distinguish the autonomy that this self-management by the university community entails from the sort of autonomy that St. Stephens College seeks, or the one that a private college has. Unlike privately owned colleges, which in the final analysis put everything aside for private profit, this university, managed by those who work in it, will not run by some logic utterly alien to what the social role of such an institution should be. It will take into account the needs of those who seek education. It may even be possible to imagine a situation in which a part of the university's elected governing body is made up of representatives (once again elected) from other sections of society. If the idea behind a central university is to provide "planned education" to the people, then this university would do just that, but bureaucrats who are far removed from the realities of teaching and learning will not be the ones doing this planning.

An objection immediately raised is of impracticality: a vicious circle of ideology and bad/compromised reasoning. As has already been said, if the goals are determined not in terms of local resolutions, but in terms of generalization this question would never come up. The demand will never be fulfilled precisely because it is fundamental. If the state gives in to the demand for complete self-management in one sphere or sector, the ball is set rolling in a direction that it would like to blast out of existence. Furthermore, if a major university like the Delhi University (DU) goes this way, it would be a huge blow to the state, not the least financially—the prospective privatization of these colleges is probably expected to bring in a great amount to revenue for the state, not to mention eventual profits for the bidders. If the university community is actually able to raise the demand strongly enough, it would, on the one hand shake up the state, and on the other could open up a horizon of possibilities that transcends the logic of the current social structure and one that can also be seized in other spaces.

Some communist interlocutors often pose another question, a seemingly uncomfortable one, whenever talk of workers' self-management and such issues come up (in this case, in the university). If the university community does manage to win some sort of autonomy, does it not merely become another interest in the market? A bureaucracy too is inevitable. So in the end what difference does it make? But comrades here are jumping the gun, sort of. The attempt is not to set up, metaphorically speaking, socialism in one country. The end is not the autonomy of the university—that would be, once again, only a defense of privilege, or an attempt to create an exclusive space. The end is to raise a demand that is so fundamental that it can be raised in all workplaces, so that solidarity can easily be achieved. Should the situation actually arise in which the university community is able to snatch some autonomy from the state, it would indeed lead to further contradictions. The way out of which, like the way out of any contradiction, is to move to the next dialectical level—in this case, to repeat what has to be one of our most important slogans, *generalization*. The autonomy of one sector cannot be maintained so long as other spheres are also not autonomous, and so long as these autonomous sectors are not mutually dependent. The sort of "combined governing body" earlier suggested, cannot be imagined without the emancipation of all sectors. This dependence, however, begins with the reliance of different struggling sections of the working class upon each other.

Class Composition and Generalization

We have already introduced and elaborated upon the notion of "generalization," and the previous section ended with the idea of mutual dependence of various parts of the working class. It is necessary now to clarify certain theoretical underpinnings of the argument being made here.

Some of the best contributions to the development of a Marxian understanding of students' struggles and interventions in the university have been made by Marxists associated (often very loosely) with what is called the "Autonomist school." Harry Cleaver (who wrote "Schoolwork and the Struggle Against it," accessible online at www.libcom.com) and George Caffentzis (who wrote, "Throwing away the Ladder: The Universities in Crisis," once again accessible at www.libcom.com) are two very significant names in this context. Some of their ideas have contributed to the formation of a lot of my own understanding, which informs the current chapter. So, very briefly, I will introduce certain fundamentals of this framework so as to contextualize all that has already been said.

In an essay titled "Marxian categories, the crisis of capital, and the constitution of social subjectivity today" (2003), Harry Cleaver explicates the notion of "class composition," "designed to grasp, without reduction, the divisions and power relationships within and among the diverse populations on which capital seeks to maintain its dominion of work throughout the social factory—understood as including not only the traditional factory but also life outside of it which capital has sought to shape for the reproduction of labor power" (Cleaver 2003, 43). In various spaces of the capitalist world system, work is imposed upon individuals in various ways, and this constitutes the identities of different sorts of workers. When using the concept of class composition these identities are called "sectors of the working class."

These "sectors of the working class," through the circulation of their struggles, "recompose the relations among them to increase their ability to rupture the dialectic of capital and to achieve their own ends" (Cleaver 2003, 43). Only when different sectors of the working class, separated from each other by various forms of internal differentiation that capitalism introduces, struggle and generalize their struggles through the inclusion of other sectors, the possibility of radical transformation arises. The sort of dialogue needed for the recomposition that Cleaver speaks of would need to take the form of a direct, political confrontation, an engagement that would leave nothing unchanged; one's identity and the ideology constituted by one's own experience changes in this encounter, even as the other is made to take into account one's identity. "A double agenda," as Cleaver (2003, 55–56) puts it: "the working out of one's own analysis and the critical exploration of 'neighboring' activities, values and ideas."

My chapter, it should be easy enough to recognize, was a representation of the material ground in which these conceptualizations are immanent. Which is also to say that the representation itself has been modeled with the help of these abstractions.[15] Our discussion of the events surrounding the Commonwealth Games in the first section introduced the notion of generalization, and throughout the chapter we have had to return to it again and again. We saw that ways of raising demands, that is tactical choices, are determined by larger strategic goals. From the perspective of somebody who seeks to contribute to the transformation of social totality, the only real goal is generalization of struggle. Generalization entails the sustained questioning of capitalism in all terrains of society.

A crucial lesson that we can draw is that generalization is not possible without destroying segmentation within the working class. Relatively more privileged sections of the working class, which have greater control over the labor process, whose incomes are higher, in whom very often, the petty-bourgeois tendency is strong, habitually, even naturally, (insofar as socialization constructs what seems natural) tend to aim for local resolutions that maintain their privileged status in society. It is exactly this tendency that they need to overcome to be able to stand with other, less privileged, sections of the working class.

Conversely, working class organizations should not, a priori, reject these privileged segments as "petty bourgeois," because what Marx called the "absolute general law of capitalist accumulation," implies that their situation keeps changing continuously; objective proletarianization is a situation they can be faced with around any corner. Objective proletarianization, together with efforts to proletarianize their subjectivity, can definitely lead them to radicalization. When the defense of privilege fails, and, as we have seen, at many crucial junctures it does and will continue to fail, internal necessity can push these gentrified proletariats to a full-fledged questioning of the capitalist system.

Notes

1. A useful passage to describe the method aspired for: "...only Hegel's is a dialectical philosophy...In Marx, those abstractions and those concepts have gone underground, they are still active and they still give form to the developments in which they are somehow materialized, but they are no longer present in their own name. Marx's text [*Capital*], to use another current word, may be seen as a practice of dialectical immanence." (Jameson 2011, 136)
2. See P. Chandra (2010a).
3. See KYS pamphlets (2010a & 2010b).
4. See KYS (2010c).
5. Although I will make some comments on how I understand the working class toward the end of the chapter, I will not enter into a full conceptualization of the space of students within the working class at large. For this see P. Chandra (2011a).
6. Actually the "Joint Action Body Against the Semester System," funnily abbreviated as "JABASS."
7. The court order can be found on the university website (University of Delhi, 2011a).
8. Show cause notices were served to teachers from the department of English overnight, after they opposed the introduction of the semester system. See "DU Show-Cause Notice to 11 Professors After Mass Resignation" (*Indian Express*, 2011).
9. The Bologna Agreement, or Bologna Process began as attempt to standardize educational standards across Europe, but increasingly it has also aimed at aligning countries outside the European Higher Education area with its standards. As I write this chapter a seminar

is being organized (by the state) to discuss this process in the Indian context. "A two-day international conference is planned to be organized by Manipal Centre for European Studies, under the aegis of India EU Study Centres Program (IESCP) at Manipal University on August 25–26, 2011 at Manipal. The is an initiative of IESCP and Manipal University to better acquaint Indian academia with the working and implications of the Bologna Process, keeping in view the increasing collaboration of Indian universities with European universities over the last few years." (IESCP, 2011)
10. Krishna Iyer was sworn in as a judge in the Supreme Court of India in 1973, and is famous for having passed many "pro-labour" rulings.
11. For more on such bills, see N. Chandra (2011).
12. All information comes from the "Act of the University" downloaded from the university website (University of Delhi, 2011b).
13. See P. Chandra (2010b).
14. To be understood here in terms of the loss of control over the labor process.
15. See note 1.

References

Caffentzis, George. 2011. "Throwing Away the Ladder: Universities in Crisis." Accessed on August 24, 2011 at http://libcom.org/library/throwing-away-ladder-universities-crisis-george-caffentzis-zerowork.

Chandra, Nandini. 2011. "Private Nation, Public Funds: The Case of the Foreign Education Providers (Regulation of Entry and Operation) 2010 Bill." Accessed on September 16, 2011 at *Sanhati*. http://sanhati.com/excerpted/4108/.

Chandra, Paresh. 2010a. "Liberal or Radical: A Dialectical Appraisal of Students' Politics." Accessed on August 10, 2011 at *Radical Notes*. http://radicalnotes.com/content/view/143/1/.]

Chandra, Paresh. 2010b. "Through and Beyond: Identities and Class Struggle". Accessed on August 10, 2011 at *Radical Notes*. http://radicalnotes.com/content/view/136/39/.

Chandra, Paresh. Forthcoming—1. "The Politics of Studenthood: The Student as a Worker" in *Social Movements, Dissent and Transformative Action* edited by Savyasaachi. New Delhi: Routledge.

Chandra, Paresh. Forthcoming—2. "Some Problems of the Students' Movement in India". In *The New Student Rebellions* edited by Carlos Sevilla. Madrid: Akal.

Cleaver, Harry. 2003. "Marxian Categories, the Crisis of Capital, and the Constitution of Social Subjectivity Today" in *Revolutionary Writing: Common Sense Essays in Post-Political Politics* edited by Werner Bonefeld. New York: Autonomedia.

Cleaver, Harry. 2011. "On Schoolwork and the Struggle Against It." Accessed on August 24, 2011 at http://libcom.org/files/On%20Schoolwork1.pdf.

Indian Express. 2011. "DU show-cause notice to 11 professors after mass resignation". Accessed on August 28, 2011 at http://www.indianexpress.com/news/du-showcause-notice-to-11-professors-after/777952/.
IESCP. 2011. "Conference on Bologna Process". Accessed on August 27 at http://www.iescp.net/events.html.
Jameson, Fredric. 2011. *Representing* Capital: *A Reading of Volume I*. London, New York: Verso.
Krantikari Yuva Sangathan (KYS). 2010a. "What Is Ailing University Democrats?" Accessed on August 10, 2011 at *Radical Notes*. http://radicalnotes.com/journal/2010/08/28/what-is-ailing-university-democrats/.
Krantikari Yuva Sangathan (KYS). 2010b. "More on What Continues to Ail University Democrats?" Accessed on August 10, 2011 at *Radical Notes*. http://radicalnotes.com/journal/2010/09/15/more-on-what-continues-to-ail-university-democrats-and-the-likes/.
Krantikari Yuva Sangathan (KYS). 2010c. "No Room of One's Own: House Question in Delhi". Accessed on August 10, 2011 at *Radical Notes*. http://radicalnotes.com/journal/2010/08/19/no-room-of-ones-own-the-housing-question-in-delhi/.
Sharma, Vijender. 2010. "Yashpal Committee Report: Prescriptions Not for Renovation and Rejuvenation of Higher Education." *Sahmat*: *Debating Education* (Against Neoliberal Thrust) 4: 46–54.
Sharma, Vijender. 2010. "FEI Bill Jeopardizes Our Higher Education System". *Sahmat*: *Debating Education* (Against Neoliberal Thrust) 4: 54–60.
University of Delhi. 2011a. "DUTA order". Accessed on August 28 at http://du.ac.in/fileadmin/DU/Events/DUTA_order_8feb2011_2322011.pdf.
University of Delhi. 2011b. "Act of the University". Accessed on July 10, 2011 at http://du.ac.in/fileadmin/DU/DUCorner/act-i.pdf.

Chapter 9

Learning Truth Telling: Beyond Neoliberal Education

Savyasaachi

In an education system, the curriculum and modes of its transaction need to determine the design of the infrastructure—the size and shape of classrooms, the look of the building, the library, the student-faculty-administration interface, the equipment and so on.

What is the nature of curriculum space and what goes into its making?

We are all familiar with the idea that everything is woven around and into the curriculum—everything here includes not merely all aspects of an institutional system but also the larger society; the history, culture, economy, politics and so on. It is one of most contested spaces—what should be included has been debated across the table and has also been a source of conflict and violence between the left, liberal, and right persuasions in the fields of politics, economy, and culture. Each of these has wanted its agenda to be pushed in.

All contestations are for being "included"—that is against a one-sided view of history and society. There is a diversity of voices, the body of knowledge has grown over the past several decades, and the objective conditions have changed rapidly and that process continues. How are these to be accommodated in the curriculum and from whose perspective?

The perspective of the student is most important. From this perspective, contestations are concerned with finding ways to learn from a plurality of visions and knowledge systems. This is about the dynamism of studentship as opposed to the authoritative figure of the "teacher." This is a shift toward opening the question of what is "learnable" and free knowledge from the monopolist control of the "authoritative teacher" (one who has the authority over the text and the body of knowledge that should be transacted in class) and the ideological ally (from any of the three persuasions mentioned above).

The neoliberal economy has been monopolizing the curriculum space. It has been relentlessly instrumentalizing the space for transacting knowledge and skills required by different sectors of the corporate economy. This has been undermining the "dynamism of studentship" that is emerging alongside "plural knowledge-systems and perspectives."

The undermining of "studentship" has contributed substantially to the making of a neoliberal disaster. This, however, is creating the ground for the emergence of an even stronger idea of dynamic studentship with its concern for the "learnable."

The Neoliberal Disaster

The neoliberal regime is oblivious to the increasing technological lag. That is, it lags far behind the aspirations of the frontier people (the masses) and thereby the requirements for a just society. The masses want jobs and justice, the neoliberal economy gives more unemployment; the masses want health, the neoliberal economy creates conditions for more health hazards, the masses want "quiet time," the neoliberal economy floods their free time with loud blaring music; the masses want the truth about perpetrators of violence and brutality, the neoliberal economy creates conditions for further conflict and violence...the list is endless.

The neoliberal mindset misses the point that with each new step to boost the economy it increases the speed of the chain reaction. There is an escalation of the rate at which difference lead to conflict, violence, war, and terrorism. Under these conditions, an economy cannot function. Massive amount of energy, finance, and institutional processes are devoted to the unproductive work of containing violence and terrorism. For instance, the production of arms and ammunition adds no value to life; on the contrary it takes away a large chunk of resources from the economy. It contributes nothing to value of food, shelter, education, and health.

The neoliberal thinking is mindless of the way it erodes all theoretical spaces. In other words, it leaves no space and time for discussing questions that emerge from the dilemmas of human predicament, for questions that seek to examine the assumptions behind our beliefs and practices.

Without such theoretical spaces, blunders are bound to occur. For instance, neoliberal thinking sees terrorism as a "security" issue, trivializes the problem, and looks for technological solutions. There is little time and space to analyse how terrorism could be a product of the neoliberal economy with its emphasis on the free-market competition between industrial-military regimes that have now perforated the fabric of society all levels, from the local to the global.

To understand and deal with the problem requires a radical reexamination of the assumptions of neoliberalism, namely the use of military forces for annihilating ethnic groups that have got arms.

It not uncommon to hear, in academic seminars, policy meetings, and debates, that the theoretical is antipractical, it slows down the competition and completion of projects. There is a tacit agreement that when a discussion gets into a deadlock on account of theory, a practical decision can be taken to continue. Often, at meetings, one hears "too much of democracy is not going to lead anywhere."

Within the neoliberal dispensation, there is no time for full discussion on basic questions. Time constraints are imposed by financial considerations—"the work needs to be done within the time-frame for which the money has been sanctioned."

There is a conflict between financial time and discussion time. In this conflict, the discussion time shrinks and this obviously implies a shrinking of theoretical space.

Such conflict and shrinking has filtered down to other fields of social and political life. Debates on policy are short and snappy, what with political activists being averse to theory. They want action and have no time for reflection. In universities there are fewer students who opt for the social sciences, for social sciences do not get one a job. Such pressure has compelled the manufacturing of more market-friendly syllabi in the social sciences.

Further, on account of this conflict, the meaning of theory itself has changed. A good example is "theory for computer programs" taught in schools and institutes. It refers to a list of terms and procedures to run and not the "why," "how," and "what" of the program. Here, theory itself has become the instrument.

In social sciences, theory is more often than not envisaged as the lens or the frame (legal, conceptual, experiential, religious, etc.) through and within which we see the world. In the first instance, the world appears either smaller (as if viewed through a convex lens) or larger (seen through the concave) than what it is. In the case of theory being the frame, the world is viewed with the terms of reference specified by the task to be accomplished. In both instances, theory is the ally of fragmentation and encourages the exclusion of critical voices of people from diverse experiences and plural cultures.

The neoliberal economy has converted theory into an instrumentality for manufacturing consent.

Army Recruitment through Text Books / Shrinking Theoretical Spaces

An instance of the mindless neoliberal economic regime, is advertisements in school textbooks for recruitment to the army.

The National Council for Education Research and Training (NCERT), on the recommendation of a parliamentary committee, has given a part of the textbook space to the army. It has granted permission to the Indian army to advertise in five textbooks—creative writing and translation, computer and communication technology, human ecology and family sciences, Indian heritage and crafts, and graphic design.

A news item titled "To catch them young, Army goes to school textbooks," dated March 18, 2009, in the *Indian Express* underscores the partnership among the army, the NCERT, and the state. It is not coincidental that an advertisement from the army is included in textbooks. This decision brings forth an ideological assumption that is integral to the core of the neoliberal regime. The army is the foundational sector of the corporate economy—not only is it expected to defend industrial and civic space, it also is at the apex of the innovation chain from where technology trickles down to arm the civil society for competition and transforms its civic character.

What do the state, education, and the market share? What brings them together? What is common between the military and the NCERT? What implications does this partnership have for the future of creative writing, the rules of translation, the form and content for computer, communication and technology, the guidelines for human ecology and family sciences, Indian heritage and crafts, and graphic design?

It is true that the army and the education system are contraries.

The army is grounded in no tolerance for questioning and education is grounded in no restraint on questioning.

How different is this positioning of a recruitment advertisement in textbook from recruitment of child soldiers?

In this advertisement, the state and the NCERT have legitimized a genocidal disposition: "to catch them young" before they begin to disagree and question, and instill in them a sense of "pride and honor" that comes from unquestioning respect for authority and unquestioned faith in the superiors, from killing innocent people and not be tried in the court of justice, for destroying ecology, for escalating the arms race and contributing to the criminalization of everyday life.

According to anthropologists, the genocidal disposition exaggerates (the vision of concave lens) and underplays (the vision of convex lens) differences and arranges them as binaries. For instance, modernity is projected as larger than life and the panacea for all problems; the only way to freedom, fraternity and well-being. Its binary opposite, tradition, is ridiculed and made to appear small. The most lethal aspect of these binaries is that they cannot be copresent—it is either one or the other. Some these genocidal binaries are as follows:

> modernity-tradition; civilisation-savagery; us-them; centre-margin; humanity-barbarity; progress-degeneration; advanced-backward; developed-underdeveloped; adult-childlike; nurturing-dependent; normal-abnormal; subject-object; human-sub-human; reason-passion; culture-nature; male-female; mind-body; objective-subjective; knowledge-ignorance; science- magic; truth-superstition; master-slave; good-evil; moral-sinful; believer-pagans; pure-impure; order-disorder; law-uncontrolled; justice-arbitrariness; active-passive; wealthy-poor; nation-states–non-state processes; strong-weak; dominant-subordinate; conqueror-conquered. (Hinton 2002, Ch 1)

Genocide is the most malignant form of militarization, for it takes pride in brutalizing life—mass killings in the name of human rights. It begins with indoctrination of the self-importance embedded in using weapons. It is not so easy to shoot the bullet that will kill. It begins with killing a person.

This sense of "self-importance" is also constitutive of the neoliberal economy. The self-importance of the neoliberal economy comes from is its vast military-industrial complex. There are a large number of studies that show that the military-industrial complex of neoliberal economy has its origin in the postwar (First World War and Second World War) reconstruction effort.

Speed has been the core of neoliberal economy. Fredrick Winslow Taylor its hero.

The salient features of the economy today are as follows:

> The rate of extracting natural resources is several times faster than the rate at which nature can reproduce them. Thus this economy has destroyed nature's capacity to regenerate. There is depletion of water, climate change, pollution, destruction of the natural base for people's livelihood.... It has created a condition of technological obsolescent waste.

Militarization is necessary to sustain this economy. It refers to training to follow, without question, the line of command from the superiors to the juniors. This, it has been argued, is necessary for ensuring security and safekeeping of resources held under monopolies. Further, the conflicts this economy produces from competition for monopoly necessitates military intervention.

Learning Demilitarization and Restoration of Citizenship

Militarization of education undermines citizenship. The militarized disposition annihilates our sense of studentship and what is learnable. And this undermines the core of citizenship. Critical voices are rendered silent, public spaces become inaccessible to a diversity of people, bilingualism declines, and plural ways of knowing are destroyed.

Militarization uproots the diversity of cultures from their nurturing grounds to create space for installations of weaponry, to mine mineral resources, to construct industrial zones, and so on. Many cultures are forced to exist in "coma," paralyzed by the proximity of military cantonments, several others are customized for ornamental display before foreign dignitaries, and several are tailored by designers' consumerism.

Experience and the Learnable

There has been resistance and dissent to contain the march of this neoliberal regime. Culturally diverse people have resisted mining, refused to be paralyzed, declined to become ornamentations before foreign dignitaries.

They have been holding a mirror to the dreadful face of modernity.

What is learnable in their critical voices is studentship to disarm the mind of the genocidal terms, categories, and principles. This is critical to demilitarization of the economy and citizenship.

These dissenting voices have asked the question "what is 'learnable' in experience"?

Experience is learning of that which is learnable and letting go of the rest.

The most original notion of "the learnable," knowable from stories of origin across diverse cultures and from contemporary works in philosophy, has as its impulse the "call" to dispel the darkness of lies, falsehood, untruth, and deception, and the "yearning" for "light."

It is a call for immersion, for radical insistence, of identification, for listening, and, in contemporary works of philosophy, bringing forth the light from within the "sacred word." Common to each of these ways is "letting go."

Without letting go, the learnable is out of reach. Experience tells us of the "rest that needs to be let gone of."

There is a yearning for clarity on what to "let go of." That is constitutive of the foundational element of our being in the world. Such yearning becomes a pursuit of the "learnable." This is constitutive of studentship as a call to being in pursuit.

Letting Go and the Learnable

What can we learn from different cultures concerning genocide and the learnable? Genocide is more than the massacre of people—it destroys the foundational element of being in the world—it leaves no ground for the pursuit of the "learnable."

From discussions on this subject we know that genocide is totalizing. It has been pointed out that this is the final statement of modernity about itself. At its best and worst, modernity offers nothing other than instruments of mass destruction of nature and culture. It generates an "unstoppable vicious cycle" of violence-reproducing-violence that draws everyone in at rapid speed. It does not heal victims but pushes them to seek compensation and becomes the perpetrator of the system that made them victims, all this in the name of justice—an eye for an eye and tooth for a tooth. The distinction between the perpetrator and the victim gets obliterated and there remains no one who is not part of the vicious cycle and can thus be the judge.

This impossibility of justice is a foundational crisis. It is the loss of humanity, of faith, and of the ground for the pursuit of the learnable.

How have cultures responded to owHoeto similar occasions in history?

Here are some examples that show the learnable.

Studentship

The *sabad* is the sacred word of the Guru Granth Sahib, the holy book of the Sikhs that was compiled for a people who were being mercilessly brutalized.

The museum at the Golden Temple in Amritsar has several paintings that show the brutality of the rulers. The gurus, literally the teachers, compiled the Granth Sahib in such times.

The verses in the Granth call upon the gathering (*sangat*) to contemplate the *sabad* and learn from it compassion, sharing, and offering of the self in the service of the other. It emphasizes that a gathering of people that contemplates *sabad* is *satsang*: companionship of people who yearn to receive the truth that comes forth from the *sabad*.

There is no hate speech; there is no prompting for justice in the form of "eye for an eye and tooth for a tooth."

The fifth guru, Arjan Dev, who compiled the Granth, was tortured to death. He was made to sit on a hot plate and hot sand was poured over him. In such a moment of pain and suffering, he smiled and contemplated the *sabad*.

The sixth guru, Hargobind, after having fought a bloody war with the Muslims conferred with his *sangat* and came to the conclusion that a mosque be constructed to bring a final end to the violence and counterviolence between the two communities. To make it, Vishwakarma, the Hindu divinity for architecture, came in human form. This heritage stands in Guru Hargobindpur and is looked after by Sikhs, who welcome any Muslim who comes to pray.

The sixth guru picked up the sword, there was war without a hate speech. There was no animosity but instead there was the effort dissolve the "other" by making it an integral aspect of the "self" and this came close the notion of the "one" that was core of the *sabad*.

The ninth guru, Tegbahadur, stood up against the rulers to create a safe space for the Kashmiri pundits, who were not being allowed to follow the path of their "faith." He was beheaded.

The tenth guru, Gobind Singh, proud of his father, decided to free the text of fickleness of human interpretations. Thus the *sabad* became the guru. And he said, "*Guru appe chela*," which literally means, a teacher is himself a student. In relation to the sacred word, these words say studentship is "learning to receive the light embedded in the *sabad*." This "learnable" came forth, in the light of his life experience of several wars and the beheading of his father for defending the rights of Kashmiri pundits.

This "let go of" dissolved the authority of the teacher over the text, and cleared the ground for the diversity of people to come to the text and be "received by it" and "receive it in turn." The learning to receive is the "learnable"—to receive the "other" and become "one" with it.

To "let go," in this instance of the authority of the teacher over the text, is a radical insistence and at the same time an immersion and an identification with the One. This is an aspect of dynamic studentship—to be one's own teacher—that is learning on one's own and of One within one's own self. This "One" is at the core of dynamic studentship. It is the One, within each of us that "receives" and it is also the basis of our humanity

Eklavya—Learning to Receive

This is a story from Mahabharatha.

Dronacharya, the guru for archery, refused to teach Eklavya, the son of Hiranyadhanu, the king of Nishaad, because he was not a Kshatriya.

Eklavya went to the forest and made with his hands a figure of Drona out of mud.

He called this "mud figure" his guru. Daily, he would pay respect to this image of his guru and practice archery. In this way he learnt.

One day, Eklavya sealed the mouth of a dog with his seven arrows. The dog could not open his mouth and ran back to where Dronacharya and Arjun had camped.

Everyone was surprised by this amazing skill in archery.

While searching for this archer, they found Eklavya practicing, who confirmed he had sealed the dog's mouth.

Dronacharya was curious to know who the boy was and where he learnt archery.

Eklavya told Dronacharya his name and of his father Nishaadraaj Hiranyadhanu (an army chief in Jaraasandh's army).

He showed Dronacharya his (Dronacharya's) mud statue. Eklavya told him how he learnt archery in the presence of this image. Dronacharya was surprised. Eklavya reminded Drona how he had declined to teach him.

Dronacharya loved Arjun, and he wanted him to be the best archer. He thus asked Eklavya to give his right-hand thumb by way of *guru dakshina* (a tribute given to the teacher).

Eklavya, without any hesitation, picked up a knife and cut his right thumb and offered it to his "guru."

There are at least three important events in this story.

First, the teacher's (Dronacharya's) refusal to teach Eklavya.

Second, Eklavya's self-learning: making the mud image of his teacher, learning in the "presence of the image," and becoming a master.

Third, Dronacharya demanding his tribute and Eklavya giving it without a word of protest.

Dronacharya's refusal to accept Eklavya as his student is an assertion of the teacher's authority over the subject. It is also an example of a mode of noninclusive learning process.

Eklavya's making the mud image of his teacher is an assertion that "the presence of the teacher in person" in flesh and blood is not necessary for learning. The image is sufficient to bring forth the presence of the teacher. This opens up the possibility for self-learning. Later, when Dronacharya appears in person he only proves Eklavya's point. The person of the teacher is not only unnecessary, it is, in fact, harmful. The person of the teacher can be overbearing, it takes away from the student the most crucial condition for learning: the freedom to experiment and explore (the thumb in this case).

Eklavya includes himself in the learning process. The making of the image undermines the teacher's claim to authority on the subject.

The "image" of the teacher is, in fact, profound—reaching far more within the student than the physical person of the teacher.

Who then is the teacher? Who is it one learns from? What is the interplay between the image and the person in the making of dynamic studentship?

Eklavya is an example of dynamic studentship.

He is ready to receive and this yearning springs forth from an inner calling to learn. Drona's refusal does not undermine either the yearning or the calling. Further, the giving of the thumb underlines the preparedness to "receive" learning unconditionally. This is as an important element of dynamic studentship. The giving of the thumb is an acknowledgement of the worthiness of learning as well as recognition of the source from whence it comes forth. This is integral to "receiving."

Any reservation or conditionality would make learning incomplete or even impossible. The giving of the thumb undermines the intention with which it was asked, namely to destroy it. It is said that the people of Eklavya's community continued to use the bow without using the right thumb.

That which is learnable stays, and is not conditional to circumstance.

The dynamic studentship demonstrated by Eklavya opens the question about how he learnt to become better than Arjun. What is it that he learnt that made him better?

The arrow released by Eklavya did not want to kill the dog but prevented it from barking. The skill here is not just accuracy or precision but the "belonging" of the arrow to the intention of the one who releases. This is a demonstration of knowledge that belongs to itself, and this is what is the learnable. Unlike the arrow in "time flies like an arrow" this arrow goes no further than to the time and space embedded in the intention of the one who releases, to which it belongs.

Eklavya did not have to become (Arjun or a Kashtriya) someone other than himself in order to learn.

He began from wherever he was and whatever he knew. How did he proceed from here? There is nothing that can be learnt about this from the text.

What can be inferred is that he worked out the relation of learning between himself, the bow and the arrow, and the image of the guru. With the yearning to "receive" and the "calling" to be not deterred, as the heart and mind of this learning relation, the bow and the arrow were receiving Eklavya as much as Eklavya was receiving the bow and the arrow. In other words, they learnt to listen to each other and, in time, learnt to belong to each other.

Socrates and the Sophist

A sophist on his return from Asia met Socrates on the street. There began a conversation between them:

> Sophist: Are you still standing there and still saying the same thing about the same things.
> Socrates: Yes that I am. But you are so extremely smart, you are never saying the same thing about the same thing. (Heidegger 1978, 252)

The learnable is between "never saying the same thing about the same thing" and "saying the same thing about the same thing". It is the yearning and calling for truth-telling.

The sophist may not be incorrect, for there are so many different facets to the same thing across time and space. What is required is the yearning to learn that which is the same about the same thing across time and space. This is learnable about the "thing." Socrates seems to suggest that it is common sense to wonder why the same thing has the same things told about it at different times.

Self Grounding—Saying the Same Things About the Same Things

We can learn about this from Heidegger's writings and his life.

He attempts to show that the learnable is beyond the factual, the experimental, and the measurable. By "beyond" he meant that the "learnable" is not determined by any of these three concerns of science. In their absence, this the notion of the "learnable" science becomes the slave of politicians and finance capital.

What does Heidegger have to say about the "learnable".
That it is mathematical.

> The word 'mathematical' stems from the Greek expression *ta mathemata*, which means what can be learned and thus, at the same time, what can be taught; *manthanein* means to learn, *mathesis* the teaching, and thus in two-fold sense. First, it means studying and learning; then it means the doctrine taught....
>
> Learning is a kind of grasping and appropriating. But not every taking is a learning.... to take means in some way to take possession of a thing and have the disposal over it. Now, what kind of taking is learning...? The *mathemata* are the things insofar as we take cognizance of things as what we already know them to be in advance—the body as body like, the plant as plant like, the thingness of a thing...it is an extremely particular taking, a taking where he who takes only takes what he basically already has...The student is merely instructed to take for himself what he already has. If a student merely takes over all that is offered he does not learn. He comes to learn only when he experiences what he takes as something he himself really already has. True learning occurs only where the taking of what one already has is a self-giving and is experienced as such. Teaching, therefore, does not mean anything else than to let others learn, that is, bring one another to learning. Teaching is more difficult than learning; for only he who can truly learn—and only as long as he can do it—can truly teach. (Heidegger 1978, 250–251)

What is it that we already have and how do we take it as self giving?

> "We see three chairs and say that there are three chairs....We can count three only if we already know three. What we take cognizance of (number three) is not drawn from any of the things...."
>
> The question is what is the relation between experience and science? What does learning from experience mean? (Heidegger 1978, 252)

Heidegger seeks to elaborate the point by discussing Newton's axiom

> Every body left to itself uniformly moves in a straight line. (Heidegger 1978, 262)

This law is at the apex of modern science.

> Where do we find it? There is no such body. There is no experiment which could ever bring such a body to direct perception...This law speaks of a thing that does not exist. It demands a fundamental

representation of things which contradicts the ordinary... (Heidegger 1978, 265)

What we learn is that the law is freed from the bindings of experience. Heidegger learns this from Galileo's experiment.

> It becomes a decisive insight of Galileo that all bodies fall equally fast, and that the difference in the time of fall derives only from the resistance of air, not from the different inner natures of the bodies or from their own corresponding relation to their particular place. Galileo supposedly conducted this experiment from the Leaning Tower of Pisa, the city where he was professor of mathematics, in order to prove his statement. In his experiment, bodies of different weights did not arrive at the same time after having fallen from the tower, but the difference in time was slight. Inspite of these differences and, therefore, really against the evidence of experience, Galileo held his proposition.... Opposition towards Galileo increased... he had to give up his professorship and leave Pisa. (Heidegger 1978, 266)

Heidegger tells us that Galileo freed knowledge from revelation as well as from experience. He showed the "self-grounding of the form of knowledge as such.... There is new experience and formation of freedom itself, i.e., binding with obligations that are self imposed... an inner drive to establish its own essence as the ground of itself and thus of all knowledge" (Heidegger 1978, 272).

How did Galileo learn? Heidegger says "... by taking the knowledge itself from out of himself. Galileo says: "I think in my mind of something moveable that is left entirely to itself.... This "to think in the mind is taking knowledge itself from out of himself." (Heidegger 1978, 266–67)

Heidegger argues that the use of reason enables the "I" to take knowledge from out of one's self.

Experience and Experiment

Each of these instances of learning as self-giving, is an experiment with immersion, radical insistence, identification (as elements of pursuit and as modes of self-giving) that draw out knowledge from the experience(s) of what we already know. This knowledge (that comes forth by means of immersion, radical insistence and identification) is also independent of experience and is its basis.

The Sikh tradition (Guru Arjun Dev, Guru Tegbahadur, and Guru Gobind Singh) shows that contemplation is immersion, radical insistence, and identification with the *sabad* that draws out the knowledge (of the *sabad*) that is self-grounding. It needs nothing outside itself to be validated.

Eklavya, similarly, shows immersion, radical insistence, and identification with image of his guru. In a similar manner, Galileo demonstrates immersion, radical insistence and identification with "the mathematical," when he stands by his principle of falling bodies.

However, what each one has to let go of is different—the Sikh gurus had to let go of their lives; Eklavya had to let go of his thumb and Galileo had to let go of his professorship and later, toward the end of his life, was forced to recant his views and live under house arrest. Heidegger, who brings us the insight into the self-giving as a mode becoming beings in this world, supported Hitler and let go his own "I think."

A mode of drawing out from within is simultaneously "the letting go" of the "I."

The experiment is about when does the letting go become a "self giving" of "self-grounded knowledge." How finding "that knowledge that is self grounded" becomes available in a lifetime.

To what extent Galileo and Heidegger gifted to themselves "self-grounded knowledge." Did they let go of the "I," and when released from its (I) bondage to what extent did they shift to self-binding freedom that belongs to "self-grounded knowledge" (and not to the "I")?

I would to suggest that they were not fully released from the "I" and did not, therefore, belong to the "self-grounded knowledge."

In contrast, the Sikh Gurus and Eklavya were fully released from the "I" and wholly belonged to "self-grounded knowledge." They are exemplars of "studentship." In other words, self-grounded knowledge can be accessed and made available in the lifetime of the student. To belong to the self-grounded knowledge is possible when a student lets go of the "I."

Toward Intellectual Self-Reliance—Decommissioning Neoliberal Education

How can mindlessness of the increasing technological lag—far behind the aspirations of the frontier people—promoted by the neoliberal education, be decommissioned?

Earlier in this discussion, the inclusion of people's voices required a consideration of "what is learnable" because what is being learnt from neoliberal knowledge has been responsible for a series of disasters, one bigger than the other.

In the previous sections, the discussions on what is learnable shows that all learning is about ways of bring forth what we already know.

This can help us understand the lag between technology and people's aspirations.

It would be entirely erroneous to say that there is need for more technology to fill in this lag. For, more technology will only let their voices go unheard and would thus contribute to the lag, making it even wider.

The lag draws us out to consider "listening" to the voices of people. They all saying—what is learnable is to come from within; learning what we already know; finding ways to bring forth what we already know.

This is not just questioning the neoliberal monopoly of knowledge and undermining monopoly over neoliberal knowledge. More importantly, these voices are saying that learning of what we already know is core of the yearning to intellectual self-reliance. All attempts of studentship to belong to self-grounded knowledge are toward intellectual self-reliance.

What we experience in the ordinary day to day life is where learning starts. Learning to listen is the key to bring forth knowledge from within. Not all that can be heard can be retained nor can all of it be "letting go." Immersion, radical insistence, identification, will reach out to what does not need to be let gone off and this will enable us to differentiate what needs to be let gone off.

The pushing out of diversity of voices and plural knowledge systems out of the public domain by the neoliberal education system is a recipe for disaster. Their presence is to let go of the deceptions that have been promoted by neoliberal democracy. These voices are saying participation is not sufficient for democracy. Only if participation enables truth telling, can democracy be viable and citizenship be restored. This seems to be a step in the direction of mindfulness of the "lag." It is important to note here that this lag encourages deception and lies.

Studentship for Truth Telling: What Is Learnable in Truth Telling?

In our discussion so far what is learnable is letting go of the "I" and receive what is already known namely, "knowledge that belongs to itself" (and not to politicians, scientists, or corporates). These are aspects of truth telling as well. Truth telling brings forth what is already known. Truth telling dispels deception.

Intellectual self reliance and truth telling go hand in hand. Intellectual self reliance is the preparedness for truth telling. Reciprocally, learning truth telling leads to intellectual self- reliance.

How is studentship of truth telling possible?

Truth telling can begin from the experiences of everyday life.

What curriculum and modes of its transaction need to put in place? This is important for it will determine the contours of the education system. This includes design of the infrastructure—the size and shape of classrooms, the look of the building, the library, the student-faculty-administration interface, the equipment and so on.

What is the nature of curriculum space and what goes into its making?

Based on the discussion so far, the key principles of the curriculum are "learning as self-giving;" listening (includes immersion, radical insistence, and identification) as ways of bringing forth that which is already known (this is self-grounding of knowledge); and letting go of the "I".

What can we learn regarding this from our exemplars, discussed earlier?

As regards learning as self-giving, we learn from the Sikh gurus that this is possible when the text is free from the authority of the teacher and the "word" is accessible to all. This is possible when a teacher himself lets go of his authority. This allows for the student to be his/her own teacher.

With respect to the teacher's readiness to let go of authority over the text, we learn from the Eklavya tale that not all teachers are ready to do that. But learning can even then become self-giving. With due deference, the student lets go of the personhood of the teacher. The importance of the "image" of the teacher is crucial to the "self-giving." Image here refers to the teacher within one's own self. It demonstrates that the role of a teacher is not to offer, but to enable recognition of the teacher within.

Without the letting go of the "I", self-giving is not possible. So, self-giving can often strengthen the "I"—"It is 'I' who learnt by myself." Until such time that the "I" is let gone of, it is not clear whether the student has learnt the learnable—that self-grounding of knowledge. The letting go one's own being in the world is the most profound letting go of the "I" (the examples of Sikh gurus). There are other ways of letting go of the "I"—the willingness to let go of the institutional definition of the "I." Galileo, giving up his professorship, did not disprove the principle he stood by.

The question, however, is does Heidegger's support for Hitler undo his work as a philosopher and his radical thought? Is support an unwillingness to let go of his "I"? Is it also a reflection of the state not willing to let "learning as self-giving" be legitimized within its own institutional structures?

The curriculum for truth telling is continuously challenging boundaries, not letting them fructify.

Can neoliberal educational institutions be transformed to facilitate truth telling?

Over the past few decades there have been several attempts at truth telling. Each of these has experimented with institutional ways to listen to the truth. What are the implications of these for the education system?

The neoliberal destructions are appropriately described as ecocide and ethnocide. There is now a growing concern over making development processes transparent and accountable.

This is in fact an expression of the yearning for truth telling.

This yearning has now legitimized social audits, environmental audits, public hearings, truth commissions, and world social fora. In each of these, there is space for truth telling.

There are now in place systems for exercise of human rights, right to information and work, along with systems of transitional justice.

Simultaneously, there have evolved, in keeping with requirements of truth telling, open learning systems, free university, basic education, experiential learning, concern for resilience, and nonreductionist knowledge.

These have been preparing the ground to go beyond the neoliberal education system.

References

Heidegger, Martin. 1978. *Heidegger: Basic Writings*, edited by David Farrell Krell. London: Routledge & Kegan Paul.

Hinton, Alexander Laban. 2002. *Annihilating Differences—The Anthropology of Genocide*. Berkeley and Los Angeles, CA: University of California Press.

Chapter 10

Twenty-First-Century Socialism and Education in the Bolivarian Republic of Venezuela: An Alternative to the Neoliberal Model

Mike Cole

Introduction

We can make a distinction between schooling, on the one hand, and education on the other, with the former referring to the processes by which young people are attuned to the requirements of capitalism (both in the form and the content of schooling), and the latter, a more liberatory process from birth to death, a process of human emancipation and socialism. In many ways, the whole Bolivarian project of twenty-first-century socialism is, *in its very essence,* education in that sense of the word. As we shall see, the revolutionary president of Venezuela has described the country as "a giant school."[1]

In this chapter, I begin by looking briefly at the advent of the government of Hugo Chávez, and the ensuing ascendancy of social democracy, and the move toward socialism. I then consider the effects of the overall Bolivarian educational processes at the level of educational institutions as a whole. As a case study, I outline the work of revolutionary socialist educators in an alternative school started by residents and activists in Barrio[2] Pueblo Nuevo in Mérida, Western Venezuela.

Hugo Chávez, Social Democracy and Twenty-First-Century Socialism

Education, as what I have called "a liberatory process from birth to death, a process of human emancipation and socialism," (e.g., Cole

2011, 141) is articulated by Hugo Rafael Chávez Frías, president of the Bolivarian Republic of Venezuela. In 2010, Chávez described the nature of the Bolivarian revolution, and the role of knowledge and education as the first of three forms of power in the revolutionary process, the others being political power and economic power:

> When we talk about power, what are we talking about... The first power that we all have is knowledge. So we've made efforts first in education, against illiteracy, for the development of thinking, studying, analysis. In a way, that has never happened before. Today, Venezuela is a giant school, it's all a school.
> From children of one year old until old age, all of us are studying and learning. And then political power, the capacity to make decisions, the community councils, communes, the people's power, the popular assemblies. And then there is the economic power. Transferring economic power to the people, the wealth of the people distributed throughout the nation. I believe that is the principal force that precisely guarantees that the Bolivarian revolution continues to be peaceful. (cited in Sheehan 2010)

In Gramscian terms, what Chávez is describing is the fostering of the development of organic intellectuals of the working class.[3]

Earlier in 2010, Chávez asserted that, apart from being a Christian, he was also a Marxist (Chávez 2010), describing Marxism as "the most advanced proposal toward the world that Christ came to announce more than 2,000 years ago" (Suggett 2010). The inclusion of "the spiritual" is one element that differentiates twenty-first-century socialism from its twentieth-century incarnation (see Cole 2012).

In 1998, Hugo Chávez won the presidential elections in Venezuela by a landslide, and inaugurated a participatory democracy. In representative democracies such as the UK and the United States, political participation is by and large limited to parliamentary politics—which represent the imperatives of capitalism, rather than the real needs and interests of the people.[4] Participatory democracy, on the other hand, involves direct decision-making by the people. Maria Paez Victor (2009) concisely summarizes Chávez's impact:

> Immediately the elites and middle classes[5] opposed him as an upstart, an Indian who does not know his place, a Black who is a disgrace to the position. Hugo Chávez established a new Constitution that re-set the rules of a government that had been putty in the hands of the elites. Ratified in overwhelming numbers, the Constitution gave indigenous peoples, for the first time, the constitutional right

to their language, religion, culture and lands. It established Human Rights, civil and social, like the right to food, a clean environment, education, jobs, and health care, binding the government to provide them. It declared the country a participatory democracy with direct input of people into political decision making through their communal councils and it asserted government control of oil revenues: Oil belongs to the people.

Vast oil revenues and reserves, Victor (2009) goes on, have been used to meet the real needs of the Venezuelan people. A little over ten years have seen the virtual eradication of illiteracy, a dramatic lowering of infant mortality, the lowest rate of malnutrition in South America, and the lowest unemployment in decades. At the same time, "the great majority of the people have
direct access to free health care, free schools, a network of daycare, a subsidized food distribution network, and subsidized medicines" (Victor 2009; see also Willgress 2010, 4–5 for the statistics). The "missions," a series of social justice, social welfare, antipoverty, and educational programs, have massively reduced poverty and greatly increased educational opportunities, all essential in the creation of organic intellectuals of the working class (for a discussion of the missions, see, for example, Cole 2009, 125–127).

These measures, of course, entail a massive educational project *for* the Venezuelan people, and other peoples in the region, and, indeed, the world. They represent a major challenge to US imperial hegemony, and its attendant ideological and repressive apparatuses (Althusser 1971).

However, while the innovations allow the export of socialist ideas and ideals, they are, of course, in themselves classic social democracy rather than socialism, somewhat akin to the policies and practice of the post–World War II Labour governments in the UK. What makes Venezuela unique, however, is that whereas these British Labour governments were posing social democracy as an *alternative* to socialism, and, indeed, attempting to fight off attempts by revolutionary workers to move toward socialism, Chávez is presenting reforms as a *prelude* to socialism.

These reforms are seen both by sections of the Chávez government and by large sections of the Venezuelan working class[6] as a step on the road to true socialist revolution. At the same time, Chávez is promoting genuine participatory democracy that is laying the foundations for the socialist project. Thus for Chávez, "[t]he hurricane of revolution has begun, and it will never again be calmed" (cited in

Contreras Baspineiro 2003). On another occasion, Chávez asserted: "I am convinced, and I think that this conviction will be for the rest of my life, that the path to a new, better and possible world, is not capitalism, the path is socialism, that is the path: socialism, socialism" (Lee 2005).

As Victor (2009) argues, one of the biggest achievements of the Bolivarian revolution is existential:

> a new sense of identity, a new sense of belonging...The great majority of Venezuelans feel they are now in control of their own government and destiny—despite the continuous attacks from the oligarchy and its satellites. Now the Chávistas frame all the political discourse and its name is Socialism of the 21st Century.

Socialism cannot be decreed from above (see the comment on this by Gerardo in the case study toward the end of this chapter). The people discuss Chávez and they support him, but they are aware that they are the motor of the revolution. It is worth quoting Victor (2009) at length:

> For the first time since the fall of the Berlin Wall, a country in the world repudiates the barbaric version of capitalism that has prevailed since Ronald Reagan and Margaret Thatcher, and embraces a new socialism, one that has its roots in the indigenous people's socialism, in Liberation Theology[7] which was born in Latin America, in Humanism, in the inspiration of Cuba, as well as the works of Marx, but not exclusively in European socialism. It is not Stalinism,[8] it is not a copy of what has passed for socialism to date, but Venezuela's own brand infused with the idea that the people are the protagonists of democracy, that the economy should serve people, not the other way around, and that only their active and direct participation in political decision making will free the country from corruption and inequality.

Writing toward the end of 2009, Luke Stobart (2009) argues that there were positive developments in that year when organized workers at the biggest factories in the country won several major battles for nationalization, including partial or total workers' control. Chávez supported the struggles, arguing that nationalized "state capitalist" firms need workers' democracy to become "socialist."

More recently (October 2010), Chávez announced the nationalization of the Spanish agro company, Agroisleña, which is renamed Agropatria; the privately owned oil and derivatives company, Venoco; and the agro industrial company Fertinitro. In addition, complete control will be taken of hundreds of thousands of hectares of land, including some 130,000 head of cattle, owned by La Compañía Inglesa (The English Company), which is controlled by the Vestey Group (Rosales, 2010). Chávez also announced a new housing program, and repeated calls to "banish bureaucracy and inefficiency" in the state apparatus. Also in 2010, five new "revolutionary laws" were announced: the Organic Law of Popular Power; the Organic Law of Popular and Public Planning; the Organic Law of Communes; the Organic Law of Social Auditing; and the Organic Law for the Development and Promotion of the Communal Economy. Finally, five new PSUV (the United Socialist Party of Venezuela) strategies were announced for 2011–2012, encapsulated in the following directives: "from political capitalist culture to socialist militancy;" "convert the machinery [of the PSUV] into a party-movement at the service of the struggles of the people;" "convert the party into a powerful means of propaganda, agitation and communication;" "the PSUV as a platform of development and strengthening of popular power;" and "the development of the Patriotic Pole" (a coalition of left-wing political parties and social movements) for the 2012 presidential election. This election is scheduled for October 7, and, at the time of writing (October, 2011), after over 12 years in government, two opinion polls show that Chávez commands nearly 60 percent support among the electorate (*Venezuela Analysis Newsletter*, October 11, 2011)

Education in Venezuela

Venezuela as "a giant school" and "education for socialism" is exemplified by the Revolutionary Reading Plan launched by Chávez in 2009 (Pearson 2009). "A change in spirit hasn't been achieved yet," Chávez suggested, and argued that the plan will be the "base for the injection of consciousness through reading, with which our revolution will be strengthened even more" (cited in ibid.).

The plan involves the distribution by the government of 2.5 million books to develop the communal libraries. Chávez said that part of the plan was a "rescuing of our true history for our youth," explaining that many standard textbooks do not acknowledge the European imperialist genocide of the indigenous peoples and their resistance (Pearson 2009). Chávez went on to recommend that people do collective reading and exchange knowledge, mainly through the communal councils and the popular libraries. He called on communal councils as well as "factory workers, farmers, and neighbors, to form revolutionary reading squadrons," one of whose tasks is to have discussions in order to "unmask the psychological war...of the oligarchy" (cited in ibid.).

"Read, read and read, that is the task of every day. Reading to form conscious and minds," Chávez noted, "[e]veryday we must inject the counter revolution a dose of liberation through reading" (cited in MercoPress 2009). Moreover, the revolutionary reading plan is intended to reaffirm values leading to "the consolidation of the new man and the new woman, as the foundations for the construction of a Socialist motherland, unravelling the capitalist imaginary" (ibid.).

As far as more "formal" education is concerned, the Venezuelan ministry of culture stated on its website that the plan will help schoolchildren get rid of "capitalist thinking" and better understand the ideals and values "necessary to build a Socialist country and society" (ibid.). Education is increasingly put forward by the state as a social good, and a central factor in shaping the system of production (Griffiths and Williams 2009, 37). In line with the Bolivarian constitution, in addition to the urban and rural poor, access has been extended to traditionally disadvantaged or excluded groups, such as those of African descent and indigenous communities. As argued in Cole (2011, chapter 5), while these are welcome developments, there is still much to do.

Tom Griffiths and Jo Williams (2009) outline the essential factors in the Bolivarian revolution's approach to education that make it truly counterhegemonic. The Venezuelan approach, they argue, draws on concepts of critical and popular education within the framework of a participatory model of endogenous socialist development (Griffiths and Williams 2009, 41). At the forefront, they note, is "the struggle to translate policy into practice in ways that are authentically democratic, that promote critical reflection and participation over formalistic and uncritical learning" (ibid.).

As in the UK and the United States, formal school education in Venezuela is based on an explicit, politicized conception of education and its role in society (ibid., 41–42). However, whereas in the UK (e.g., Beckman et al. 2009) and the United States (e.g., Au 2009), the capitalist state increasingly uses formal education merely as a vehicle to promote capitalism, in the Bolivarian Republic of Venezuela, "the political" in education is articulated *against* capitalism and imperialism and *for* socialism. In 2008, a draft national curriculum framework for the Bolivarian Republic was released. It stated that the system is "oriented toward the consolidation of a humanistic, democratic, protagonistic, participatory, multi-ethnic, pluri-cultural, pluri-lingual and intercultural society" (Ministerio del Poder Popular Para la Educación 2007, 11, cited in Griffiths and Williams 2009, 42). It went on to critique the former system for reinforcing "the fundamental values of the capitalist system: individualism, egotism, intolerance, consumerism and ferocious competition...[which also] promoted the privatization of education" (Ministerio del Poder Popular Para la Educación 2007, 12, cited in ibid., 42).

One central message of the Bolivarian revolution is that a fundamental counterhegemonic shift in the political economy toward socialism, including *universal* free access to education, with a high degree of equity in terms of opportunity and outcomes, can be achieved quite quickly (Griffiths and Williams 2009, 34). As Griffiths and Williams conclude, the Bolivarian system consistently refers these back to the underlying project to promote the formation of new republicans, with creative and transformational autonomy, and with revolutionary ideas; and with a positive attitude toward learning in order to put into practice new and original solutions for the endogenous transformation of the country (Ministerio del Poder Popular Para la Educación 2007, 16, cited in ibid. 2009, 42–43). It should be stressed at this stage that in terms of actual practice in the schools and universities, education based on the above revolutionary principles is by no means universal. Indeed, as Griffiths and Williams (2009, 44) point out, discussions with education academics and activists during fieldwork in Caracas in 2007, 2008, and 2009, repeatedly raised the challenge of the political and pedagogical conservatism of the existing teachers, often in opposition to the government's Bolivarian socialist project (e.g., Griffiths 2008).

Revolutionary Education in an Alternative School in Barrio Pueblo Nuevo, Mérida *Creating Space*[9]

The school is a small project, started by committed socialist revolutionary residents and activists of Barrio Pueblo Nuevo, perhaps the poorest community in the city of Mérida in western Venezuela. It caters to students aged between eight and fifteen, and since, at the time of the research, it had been operating for only six months, it was very much in its initiatory phase. The teachers want to create an alternative for young people who have been left behind in the public school system and re-engage them in participatory pedagogy consistent with socialist and democratic values. The school is currently linked to the ministry of education under the title of "alternative school" and receives some state funding.

Reflecting on the overall context of his fieldwork at the school, Edward Ellis (2010) points out that the fact that the school is the exception rather than the rule as far as education in the country as a whole is concerned "need not be understood as distressing. It can be seen...as a great opportunity to empower and encourage new forms of change." He underlines the spaces that the Chávez government has opened up—in this case for "independent and autonomous...new projects to grow and develop." As Gerardo, a part-time collaborator at the school, a long time community activist from the barrio, and an organic intellectual of the working class par excellence states: "ten years ago this wouldn't have been possible. This would have been called 'terrorist' and would have to be underground." As he puts it, revolutionary teachers, unlike before, can advance faster, no longer having "to worry about being hunted down."

Gerardo points out that the school has opened many doors for people and that there are "a lot of expectations" from the ministry of education, which is hoping that the school might work as "a model for other schools."

Twenty-First-Century Socialist Praxis

Gerardo is committed to socialist praxis, noting that "socialism is done, not decreed." Given that the words "revolution" and "socialism" are omnipresent in Venezuelan society, and can be used "without much thought," Gerardo is working on the *construction* of socialism in the school, being "a bit more responsible in this sense." As he explains, "here we practice socialism with concrete elements from everyday life...sharing, working in a collective way, friendship, getting along, the fundamental bases of socialism with praxis." Having seen societies torn apart in a capitalist system based on consumption, and underlining Chávez's stress on participatory democracy, Gerardo notes that the teachers are trying to teach the children to be "critical and proactive"—"not just criticism but how things can be changed," "we are trying to show that the children have a participatory role in society, and that this role can be transformative."

Communication tools are crucial in this process—"the radio, the television, the written word...these things can lead to the transformation of society."

Lisbeida, a university student studying criminology, and a dance instructor, working at the school and in the community as a volunteer, says of twenty-first-century socialism, it "is being redefined, something that is flexible. I believe there are new understandings of what socialism is and how it can be implemented":

> But basically, the core concepts are the same: equality, social justice, elimination of class differences, more horizontal processes, all of this inside our school is an intrinsic part of what we are doing. It's our base... So we are trying to transmit these values of equality, solidarity, cooperation, collective work.

James Suggett, a writer for venezuelanalysis.com,[10] who is also a community activist and a volunteer at the school, reflects Freireian[11] analysis when he says he is critical of those teachers who view socialism as being authoritarian, those who believe they should be getting students into line. For Suggett, "socialism means creating a democratic space in the classroom," encouraging people "to recognize oppression and overcome it."

Communal, Cooperative, and Democratic Living and Learning

At the alternative school in Barrio Pueblo Nuevo, each day starts with a communal breakfast, after which students are brought together to discuss what will take place that day. Sometimes communal cleaning of the community center where the classes are held ensues; sometimes the day starts with group activities, focused on reading, writing, or mathematics, depending on what students wish to work on, or need to improve.

Addressing the socialist roots of Venezuela's indigenous communities, Gerardo illustrates Freire's process of conscientization (the pedagogical process by which counterhegemonic awareness is achieved) as he points out that indigenous people have a tradition of companionship, solidarity, respect, and sharing, and do not have the concept of private property, and how the teachers are trying to break the paradigms of Western society that value "capital more than people," and that prioritize individualism and competition. The school aims to provide the children with a point of departure so that they can all advance together toward socialism. Gerardo points to the use of a pedagogy that "involves the children in collective work and thinking" and includes cooperative games. When the teachers meet with the children, as Jeaneth (the main teacher of the school, a member of the community whose children are studying at the school) explains, the teachers try to emphasize "that we are a collective and if something happens to the group it affects us all."

Learning at the school is in line with Freire's advocacy of "dialogic education," which entails a democratic learning environment and the *absence* of authoritarianism, of "banking education" (where teachers deposit "facts" into empty minds) and of grades. As Jeaneth puts it:

> we plan activities and then ask the children which they would like to work on. They choose the area. We have some basic parameters that they need to work in but they choose. Also, when we leave the school for a trip, we propose the idea to them and they take part in the discussion about how to plan the trip.

Tamara Pearson, like Suggett, a writer for venezuelanalysis.com, and also a volunteer teacher of reading at the school, points out that:

> no one is forced to do anything and there are no punishments. If they don't want to participate in an activity, they can simply go somewhere else, or sit and watch. Hence, the weight is on the teacher to properly motivate the students and draw them in through the activity rather than discipline and threats of lower grades or whatever.

"There is no grading or competition," Pearson explains, "there's simply no sense of them competing with others." "The idea of the school," she believes, "is to teach using more creative and dynamic methods, without the usual competition and grades and failure and passing and who is first etc, with teachers who are very supportive and friendly, while also involving the community in school life, and vice versa."

Socialism and the Community

As Edward Ellis states, "there is a real emphasis on trying to increase students' participation in all activities." He gives the example of how "the students watched a movie and then discussed how to organize a screening of that same film in their community. A group conversation was held to identify what the steps necessary would be to put on this screening." As Ellis explains, "there is a lot of collaboration on the part of the community and different activities are led by different folks...It is quite common for the students to leave the classroom to attend an event in the community." In addition, as Lisbeida points out, the school's "activities [are] open to the entire community so that the community is a protagonist in what happens in the school. In that way, the dance group which is part of the school is also part of the community." Emphasizing how Participatory Action Research (PAR)[12] works in the community and school, Lisbeida explains:

> the idea is that the children have an impact in their community, carrying with them this experience to their homes and to their families so that their families also become integrated in the educational process that the school is trying to carry out. So there's a kind of feedback that we are trying to accomplish between the community and the school. And school-community means family, workers, etc. There is an important interaction which is very relevant to the educational process in the school.

This is not to glamorize the students' community. As Gerardo explains, some of the students come from homes where there are problems of violence, alcohol, or drugs, or unemployment and its attendant problems. However, as Lisbeida believes, this can also be a source of strength for the students:

> As these students come from backgrounds that are very difficult, I think that this gives them the ability to see certain social realities with more clarity: justice, the marked differences between violence and love. I see this as a potential to create criticisms and questions with more meaning. Because they have experienced very difficult things, they are not going to be afraid and they are going to have a very strong base to be critical of things.

Gerardo points out that there is help from some government missions, such as Mission Barrio Adentro (literally "mission inside the barrio"), which provides comprehensive publicly funded health care, and sports training to poor and marginalized communities. Barrio Adentro delivers de facto universal health care from cradle to grave.

In addition, the teachers are trying to improve human relations, not only with cooperative games, from which the teachers are also learning, but there are physical spaces "with a community vision," such as a community library and a community radio station. As Lisbeida puts it:

> we've noticed that the children are arriving at their house with new attitudes, and although we don't have a way to scientifically measure it, we can feel a difference in the attitude of the parents as well... how they treat their children. Something very interesting is happening.

> Things are changing...[the children] learn things based on what they already know and live. In this way, they can also learn that they have the potential to change the reality that surrounds them.

The students at the alternative school in Barrio Pueblo Nuevo are clearly being empowered, and already there are signs of progress. As Lisbeida enthuses, "one of the things that we have seen with this process in the school is that the ones who were thought to be completely without potential or capacity to learn are making people turn their heads. They are doing some incredible things." As Gerardo concludes:

> we've only had a short time operating but I have noticed a change in the way the children see things. Before, their world was just the barrio, but now they are looking a little bit beyond this. And I have seen that the children are speaking now, they are conversing...Before everything was resolved through violence. Now there is more talking. There are still some very sharp words, but we are working on it. This has opened many doors for people. There are a lot of expectations...And there are many things that we have learned about ourselves due to the students.

Conclusion

The government of the Bolivarian Republic of Venezuela, led by Hugo Chávez, represents, I believe, the best currently existing model in the world for a future socialist society. However, as stressed by Gerardo, the part-time collaborator in the alternative school in Barrio Pueblo Nuevo, and by Chávez himself, the revolution will not be decreed from above. From a Marxist perspective, it is important to stress the Chávez government's dialectic and symbiotic relationship with the Venezuelan working class.

However, as Martinez et al. (2010, 2) argue, President Chávez continues to be "the defining political factor" as revealed "by the typical political labels that...divide many Venezuelans between *Chavistas* and *anti-Chavistas*." It is "precisely in the relationship and tension between the Venezuelan government and the social movements that the process of building a participatory democracy comes alive most vividly." Greg Wilpert (2010, viii–ix) underlines this fact:

> To learn about...the movements that stand behind the Chávez phenomenon is...as important as learning about the Chávez government

itself. One cannot truly make sense of one without the other. And making sense of and defending what is happening in Venezuela is perhaps one of the most important tasks for progressives around the world today, since Venezuela is at the forefront in the effort to find a real progressive alternative to capitalism, to representative democracy, and to U.S. imperialism.

Central to the Bolivarian Revolution, as we have seen, is the idea of participatory democracy, as opposed to representative democracy, which has been a pillar of Chávez's philosophy since his first election victory in 1998.

While much remains to be done, particularly with respect to the full implementation of indigenous and Afro-Venezuelan rights (consistently acknowledged by Chávez, though not the whole of the Chávez government), there seems to be an abundance of hope for the future at the local and societal levels *despite* the forces opposing the revolution (see Cole 2011, 146–149).

With respect to education, we have witnessed that, viewed as a lifelong liberatory process, education is a key pillar of the revolution. I have noted how this is manifested in Chávez's concept of Venezuela as "a giant school." At the "formal" institutional level of education, the principles of the revolution have not been fully put into practice. Moreover, given the aforementioned conservatism of many teachers discovered by Griffiths and Williams, the challenge for Venezuelan revolutionary teachers to continue their counterhegemonic struggle against capitalism, racism, and imperialism remains paramount.

As noted earlier in this chapter, the overall societal reforms with respect to the "missions" and the other ameliorative measures are precisely that— *reforms*. However, just as these societal reforms need to be seen in the context of the country having a revolutionary socialist president and millions of pro-Chávez workers, who are *or have the potential to become* revolutionary socialists, so do the reforms at the level of education in general, and at the level of the alternative school in Barrio Pueblo Nuevo. In the same way that the societal reforms are reminiscent of those of the post–World War II Labour governments in the UK, the educational reforms being carried out in Barrio Pueblo Nuevo recall those that took place, for example, in the Inner London Education Authority (ILEA) and other progressive authorities. Indeed, in some ways these UK-based educational reforms were more progressive, particularly with respect to equality policies, as are equality policies embedded in UK equalities legislation today (see chapter 4 of Cole 2011 for a discussion).

In Mérida, there are, however, revolutionary teachers fostering, in Freire's terms, a deepening awareness of the sociocultural reality that shapes their students' lives, including the racism still institutionalized in Venezuelan society. To reiterate, unlike the UK and the United States, either historically or contemporaneously, the promotion, in future workers, of the consciousness that they have the capacity and the power to transform that reality, is supported in Venezuela by a revolutionary movement and a revolutionary president.

Good socialist education in the UK tends to get undermined or banned, as was ILEA, against the wishes of the parents/carers, by the undemocratic government of Margaret Thatcher. In the Bolivarian Republic of Venezuela, socialist education is promoted by and is pivotal to the revolutionary process.

Whereas the liberation of the working class in the UK and the United States is, for the foreseeable future, forestalled,[13] in Venezuela, for Chávez, the epicenter of the revolution, socialism is unstoppable. Whatever the final outcome of twenty-first-century socialism, in Venezuela's "giant school," conscientization is providing the working class, current and future, with the certainty that a different world is possible.

In the words of one resident in the Caracas barrio of Baruta, who joined the hundreds of thousands of people, maybe a million, descending from the barrios around Caracas, successfully demanding the reinstatement of Chávez after the military coup in 2002 (Blough, 2010):

> We love our president, but this is not his revolution. This is our revolution and it will always be the revolution of the people. If President Chávez goes, we will miss him dearly but we will still be here. We are revolutionaries and we will always be here. We will never go back! (cited in Blough 2010)

In various ways, we all have much to learn from each other. The revolutionary teachers in the school in Mérida have expressed a desire for open collaboration with revolutionary pedagogical scholars and theorists outside of Venezuela (personal correspondence). The UK has a history of working-class militancy, currently hindered by the ideological and repressive apparatuses of the British state, particularly since the advent of the Thatcher government, and accelerated under Tony Blair, and under the ConDem government (see Cole, 2011). Blair's mantra, "education, education, education," in essence creating a flexible workforce for capitalism, represents the antithesis of the forms of popular education advocated by Chávez.

With respect to the United States, San Juan Jr. (2010, p. xiv) has suggested that among other factors, the lack of a viable labor union tradition has distorted historical materialist principles[14] in that country.[15] Hence, among many leftist academics, "there is no mention of the working class as a significant force for overthrowing capitalism, much less initiating a socialist revolution" (San Juan Jr. 2010, xiv). Nevertheless, despite all this, revolutionary thought continues to exist among some key educationists in the United States (see Cole 2011, chapter 4).

San Juan Jr. (2010, xiv) shows awareness of how events in Venezuela may serve as a positive example to people in the United States, when he suggests that it is instructive to contrast the trend among those leftists in the United States who have abandoned the socialist cause, with the revolutionary promotion of popular literacy in Venezuela, "a pedagogical experiment of historic significance for all anti-capitalist militants" (San Juan Jr. 2010, xiv).

As part of the more general process of conscientization for all workers, intercontinental collaboration between revolutionary teachers and revolutionary academics surely captures a key element in the spirit of internationalism, a fundamental tenet of Marxist praxis. Writing about the significance of the 2012 Venezuelan presidential elections, Correo Del Orinico International (2011) notes:

> the results of next year's presidential elections will greatly affect the future of Venezuela's democratic, socialist and participatory revolution, as well as regional integration efforts across Latin America and the Caribbean and global initiatives to consolidate a multi-polar world.

Notes

1. This chapter is based in part on chapter 5 of Cole 2011.
2. "Barrio" is a Spanish word meaning district or neighborhood. In the Venezuelan context, the term commonly refers to the outer rims of big cities inhabited by poor working-class communities.
3. As the Marxist writer and political activist Antonio Gramsci argued, traditional intellectuals regard themselves as an autonomous and independent group, and are seen as such by the public, whereas in fact they tend to be conservative and allied and supportive of the ruling group. Organic intellectuals, on the other hand, grow organically with both dominant and subordinate group classes in society, and are their thinking and organizing elements. For Gramsci, organic intellectuals are produced by the educational system to perform a function for the dominant social group in society. It is through organic intellectuals that the ruling class maintains its hegemony over the rest

of society. Gramsci argued that it was important for the working class to produce its own organic intellectuals, and also that a significant number of "traditional intellectuals" come over to the revolutionary cause (see Burke 2005 for an analysis).
4. Vladimir Illyich Ulyanov (commonly known as Lenin), one of the founders of the Russian Revolution, characterized capitalist democracy as the process by which oppressed workers are allowed once every few years to decide which particular representatives of the oppressing class will represent them and repress them in parliament (1917 [2002], 95).
5. "Middle class" is used here in the sociological sense of relatively rich people in relatively high-status jobs.
6. The Venezuelan working class should not be viewed as constituting a traditional industrial proletariat, akin to the working class that constituted the driving force of much of twentieth-century socialism (see Cole 2011, chapter 1 for a discussion). Some 60 percent of Venezuelan workers are involved in the informal economy (street vendors and so on), primarily in the barrios from where Chávez draws his support (Dominguez 2010).
7. Liberation theology began as a movement within the Catholic Church in Latin America in the 1950s, achieving prominence in the 1970s and 1980s. It emphasizes the role of Christians aligning themselves with the poor and being involved in the struggle against economic, political, and social inequalities. In Chávez's view, "[t]he people are the voice of God" (cited in Sheehan 2010). Chávez is referring to the Venezuelan revolutionary masses.
8. Stalinism refers to political systems that have the characteristics of the Soviet Union from 1928, when Joseph Stalin became the leader (his leadership lasted until 1953). The term refers to a repressive and oppressive from of government by dictatorship, which includes the purging by exile or death of opponents, mass use of propaganda, and the creation of a personality cult around the leader.
9. The fieldwork at this school was carried out on my behalf by Edward Ellis. I am most grateful to him for this. The subheadings in this section of the chapter reflect the main issues and concerns that arose in Ellis's interviews. The issue of racism was also raised (see Cole 2011, chapter 5). Cole (2011), as a whole, specifically addresses racism, and chapter 5 of that volume also considers racism and antiracism in Venezuela.
10. Venezuelanalysis.com, in its own words:is an independent website produced by individuals who are dedicated to disseminating news and analysis about the current political situation in Venezuela. The site's aim is to provide ongoing news about developments in Venezuela, as well as to contextualize this news with in-depth analysis and background information. The site is targeted toward academics,

journalists, intellectuals, policy makers from different countries, and the general public.

11. For Paulo Freire, learning environments, as democratic spaces, entail an absence of authoritarianism (Freire 1987, 102, cited in Freire and Shor 1987). Such an absence is not to be confused with a lack of authoritativeness. As Peter Ninnes (1998) points out, Freire (1998b) explains the importance of teachers being authoritative, rather than being weak and insecure or being authoritarian. In addition to democracy, dialogic education centralizes the need to develop an open dialogue with students, and requires a balance between "talking to learners and talking with them" (Freire 1998b, 63, cited in Ninnes 1998). Freire maintains that only through talking with and to learners can teachers contribute to the "[development of] responsible and critical citizens" (ibid., 65, cited in Ninnes 1998). Freire makes a distinction between the progressive and democratic teacher, on the one hand, which he favors, and the permissive or authoritarian teacher, on the other, which he rejects.

12. Participation Action Research (PAR) involves respecting and combining one's skills with the knowledge of the researched or grassroots communities; taking them as full partners and coresearchers; not trusting elitist versions of history and science that respond to dominant interests; being receptive to counternarratives and trying to recapture them; not depending solely on one's own culture to interpret facts; and sharing what one has learned together with the people, in a manner that is wholly understandable (Gott, 2008).

13. This is not in any way to undermine the significance of the ongoing (at the time of writing—October, 2011) "Occupy Wall Street" phenomenon, nor the movements worldwide which are following in its wake. "Occupy Wall Street" self-describes as: a people powered movement that began on September 17, 2011 in Liberty Square in Manhattan's Financial District, and has spread to over 100 cities in the United States and actions in over 1,500 cities globally. OWS is fighting back against the corrosive power of major banks and multinational corporations on the democratic process, and the role of Wall Street in creating an economic collapse that caused the greatest recession in generations. The movement is inspired by uprisings in Egypt, Tunisia, Spain, Greece, Italy, and the UK, and aims to expose how the richest 1 percent of the people are writing the rules of the global economy and are imposing an agenda of neoliberalism and economic inequality (occupywallst.org/).

14. Marx argued that societies progress through various stages. Moreover, all past history, with the exception of its most early stage (primitive communism—the original hunter-gatherer society of humanity) is, according to Marx and Engels, the history of class struggles. These warring classes are always the products of the respective modes of

production, of the *economic* conditions of their time. Thus slaves were in class struggle with their masters in the historical epoch of ancient slavery; feudal serfs with their lords in times of feudalism; and in the era of capitalism, workers are engaged in a class struggle with capitalists. Like ancient slavery and feudalism, capitalism is viewed merely as a *stage* in human development. Marxists see such stages as containing a number of *contradictions*, which resolve themselves dialectically. Thus when these contradictions become too great, a given stage gives way to another. For example, just as the privileges that feudal lords held and the hereditary basis of subordinating serf to lord in the feudal societies contradicted the need for "free" labor power in emerging capitalism ("free" in the sense that workers were not needed to be indentured to the capitalists; they were, of course, forced to sell their labor power in order to survive), present-day capitalism contains contradictions that Marxists believe, *given the right circumstances*, can eventually lead to its demise, and be replaced by socialism.
15. It is, in part, for this reason that a non-Marxist interpretation of Critical Race Theory (CRT) is so preeminent among US antiracist academics (for a Marxist critique of CRT, and a discussion of some of its strengths, see Cole 2009).

References

Althusser, Louis. 1971. "Ideology and Ideological State Apparatuses" in *Lenin and Philosophy and Other Essays*, London: New Left Books. Accessed on December 19, 2009 at http://www.marx2mao.com/Other/LPOE70NB.html.

Au, W. 2009. "Obama, Where Art Thou? Hoping for Change in U.S. Education Policy." *Harvard Educational Review*, 79 (2) (Summer): 309–320.

Beckman, A., C. Cooper, and Dave Hill. 2009. "Neoliberalization and Managerialization of 'Education' in England and Wales—A Case for Reconstructing Education." *Journal for Critical Education Policy Studies*, 7 (2) (November). Accessed on April 16, 2010 at http://www.jceps.com/PDFs/07-2-12.pdf.

Burke, B. 2005. "Antonio Gramsci, Schooling and Education." Accessed on August 19, 2010 at http://www.infed.org/thinkers/et- gram.htm.

Chávez, H. 2010. "Coup and Countercoup: Revolution!" Accessed on April 17, 2011 at http://venezuela- us.org/2010/04/11/coup-and-countercoup-revolution.

Cole, Mike. 2009. *Critical Race Theory and Education: A Marxist Response.* New York: Palgrave Macmillan.

Cole, Mike. 2011. *Racism and Education in the U.K. and the U.S.: Towards a Socialist Alternative.* New York and London: Palgrave Macmillan.

Cole, M. 2012. "Marx, Marxism and (Twenty-First Century) Socialism" in *Teaching Marx Across the Curriculum: The Socialist Challenge* edited by M. Cole, and C. S. Malott. Charlotte, NC: Information Age Publishing Inc.

Contreras Baspineiro, A. 2003. "Globalizing the Bolivarian Revolution: Hugo Chávez's Proposal for Our América." Accessed on April 7, 2010 at http://www.narconews.com/Issue29/article746.html.

Correo Del Orinoco International. 2011. "Chavez Campaign Prepares Nationwide Grassroots Coalition for 2012 Elections". Accessed on August 5, 2011 at venezuelanalysis.com/news/6544.

Dominguez, F. 2010. "Education for the Creation of a New Venezuela." Paper presented at Latin America and Education, Marxism and Education: Renewing Dialogues XIII, Institute of Education, University of London, July 24.

Freire, P. and I. Shor 1987. *A Pedagogy for Liberation: Dialogues on Transforming Education*, London: Macmillan Education.

Gott, R. 2008. "Orlando Fals Borda: Sociologist and Activist Who Defined Peasant Politics in Colombia," *The Guardian*, August 26. Accessed on October 17, 2011 at http://www.guardian.co.uk/world/2008/aug/26/colombia.sociology.

Griffiths, T. G. 2008. "Preparing Citizens for a 21st Century Socialism: Venezuela's Bolivarian Educational Reforms," Paper presented at the Social Educators Association of Australia National Biennial Conference, Newcastle, Australia, January 20–22.

Griffiths, T. G. and J. Williams. 2009. "Mass Schooling for Socialist Transformation in Cuba and Venezuela." *Journal for Critical Education Policy Studies*, 7 (2): 30–50. Accessed on April 12, 2010 at http://www.jceps.com/index.php?pageID=article&articleID=160.

Lee, F. J. T. 2005. "Venezuela's President Hugo Chavez Frias: 'The Path is Socialism.'" Accessed on May 4, 2007 at http://www.handsoffvenezuela.org/chavez_path_socialism_4.htm.

Lenin, V. I. 1917/2002. *On Utopian and Scientific Socialism*. Amsterdam: Fredonia Books.

Martinez, C., M. Fox, and J. Farrell. 2010. *Venezuela Speaks: Voices from the Grassroots*. Oakland, CA: PM Press.

MercoPress. 2009. "To School for Reading Classes with Karl Marx and Che Guevara," MercoPress, May 17. Accessed on February 10, 2011 at http://en.mercopress.com/2009/05/17/to-school-for-reading-classes-with-karl-marx-and-che-guevara.

Ministerio del Poder Popular Para la Educación. 2007. "Currículo Nacional Bolivariano: Diseño Curricular del Sistema Educativa Bolivariano." Accessed on August 10, at http://www.me.gov.ve/media.eventos/2007/dl_908_69.pdf.

Ninnes, P. 1998. "Freire, Paulo's Teachers as Cultural Workers: Letters to Those Who Dare Teach," translated by D. Macedo, D. Koike, and

A. Oliveira. Boulder: Westview Press, *Education Review*, August 4. Accessed on September 12, 2010 at http://www.edrev.info/reviews/rev28.htm

Pearson, T. 2009. "Venezuela Opens National Art Gallery and Launches National Reading Plan," Accessed on April 7, 2010 at http://venezuelanalysis.com/news/4402

Rosales, A. 2010. "Chávez Revving Up Revolution with Land Takeovers." Accessed on October 24, 2010 at http://venezuelanalysis.com/analysis/5716.

San Juan J r., E. 2010. "Foreword" to D. Kelsh, D. Hill, and S. Macrine (eds.), *Class in Education: Knowledge, Pedagogy, Subjectivity*. London and New York: Routledge.

Sheehan, C. 2010. "Transcript of Cindy Sheehan's Interview with Hugo Chavez." Accessed on August 1, 2010 at http://venezuelanalysis.com/analysis/5233.

Stobart, L. 2009. "Letter from Venezuela," Socialist Review, October. Accessed on October 25, 2009 at http://www.socialistreview.org.uk/article.php?articlenumber=11001.

Suggett, J. 2010. "Chávez's Annual Address Includes Minimum Wage Hike, Maintenance of Social Spending in Venezuela." Accessed on August 5, 2010 at http://venezuelanalysis.com/news/5077.

Victor, M. P. 2009. "From Conquistadores, Dictators and Multinationals to the Bolivarian Revolution," Keynote speech at the Conference on Land and Freedom, of "The Caribbean Studies Program," University of Toronto, October 31.

Willgress, M. 2010. "Venezuela under Threat from US Intervention," *Latin America Forward! Adelante!* Accessed on April 9, 2010 at http://www.venezuelanalysis.com/analysis/4979.

Wilpert, G. 2010. "Prologue" in C. Martinez, M. Fox, and J. Farrell, *Venezuela Speaks: Voices from the Grassroots*, Oakland, CA: PM Press.

Chapter 11

Being, Becoming, and Breaking Free: Peter McLaren and the Pedagogy of Liberation

Peter McLaren in conversation with Ravi Kumar

I

Ravi Kumar: You have been in the forefront of revolutionary critical pedagogy along with other social scientists. Where does the break happen in the works of revolutionary critical pedagogues from that of earlier educationists—the neo-Marxists like Michael Apple or critical pedagogues such as Henry Giroux?

Peter McLaren: I don't see it so much as a break or rupture as coming to a fork in the road, a fortuitous crossroads of sorts—and deciding to take a different path, recognizing that the journey I had taken with fellow critical educators had been a long and arduous one, freighted with travails and tribulations, a voyage where a lot of learning had taken place and many important struggles had been initiated. Apple's work was important to me as a graduate student because it was a clear exposition of a neo-Marxist analysis of the North American curriculum and policy initiatives and Giroux's work—where I find more similarities to Zygmant Bauman, Castoriadis, and the Frankfurt school than to the revolutionary Marxist tradition out of which my more recent work has emerged—remains important to me to this day; I consider Henry one of the most insightful and protean scholars on the topic of youth culture and one of the most illuminating critics of contemporary social formations, including the blood-sucking behemoth we refer to as neoliberal capitalism. His creative and brilliant work on so many topics has inspired an entire generation of intellectuals. What's different among us? Well, I think many things, and I would point to the most significant as my preoccupation with the writings of Marx, my hoisting of class as a central concept in teacher education, and the creation of socialism for the twenty-first century and linking education to the worldwide struggle for socialism, and working toward the instauration of Marxist educational theory in North America, along with a few fellow travellers. That path was opened up to me, in part, by the work of British educationalists Dave Hill, Mike Cole, Glenn Rikowski, and Paula Allman. Back in the mid-1980s, Mike Cole challenged me to subject my own work to a Marxist critique and I am glad that I obliged. Now I think your question leads to a more important question—what differentiates my work in general from the progressive tradition in North America? In the early-1990s I was working from a perspective I called critical postmodernism—the term critical postmodernism or resistance postmodernism was used, after Teresa Ebert, to distinguish it from "ludic postmodernism" or the postmodernism of the spectacle, of the theatrical apparatuses of the state, the politics of representation, and the propaganda of desire, a pedagogy of "arousal effect," a kind of microresistance linked to a secret museum of academic codes and codices that existed within culture where culture's mystified nature could be explored and a politics of negation unleashed, the aim of which was to produce a well-tempered radical where the alienation of everyday life under capitalism was seen as not so bad because it was suffered by good people. I was concerned that, among the cultural avant-garde, questions of class became ideationally sequestered from internal scrutiny—there existed a proclivity to self-censorship related to questions of class because the working class, in their role as organic intellectuals, were relegated to the role of cultural workers, and needed tutelage in the spaces of the vanguard regarding questions of cultural production, whereas questions of class were deemed to be self-evident and, to some extent, too inevitable.

Now I don't want to leave you with the impression that I don't think culture is very important, since culture is linked to ways of "living out" historically specific antagonisms and relations of subordination. Given that the politics of liberation is headquartered in critical consciousness and ignited by revolutionary praxis where historical agents transform themselves through their struggles, I became interested in pedagogical spaces that could make the strange familiar and the familiar strange, more specifically in the sense of accounting for the "rich totality of many determinations" that Marx talks about. In other words, I tried to do a number of things: to understand how a distracted and indifferent subjectivity (that led to critics bemoaning the superficiality of modern life), one that remains blasé to shifts and changes within a moving modernity, can be invited into new perceptions of the social self by building a critical lexicon gleaned from the critical literature; to make the subterranean or oblivious workings of capital more conspicuous to teachers and educators, to conceive of the concept of praxis as ontologically important, and examine history not as something already written or hardwired into predicated or predictable outcomes but open to change once certain ideological and material conditions are superseded and fetishized everyday life grasped dialectically (i.e, those conditions that shape and educate our desires surreptitiously or in tacit ways). I wanted to add some dialectical flesh to the progressive bones of critical pedagogy (which had becoming increasingly domesticated, as Paulo Freire was turned into a type of benevolent, almost Santa Claus figure), and tried to give this flesh an almost raucous, ribald and garrulous physicality through an eclectic writing style—without becoming trapped in a phenomenology of sensation or seduction. I tried to understand, in theoretical terms, what gives our desires direction. And, of course: What is the direction of our desiring? I became interested in the notion that human beings form reality in the process of becoming human, that praxis determines human beings in their totality—in other words, that praxis distinguishes the human from the nonhuman, which is something Karel Kosik talked about in his work on the dialectics of the concrete. Following Kosik, I became interested in the movements of the world's totality and how this totality is uncovered by human beings, and how, in our uncovering this totality, we develop a particular openness toward being. How can we discover ourselves as historical beings? The results of our actions in and on and through the world do not coincide with our intentions. Why is this? What accounts for the disharmony between the necessity and the freedom of our actions as human beings creating and being created by historical forces? These are questions that motivated my thinking, and still do. Do we make history or does history make us? Or do both occur simultaneously? I do not believe we are summoned by some higher power to create historical outcomes but that, following Marx, we make history. Kosik saw this as the interconnection of the objectified and objectivized praxis of humankind.

This praxis in the form of production forces, forms of thought, language, and so on, exists as historical continuity only because of the activity of human beings. But this objectified and objectivized praxis has a form, and it is this form which is fixed in human history and seems over time to be more real than human reality itself and becomes the basis for historical mystification, for what Kosik refers to as the basis of the possibility of inverting a subject into an object.

So, in effect, this forms the possibility for ideological mystification, for the ideological state apparatuses, all the way to the current kind of totalitarianism we had under the Bush administration ruled by the "big lie"—a lie that enters people's heads as if it were a metaphysical being, a mystical substance in which human beings seek a guarantee against chaos, against chance, against the everyday contingency of life. So that every individual enters conditions not of their own making, and there is a dialectic we must uncover between individuals and those conditions that are given for every generation, epoch, and class. And as Kosik noted, we can transcend these conditions but not primarily in our consciousness and intentions but through our praxis. We get to know the world by actively interfering in it. We discover our revolutionary ethics in the process of our objectification and our resistance to it. I tried to convey to my students that economics is not some nomothetic discipline but an ethic—a moral philosophy—that is perverse because of the way it deals with practical human relationships through its frenzy to maximize profits. I became interested in the work of Raya Dunayevskaya and her notion of absolute negativity. Absolute negativity, in Raya's sense of the term, does not refer simply to an endless series of negations but a negation that can free itself from the object of its critique. Raya discovered this in Hegel. Hegel worked with a type of self-referential negation, which was modified by Marx. By negating itself, negation establishes a relation with itself and is freed from dependence on the external object—so this type of negativity, since it exists without relation to another outside itself, is absolute—it is absolved from dependence on the other. This type of negation has negated its dependence on an external object. Marx critically appropriated this concept to explain the path to communist society. As Peter Hudis has explained, Marx, via Hegel, understood that to negate something still leaves us dependent on the object of critique. The alienated object is simply affirmed on a different level. So when you look at revolutions of the past, you see that they were still trapped by the objects that they tried to negate. They didn't fully negate their negations, so to speak. Along these lines, Peter Hudis notes that communism is the negation of capitalism but as such it was still dependent on the object of its critique insofar as it replaced private property with collective property. Communism thus was not free from the alienated notion that ownership is the most important part of being human. Ownership was still affirmed, but on a different level. Of course, it was good to negate private property but this did not go far enough to pave the way to a truly new, a truly positive society. In order to meet this challenge, you need a human praxis that can achieve the transcendence of alienation. And this necessitates a subjective praxis connected with a philosophy of liberation that is able to illuminate the content of a postcapitalist society and convincing the popular majorities that it is possible to resolve the contradictions between alienation and freedom. Now it is clear that attempts to concretize absolute negativity as a new beginning rather than repeating the mistakes of an earlier era have been halted by the forces of colonization and imperialism. Ramon Grosfoguel, Nelson Maldonaldo-Torres, Enrique Dussel, Walter Mignolo, and Anibal Quijano and others are writing cogently and presciently about the coloniality of being in this regard, where the epistemological genocide linked to the Eurocentric forces of colonization, and economic exploitation linked to capitalism, are demonstrated to be coconstitutive of plundering the oppressed (invented nonbeings) of their alterity, their liberty, and their humanity—where, as Enrique Dussel notes, indigenous peoples have become but free labor for a colonial tributary system linked historically to European capital. I am interested in the historical process of the European ego's missionary sense (I discover, I conquer and I evangelize) and ontological sense (I think) and how this links up to the concept of the transnational capitalist class and the transnational state apparatus as developed by William Robinson.

RK: Freire, with whom you have worked and whose ideas you have critically used in your works, has been used by different shades of intellectuals and even agencies that sustain the rule of capital. What is it that allows the use of Freire's works/ideas by them and what difference does it make when you use his ideas in your works?

PM: Well, I make no claim to a "purer" interpretation of Freire's work. I think of the influence that Karel Kosik's Dialectics of the Concrete had on Freire, and I think we can understand Freire best when we see his work in terms of how he fashioned the notion of praxis. In this respect, I would argue that Freire's work has been flensed by liberals. The politics of his praxis has been pasteurized. The supreme postulate—the unity of theory and practice—is upheld by liberals and criticalists alike—but the original philosophical questioning (at least within materialist philosophy) that formed the conditions of possibility for revolutionary praxis has disappeared. Thus, as Kosik notes, the unity of theory and praxis has come to be realized and grasped in different epochs in very different ways. Liberals often deal with the pseudo concrete when utilizing praxis—they view it in terms of addressing the practical applications of pedagogical theory, or something like that, in which the focus is on the subjective consciousness of the individual. Praxis in the way I understand it, via Freire, and others, is the ontological process of becoming human. Reality manifests itself in this becoming, in this onto-formative process of becoming, in which the practice of being human forms and interprets reality. So praxis, as Kosik points out, is a specific mode of being that determines humans in their totality.

A specific mode of being, praxis becomes a way of transcending our finitude and helps us to constitute our relationship to the totality of human existence. Many approaches to knowledge limit the notion of praxis, fetishize it, and turn it into some kind of technique of learning. Here, formal logic replaces dialectical logic. This goes against a materialist philosophy of praxis in which praxis is viewed as an onto-formative process, as the historical mediation of spirit and matter, of theory and action, epistemology and ontology. Here we need to talk about revolutionary praxis, denouncing oppression and dialectically inaugurating new forms of social, educational, and political relationships. Clearly, reflecting on our practice means finding ways of organizing and activating our pedagogical relationships so that the oppressed become protagonists in their historical formation. Freirean praxis is oriented toward socialist relationships and practices, and this has been jettisoned by liberals. Revolutionary praxis is, if Marx's stresses are taken into account, not some arche-strategy of political performance undertaken by academic mountebanks in the semiotics seminar room but instead is about "the coincidence of the changing of circumstances and of human activity or self-change." It is through our own activities that we develop our capacities and capabilities. We change society by changing ourselves and we change ourselves in our struggle to change society. The act of knowing is always a knowing act. It troubles and disturbs the universe of objects and beings, it can't exist outside of them; it is interactive, dialogical. We learn about reality not by reflecting on it but by changing it. Paying attention to the simultaneous change in circumstances and self-change and creating a new integrated worldview founded upon a new social matrix—what I call socialism—is how I understand revolutionary movement as praxis.

RK: The works of revolutionary critical pedagogues have been often critiqued as nonviable, as ideals which cannot be achieved. Their works are also critiqued on the grounds that they do not talk much about curriculum, teacher training, classroom transactions or students psychology. Rather they are seen as arguing against imperialism and capitalism or resistance against capitalism. How would you respond to such critiques?

PM: I think there is some truth to this criticism. But there are several ways to look at this dilemma. First and foremost, if there are no other critical educators addressing neoliberal capitalism and imperialism, specifically from a Marxist perspective, or dealing systematically with what Anibal Quijano and Ramon Grosfoguel call the "coloniality of power" then it is obvious revolutionary critical educators need to be up to this task. Clearly, the copious offerings of the postmodern left have remained regnant in the education literature, Hardt and Negri's work on the immateriality of labor, the multitude, and Foucault's work on the archaeology of power, etc. Joining these are neo-Weberian approaches to class. There are, in my mind, too few Marxist analyses available for students to engage within the educational field, although perhaps it is different in India, and I know that it is different in England with the work of Dave Hill, Mike Cole, Glenn Rikowski, Paula Allman, and others gaining worldwide visibility. So in terms of my own work, I have been trying to address issues that you and colleagues in England and elsewhere have been addressing for a much longer time. My task, along with other North American critical educators, has been to try to give the anticapitalist movement relevance for North American educators. One theme that has dominated my work has been a Marxist critique of global capitalism. The sociologist Willian I. Robinson argues that we have a global capitalist system that has entered a new phase during the last two decades—what we have come to call neoliberal capitalism. Obviously we need to mount a politics of resistance. Social and political forces are still needed to challenge state power at the national level. It is wrong to think that there is no more need to talk about state power or the need for political organizations that can cooperate in civil society as well as in political society. We have two extremes at the current historical juncture: the old model of the vanguard party overthrowing the state (the vertical model) and the civil societarian position about changing the world without taking state power. Enrique Dussel points out that asking whether or not it is possible "to change the world without taking power" is the wrong question. Power, notes Dussel, can't be "taken" as it were a "thing." Power belongs to the political community, to the people, as it were. Power can be exercised institutionally by representative delegates of the community but the question remains—in whose interests do these institutions serve? Dussel argues,

> The package of State institutions (potestas) needs to be untied and changed as a whole by conserving what is sustainable and eliminating what is unjust—thereby creating the new. Power (as potestas) is

not "taken" en bloc. It is reconstituted and exercised critically in view of the material satisfaction of needs, in fulfilment of the normative demands of democratic legitimacy, and within empirical political possibility. But to be clear, without the obediential exercise of delegated institutional power the world cannot feasibly be changed. To attempt to do so is little more than abstract and apolitical moralism and idealism, which clearly results from practical and theoretical confusions.

And Robinson is correct in positing a crucial remaining question: What types of political vehicles will "interface" between popular forces and state structures? What's the relationship between the social movements of the left, the state, and political organizations? Previously the relationship was vertical (cultivating a top-down hierarchy), now it's horizontal (cultivating democratic social relations from the ground up). So what will eventually replace the neoliberal model? Market capitalist models? Reformist models that will sustain the rule of capital? What are the forms of organization we need to resist the rule of capital? At the level of the state as well as the public sphere. What political vehicles can the popular majorities create that can interface between popular forces and state structures? How can popular forces utilize state power in order to transform the state and bring about a socialist alternative to the capitalist law of value? According to Robinson, previously there was a vertical model. In the last 15 or 20 years, the emphasis has been on horizontal relations, networking among different social groups, and bringing about democratic relations from the ground up via participatory democratic forms of organization. Here, indigenous organizations have taken the lead. We need countervailing forces from below—popular forces and movements of popular majorities from below that can put pressure on the state (where global forces pressure even revolutionary governments to moderate structural change), even when the state is working toward socialist ideals such as the case of Venezuela. What are the pedagogical implications in all of this? How can we look at critical pedagogy as a social movement, as a broad coalition of groups? How do we define pedagogy in this context? How is critical pedagogy a force for change that exists as much outside of schools as within them? These are questions that need exploring. And there are too few of us in the field of education engaging these questions.

Let's take another important theme. In addition to challenging the neoliberal globalization of capital, revolutionary critical educators need to address the concept of colonialism. Anibal Quijano, for instance, notes that with the help of capitalism, the idea of race helped to yoke the world's population into a hierarchical order of superior and inferior people and it became a central construct in creating and reproducing the international division of labor, including the global system of patriarchy. He writes how, historically, slavery, serfdom, wage labor, and reciprocity all functioned to produce commodities for the world market—and this "colonial power matrix" ("patrón de poder colonial") came to affect all dimensions of social existence such as sexuality, authority, subjectivity, and labor. Berkeley professor Ramon Grosfoguel conceptualizes this as a historical-structural heterogeneous totality that by the late nineteenth century came to cover the whole planet. Grosfoguel has described the coloniality of power as an entanglement of multiple and heterogeneous global hierarchies ("heterarchies") of sexual, political, epistemic, economic, spiritual, linguistic, and racial forms of domination and exploitation where the racial/ethnic hierarchy of the European/non-European divide transversally reconfigures all of the other global power structures. As race and racism became the organizing principle that structured all of the multiple hierarchies of the world-system, different forms of labor that were articulated to capitalist accumulation at a world scale were assigned according to this racial hierarchy. Cheap, coercive labor was carried out by non-European people in the periphery and "free wage labor" was exercised by people of European descent in the core. Such has been the case up to the present day. Grosfoguel makes an important case that, contrary to the Eurocentric perspective, race, gender, sexuality, spirituality, and epistemology are not additive elements to the economic and political structures of the capitalist world-system, but a constitutive part of the broad entangled "package" called the European modern/colonial capitalist/patriarchal world-system. Now as revolutionary critical educators, we need to examine class struggle in the context of the production of the coloniality of power. This is an important project. So yes, this is a lot of theoretical work, and the basic arguments need to be laid out before we can build a curriculum that can address these issues and more work needs to be done before we can mine their implications for teacher education, curriculum, and a psychology of liberation. When we look at psychology, we can look to the pioneering work of Frantz Fanon and, of course, Ignacio Martín-Baró, the Jesuit priest who was murdered by the US-backed military forces of El Salvador. Of course, some educators are addressing the issue of decolonizing pedagogy at the level of the classroom, of decolonizing the curriculum, and this is important work. It is not that works addressing these themes have not been done before for many years. It's just that when new questions and configurations arise at the level of global politics, we need to examine their implications from both geopolitical and micropolitical perspectives, using new conceptual schema and utilizing empirical work being done on the ground. And putting it all together.

But, a single revolutionary critical educator would find it difficult to do everything you mention in your question all at once—to put implications for curriculum planning, for learning theory, for psychology, for teacher education, for pedagogical approaches in the classroom all in one book, or one study, for instance. I like to see revolutionary critical education as a collective enterprise. Some critical educators are writing about classroom issues, others are looking at the curriculum. I am writing more on a "macro" level, trying to develop a coherent philosophy of praxis—and of course I benefit from the work being done by critical educators worldwide. If I were a preservice student in a teacher education programme, obviously reading a book by McLaren would not be enough to answer so many important pressing questions that classroom practitioners need to address. The key would be to read educators who can give you some philosophical foundations, including the concept of revolutionary praxis, some historical foundations, ethical and epistemological foundations, and some multicultural foundations that include issues around gender and patriarchy and sexuality and disability, and foundations for developing critical classroom practices, including ecopedagogy and teaching for a sustainable biosystemic future. We are a collective effort. People sometimes want me, or some other revolutionary critical educator, to do everything in a single text. The key is not to look for a single source but to appropriate critically from a wide expanse of revolutionary critical discourses—inside and outside of the educational literature. Here in the United States we have a field called educational foundations. But you don't see programmes called educational foundations as much today as when I began teaching in schools of education a number of decades ago. I think we need to revive educational foundations, and try to revision them as critical educational foundations programmes.

The state is not a neutral site, and what we need to challenge is how capital has shaped it and how it is shaping capital. Civil society is part of the state and is not an autonomous region that miraculously floats above the messy world of class antagonisms. Many progressive educators fail to realize this. So what happens? In their refusal to move beyond reclamation of the public sphere and an embracing of an anaemic and abstract conception of democracy and freedom, they unwittingly reflect the leftist face of the capitalist class in which appearances are created and preserved while reality is eroded. For me, the struggle is about building a socialism of the concrete, not an abstract utopia, a radical democracy of the abstract spawned by a revivified civil society. And we all have been remiss is failing to spell out what this means, what this could be like. That is the challenge for some of us, and until we develop a coherent direction of where to go AFTER capital, we will be trapped in a leftist neoliberalism, and that is a very perilous place for humanity to be.

II

RK: How do you analyse the current recession as a pedagogue? How do you see it as a teacher-worker affecting the educational scenario?
PM: Teachers need to develop anticapitalist pedagogies. They need to involve their students in a discussion of the current global economic crisis—and not be afraid to use the word "capitalism." We need to stress the "class" dimension of the crisis in Marxian terms. We need to enter into discussions about how capitalism works and how the question of politics pervades questions of the economy and the distribution of wealth and class power. And how all these questions have a moral dimension (can morality exist within capitalism?) as well as a political basis. There is a tremendous fear about socialism in the United States these days, but we must remember that the ruling class only fears socialism for the poor because the entire system is protected via socialism for the rich, a system that is comfortably in place—although it needs to be unmasked as socialism for the rich. The great US polymath, Gore Vidal, pointed out that the US government prefers that "public money go not to the people but to big business. The result is a unique society in which we have free enterprise for the poor and socialism for the rich" and we can clearly discern the truth in that statement when we look at the recent nationalization of Fannie Mae and Freddie Mac where you can see clearly that the United States is a country where there exists socialism for the rich and privatization for the poor, all basking in what Nouriel Roubini calls "the glory of unfettered Wild West laissez-faire jungle capitalism"—and what Marxist theorist David Harvey argues has led to "a financial Katrina"—that has allowed the biggest debt bubble in history to fester without any control, causing the biggest financial crisis since the Great Depression. Indeed, socialism is only condemned when it profits the poor and the powerless and threatens the rich. But capitalists are quick to embrace a socialism for the rich—which really is what neoliberal capitalism is all about. But of course, it's called free-market capitalism and is seen as synonymous with the struggle for democracy.

But free-market ideology cannot fix a crisis created by free-market ideology. I look around me to the decaying infrastructures of the cities here and I feel I am living in some kind of slow-motion demolition of civilization, in a film noir comic book episode where denizens of doom inhabit quasi-feudal steampunk landscapes of wharfs and warehouses and rundown pubs, roaches sliding off laminated table cloths, in an atmosphere of dog-eat-dog despair. Those whose labor is exploited in the production of social wealth—that is, the wage and salaried class—are now bearing most of the burden of the current economic crisis in the United States and, quite simply, what is called for is a mass uprising like we saw in Argentina in 2001–2002 when four presidents were forced out in less than three weeks, like we saw in Venezuela when the popular majorities rescued President Hugo Chavez during a CIA-supported coup, or like we saw in Bolivia, when the indigenous peoples put Evo Morales in power or what we are seeing in Iceland, in Latvia, in Greece, in South Korea today. We need to cry "¡Que se vayan todos!" ("All of them must go!") And flush contemporary deregulated capitalism down the toilet. But the interminably overcast political world and the media/videosphere in the United States provide the US public with what Paul Valéry described as "the succour of that which does not exist"—in this case, a belief that free-market capitalism is still the best of all possible systems and needed to keep democracy safe from the feral hordes of barbarians who might turn to the evil of socialism if we are not vigilant in protecting our way of life. As educators, we are faced with a tough challenge in teaching about and against capitalism.

William Tabb notes that the system itself created this crisis by floating the stock of new companies that promised to invest in high technology. Prices rose so high that the stock market came crashing down. When the Federal Reserve lowered interest rates and kept lowering them, it became easier for companies and individuals to borrow and it helped people pay off debt and borrow more and low-interest mortgages made home ownership cheaper. As housing prices rose and kept rising, mortgage originators gave out easy loans with little or no down payment as well as low teaser-rate loans, which would reset in the future, were offered, and interest-only mortgages became common. Adjustable-rate mortgages allowing borrowers to make very low initial payments for the first years became popular. The banks learned to securitize these loans by selling the collateralized debt obligations to someone else who would receive the income. You would get paid up-front with money you could lend to still more borrowers. Tabb tells us that between mid-2000 and 2004,

American households took on three trillion dollars in mortgages while the US private sector borrowed three trillion dollars from the rest of the world. Almost a half of the mortgages were financed with foreign money. And when the Securities and Exchange Commission changed the rules to allow investment banks to take on a great deal more risk, we saw the collapse of Wall Street as we have known it. When the big investment banks received an exemption from regulation limiting the amount of debt they could take on, they borrowed and invested more in relation to the actual capital the bank possessed. But they ran out of money when things went bad. This is what happens when you put your faith in the magic of the market (the market is the singular most important deity in the United States) and allow banks to self-regulate. Social regulation in the public interest is, and has always been, an anathema to the ruling class, or the transnational capitalist class, however you describe the guardians of the interest of capital. The ruling class and its powerful factions of capital put the blame on too much governmental regulation—not too little—with respect to the current crisis just at a time when we need strong government action.

Because of the credit squeeze, businesses cannot get sufficient credit and so are cutting back on investment, on payroll, on employees and are not pursuing strategies to help working people—why aren't mortgage rates being lowered to let people stay in their homes? Why is money being thrown at the banks when they need to be nationalized and reorganized? We need to move to direct job creation, not giving tax breaks to corporations doing business in the United States. As Tabb notes, minimizing or eliminating their tax burden leaves the working people to pay more. Tabb is correct in arguing that the issue of class power and the structural nature of capitalism as a system of class domination have to be brought front and center—we need to critique the very class structure of capitalism. If we wish the patterns of taxation and procorporate policy we need greater social control over capital with its recurring crises and unpredictable cycles and chronic instability and a complete rethinking of the system in terms of what economic democracy really means for the wretched of the earth.

Given the nature of capitalism, and primed by the laws of capitalist competition and accumulation, capitalists are forced to produce a surplus product in order to produce surplus value; and in order to generate even more surplus value, must be reinvested and this continued reinvestment expands surplus production and there exists a continual need to discover spaces for surplus production. Capitalists are in continual search for new means of production as well as natural resources and the necessity of raw material extraction has led to what some have called the new imperialism. What we need, obviously, is a noncapitalist class structure.

We are entering a period where leftist educators must play an important role in the global struggle with finance capital.

The most important approach to discussing the crisis in capitalism has been developed, in my view, by Glenn Rikowksi in his discussion of the social production of labor-power as this relates to education. "Labor-power" is the potential or ability of workers to work, it is the latent value (or the promise of creating value possessed by human labor) that has not yet been expended. "Labor" is the actual activity of producing value. The profit, or what Marx refers to as surplus value, arises when workers do more labor than is necessary to pay the cost of hiring their labor-power.

Exploitation is normalized institutionally when a small minority (the capitalists) monopolize the means of production, and workers must rely on wage labor at the behest of the capitalists. This inequity is preserved and reproduced by the state. The presence of the unemployed pressure employed workers, ensuring that they will work unremittingly hard to produce for the capitalists. So an anticapitalist curriculum begins with the struggle for morality, which can only occur outside of capital's value form. Equality is impossible under capitalism since under capitalism it is the quality of labor-power that is paramount, not the equalization of labor-power. These are issues that need to be explored. Glenn Rikowski puts it this way:

> In capital's social universe, "values" have no substance, but value is the substance. Morality, is the struggle for morality, the struggle to make it real, and this can only be a possibility (still only a possibility) in the movements of society post-capitalism. Moral critiques of capitalism are in themselves insufficient, as Marx held (though they are understandable, and may energize people and make them angry against the system, and this anger may lead to significant forms of collective struggle). However, the struggle to attain morality, the struggle to make values possible, continually crashes against the fabric of society. It is this that makes struggles for gender equality, "race" equality and so on so explosive. In capitalist society, these forms of equality (like all other forms of equality) are impossible. But the struggle for their attainment exposes their possibility, a possibility that arises only within a post-capitalist scenario.
>
> On this analysis, collective quests for gender and "race" equality are a threat to the constitution of capitalist society; they call forth forms of equality that can have no social validity, no existence,

within the universe of capital—as all forms of equality are denied except for one. This is equality on the basis of exchange-value. On the basis of exchange-value we are all equal. There are a number of aspects to this.

First, our labours may be equal in terms of the value they create. However, as our labour-powers have different values, then 10 weeks of my labour may be equal to a single day of the labour of some highly paid soccer player. Equality here, then, operates on the basis of massive substantive inequality. Second, the value of our labour-powers may be equal; so one hour's labour of two people with equal labour-powers (in terms of labour-power quality) creates the same value. In a paper of last year, I go on to show that although these are the only forms of equality socially validated within the social universe of capital, practically they are unattainable as other social drives break these forms of equalisation.... For example, the drive to enhance labour-power quality as between different capitals, national capitals and between individuals pursuing relative "self-investment" in their own labour-powers would constantly disrupt any systematic attempt to create equality of labour-powers through education and training. Although forms of equality on the basis of exchange-value are theoretically possible, the first (equality of labour) is abominable as it is compatible with massive inequalities of income and wealth, whilst the second (equality of labour-powers) is practically hopeless. The outcome of all this is that struggles against inequalities in capitalist society are struggles for forms of equality that cannot exist within capitalism. Yet they nevertheless constitute struggles against the constitution of capitalist society, and also for equality than can attain social existence on the basis of the dissolution of the social universe of capital.

Rikowski explains, after Marx, how labor-power is transformed into labor in the labor process, and how, in this movement value, and then, at a certain point, surplus value is generated. He illustrates that there are two aspects to labor: it is a process of producing use-values and also value (a valorization process). These are not two separate processes but both are expressions of the one and same set of acts within the labor process. Rikowski puts it thus:

If the product is useless then value is not realized at the point of sale. Labor power consists of those attributes of the person that are used in creating a use-value (the use-value aspect of labor power), but labor power also has a quantitative, value-aspect too. Through the activity of the worker (labor) in the labor process, some of our personal powers (labor power) also become expressed as value-generation. Thus: labor power is the unique, living commodity that is the foundation of value, the substance of the social universe of capital. We create the social universe of capital.

Rikowski goes on to argue that education and training play a key role in the social production of labor-power. There exists a social drive to reduce all education and training to labor-power production and, according to Rikowksi, this reflects the deepening capitalization of the whole of social life. In contemporary capitalist society, education and training play an incredibly key role in the social production of labor power—which Rikowski reminds us, is the single commodity on which the expansion of capital and the continuation of capitalist society depend. Thus, it behooves us mightily as critical educators to understand the processes by which education and training increasingly operate as vehicles of labor-power production, and—and this is crucial to remember—it is not labor but rather labor-power that generates value when it is expressed as labor in the capitalist labor process. Value is the substance of the social universe of capital. Education and training thus have a key role to play in the maintenance and expansion of the social universe of capital. As educators, as students, we are all involved in socially producing labor-power, although teachers have more social power in this regard than do students. If we are part of the endless social drive to enhance labor-power quality then we are at the same time participating in a process that necessarily creates an inequality of labor-power values, and works against what education in capitalist society should be about, which is labor-power equalization. I am brought back to one of Marx's reflections, "The realm of freedom begins where the realm of necessity is left behind," and also, "limiting the length of the working day, is a crucial demand."

The key here is to recognize the fundamental contradiction between the drive to enhance labor-power quality, and the real necessity of labor-power equalization. And the latter is not possible within the social universe of capital. Rikowski is at the forefront of this idea, and here his contributions to critical pedagogy are of inestimable importance. Business and corporate leaders realize that education is all about the reproduction of labor-power for capital although, as Rikowski notes, they call it "human capital," and this is a very scary term indeed. But it is accurate. In my writings I try to capture the alienation and fetishization and commodification of human life, of capitalism turning living laborers into abstract laborers. Here in the United States, the process of educating students' labor-power for capital is increasingly standardized—we make sure students can take standardized, multiple-choice exams that stifle their thinking and make them less able to develop the critical skills that can help them figure out that they are fodder for the reproduction of capitalist social relations. Rikowksi notes that "teachers and trainers have huge strategic importance in capitalist society: they are like 'angels of the fuel dump', or 'guardians of the flame', in that they have intimate day-to-day responsibility for generating the fuel (labourpower) that generates what Marx called the 'living fire' (labour)." God forbid that students might question the representatives of capital! So the task becomes: Who can compete best in enhancing the quality of labor-power of students to further the efforts of neoliberal globalization? We, as teachers, labor for labor-power production! We are learning to labor for labor-power enhancement, not labor-power equalization.

So how can we disturb this process? How can we subvert, unsettle, resist, rupture, and confound this process? Well, Rikowski argues that we can "work to enshrine alternative educational principles and practices that bring into question the constitution of society and hint at ways in which expenditure of labour-power does not take a value form." We are constituted by labor and capital and this contradiction plays itself out within the deep recesses of our psychologies (as psycho-Marxism has shown us).

We are constituted by the concrete, qualitative, use-value aspect; and second by the quantitative, abstract value-aspect of labor and we are produced, necessarily as "living contradictions." We are, assuredly, propelled by the movement inherent in this living contradiction in the direction of transforming ourselves by changing society (by the coincidence of changing circumstances and self-change, as Marx would put this notion we call revolutionary praxis), and through this by struggling to build a social universe outside of capital's value form. So we can begin this task when we acknowledge how we can't have real equality through exchange-value, but only on the basis of the equalization of labor-power, or the equality of valorization of labor-powers. And why? Rikowski hits the socialist nail into the capitalist coffin when he says:

> This is because the inequalities of labour-power quality generated within the capitalist labour process require re-equalisation to the socially average level in order to attain the equalisation of labour-power values that is the foundation of social justice in capitalism. As individual capitals are responsible for generating these inequalities, then they are responsible for re-engineering labour-power equality. Thus, capitalist enterprises are responsible for providing compensatory education and training in order to equalise labour-power values. As

this process has indeterminate effects regarding surplus-value creation, which is the basis of capitalist profit, it is unlikely that, in practice, representatives of capital (employers) would pick up the tab.

Now here we can see why Rikowski notes that "social justice on the basis of capital exists only in the form of a mode of social life denied" precisely because the struggle for labor-power is annulled by capital's social drive to enhance labor-power. We need to focus not only on social relations within the classroom but to take into serious account the quality of social relations in all organizations seeking to transform capitalist society. Here, all of us—whether we are teachers in classrooms, or workers in factories, or working in retail at the local boutique—are encouraged to become critical revolutionary educators. So, along with Rikowski, Paula Allman, Dave Hill, and Mike Cole, and others, I would like to see educators put into practice the critique of capitalist production and this should include, as Rikowski emphasizes, the production of teacher work and its relationship to social domination in capitalist societies. And, of course, needed are theorizations and strategies of how labor-power can be used by workers in the service of anticapitalist activity. As Rikowski notes:

> "Labor power is the supreme value-creating power on which capital depends for its existence, and it is incorporated within laborers, who have the potential to withhold this wonderful social force (through strikes or leaving the employment of a capital) or worse, to use labour-power for anti-capitalist activity and ultimately for non-capitalist forms of production. Together, these features make labour-power capital's weakest link. Capital depends on it, yet has the capacity to be used by its owners against capital and to open up productive forms which capital no longer dominates. Marx and Marxist analysis uncovers this with a great force and clarity as compared with any other critical social theory."

So, insofar as we are able to, as Rikowski puts it, "critique the ways in which human labour constitutes capitalist society (how we become dominated by our own creations) and the constitution of capitalist society in terms of its basic structuring features" we are building the foundation for a truly critical pedagogy. Here we can ask ourselves how we become constituted—I would even use the word "enfleshed"—by the following aspects of labor-power summarized by Rikowski, below:

1. The value aspect of labor (power): the quantitative aspect
2. The use-value aspect of labor (power): the qualitative aspect

3. The exchange-value aspect of labor (power): the aspect that determines the equality of labors and labor-powers
4. The subjective aspect of labor (power): the will determined aspect
5. The collective aspect of labor (power): the cooperative aspect (involved in workers working together)
6. The concrete aspect of labor (power): the particularities and peculiarities of labor and labor-power attributes involved in specific labor processes and in specific work roles

Second, and here I am following Rikowski's typology of what a truly revolutionary critical pedagogy would look like, I would explore how inequalities are generated by capitalist society—racialized inequalities, patriarchal inequalities, inequalities based on differential treatments of various social groups. The third moment in Rikowski's architectonic is his recommendation that we critique all aspects of capitalist life. Rikowski summarizes this as follows:

- It is based on the works of Marx and Marxism, first and foremost;
- The starting point is the critique of the basic structuring phenomena and processes of capitalist society—which involves a critique of the constitution of capitalist society;
- The second most significant level of critique is the host of social inequalities thrown up by the normal workings of capitalist society—and issues of social justice can be brought in here;
- The third level of critique brings in the rest of capitalist social life—but relates to the first and second levels as frequently as possible;
- Two keys fields of human activity in contemporary society stand in need of fierce critique: capitalist work and capitalist education and training (including the social production of labor power);
- Labor-power—as capital's "weakest link"—deserves special attention as it has strategic and political significance.

I would add another feature to the schema Rikowski has provided. For me, since the value form of labor (abstract labor) that has been transmogrified into the autonomous moment of dead labor, eating up everything that it is not, can be challenged by freely associated labor and concrete, human sensuousness, we need to develop what I call a philosophy of revolutionary praxis. This involves envisioning a noncapitalist future that can be achieved by means of subjective self-movement through absolute negativity so that a new relation between theory and practice can connect us to the idea of freedom. As Peter

Hudis argues, the abolition of private property does not necessarily lead to the abolition of capital so we need to push further, to examine the direct relation between the worker and production. Here, our sole emphasis should not be on the abolition of private property, which is the product of alienated labor; it must be on the abolition of alienated labor itself. As I have mentioned before, Marx gave us some clues on how to transcend alienation, ideas that he developed from Hegel's concept of second or absolute negativity, or "the negation of the negation." I've written about his, and it comes mainly from the work of the founder of Marxist humanism in the United States, Raya Dunayevskaya. In addition to this, we need an approach to decolonizing pedagogy, and it's not just a question of the epistemicide—the epistemological violence visited upon pedagogies (including pedagogies of liberation) via Eurocentric teaching philosophies and practices—but a question of pedagogies driven by neoliberalization, involving themselves, both in tacit and manifest ways, in spreading market ideology. This is where I support President Hugo Chavez, and movements in Latin America that are antineoliberalization.

RK: Barack Obama's election as US president has reintroduced the debates on race and whether class can be termed the primary category and fundamental basis of social structure. Obama in a recent interview said, "...everybody's learned their lesson. And the answer is not heavy-handed regulations that crush the entrepreneurial spirit and risk-taking of American capitalism. That's what's made our economy great. But it is to restore a sense of balance." Given such deep commitment to capitalism one cannot expect him to revert back on what neoliberal assault has done, even though majority of African Americans are poor and pauperized, and worst hit by recession. In such a case, Obama would not have greater sympathies for his race. Private capital, which helped him amass the largest ever election fund, will remain his priority. How do you see this situation?
PM: Well, I am going to answer this using some comments I made in a recent article about the election that is in press here in the United States. The recent presidential election was perhaps little more than a rehearsal for a return of the same, a pretext for the restatement of business as usual in a different voice, whose message is more about timbre and pitch than policy—a rewriting of the old (the Leibnizian "we live in the best of all possible worlds") in the new subjunctive language not simply of hope and possibility (what if?) but of resounding and reverberating hope and possibility ("what if" meets "we shall"), delivered in the Horatio Alger-Joins-the-Orange-Revolution aerosol discourse

of "Yes We Can!" This is because the hope of which Obama speaks is impossible to achieve under capitalism. Even if Obama has the best intentions, the rules of the game prevent the kind of difference that will make a real difference. Everything that could conceivably bring about the kind of social transformation that will dramatically change for the better the fabric of everyday life in America is unmasked as an impossible contradiction if we place it in the context of the persistence of capitalism as the only alternative way to organize the globe for overcoming necessity. Of course, we won't place it in such a totalizing context (isn't totalizing one of the bete noires of the Marxists, according to poststructuralist pundits?), but will focus on the subjective nature of the trauma or on the cultural aspects of the global crisis in which we are living rather than analyse the structural of systemic roots of the crisis.

In this regard, the election could be likened to a media virus programming its own retransmission via a well-worn template that has no entrance for the critic and no exit for the cynic. And no substance whatsoever. Participant spectators trying to use their ballot for political change find themselves sucked right back into a social universe of diminishing expectations and endless spectacle that keeps them narcotically entrained in a strange loop of sound-byte aphorisms. It's forcing them to chase their tails inside what resembles a fetishized moebius strip, and absents any counterpoints or counternarratives, devoid, in other words, of contextual or relational thinking. Or following the hands of an Escher drawing where the sketch dissolves into the artist then dissolves back into the sketch, ad infinitum; illusion and reality appear an endless dance with little chance of breaking out into a new moral, political or economic logic through some form of metacommunication or metapraxis—after all, who is there to listen except the already insane?

The unwitting victims, the popular majorities, have once again fallen prey to a contagion of manipulation, of an endless circularity of mutual determinations that spreads like a bacilli in a fetid swamp disguised as a golden pond that sports at its center a shining marble fountain spurting audacious hope like a geyser of yellow ink. Obama's fountain of national renewal.

The mainstream media coverage of the election created a vortex of political indeterminacy, of radical contingency—a multitemporal, nonsynchronous dynamic internal to the mechanisms of the election coverage as such—that encouraged antidialectical analyses of the issues facing the American public, causing its coverage to slip and slide, and remain unfastened to any coherent historical narrative of social change, making contextual thinking impossible and blurring the distinction between illusion and reality, between the cadaver and the autopsy that follows. The historical and contextual rudderlessness of the media created a conceptual field in which real transformation cannot be conceptualized. Such is the nature of the corporate media.

The election was a media spectacle that served as little more than an allegorical background for the battle for the soul of America. The media used our ballots to reproduce at the level of action the symbolic violence they export daily at the level of ideas. The goal is to get a neoliberal of the right or the left elected—somebody who will not challenge the presuppositions of the transnational capitalist class. In the interests of subverting the Bush regime, voting Democrats became organs of the body politic, subverting their own interests in the belief that their votes would matter, that they had the power to explode the limits or the self-contained subjectivity of our media-educated expectations and conditioned political agency.

The conservative recipe for economic well-being—tax cuts and low inflation through monetary policy controls and unfettered and unregulated markets—cannot succeed under global neoliberal capitalism. The overall savings rate of Americans (it's been dropping since 1997) failed to increase with tax cuts. Supply-side economics pivots on a small number of Americans controlling a significantly large amount of the nation's total income—1 percent of Americans that the GOP's tax policies have favored—and this policy has clearly failed the poor. Deficit spending did grow the economy by 20 percent during Bush's tenure but between 2002 and 2006, it was the wealthiest 10 percent of households that saw more than 95 percent of the gains in income. Deregulation simply became a criminal enterprise of making more and more profits. But the real question is whether or not the system of capitalism itself is criminal. Without answering this fundamental question, we focus on the salaries, benefits, and bonuses of the top executives that are getting taxpayer bailouts from Washington. We bristle at the executive largesse in terms of cash bonuses, stock options, and personal use of company jets (the average paid to each of the top executives of the 116 banks now receiving government financial aid was $2.6 million in salary bonuses and benefits)—the total amount would actually cover bailout costs for many of the banks (so far they have received 188 billion of our taxpayer dollars) that have accepted tax dollars to keep afloat. So, while we fume about Wells Fargo of San Francisco, which took $25 billion in taxpayer bailout money with one hand and gave its top executives up to $20,000 each to pay personal financial planners with another, we would do well to focus more on our complacency with respect to capitalism as the only system under which democracy can flourish (and that's quite an assumption about the state of democracy in this country).

The richest 400 Americans own more than the bottom 150 million Americans combined; their combined net worth is $1.6 trillion. During the Bush years, the nation's 15,000 richest families doubled their annual income, from $15 million to $30 million and corporate profits shot up by 68 percent while workers' wages have been steadily shrinking (and the workers are not the ones who are being bailed out by the government). That scenario isn't about to change radically with the election of Obama, who might possess Jeremiah's aliveness to spiritual vision (don't his hands look light lighted candles when he speaks) but is unwilling to unmask and name the powers that be because, well, for one thing, he is that power.

Predictably, the Republican spin machine, FOX News, is trying to stave off a New Deal type of depression-recovery program discussed by Obama by claiming that most historians agree that Roosevelt and the New Deal actually prolonged the Great Depression. Of course, this revisionist reading of history sounds even silly to freshmen college students, but if it gets repeated often enough, it will be received by FOX TV's hapless listeners as if it were regurgitated from the bowels of the gospel.

We haven't seen the worst of the economic crisis. And while we might not see a return to the orphan trains of the 1920s, where hundreds of thousands of homeless and orphaned "street urchins" were taken to small towns and farms across the United States as part of a mass relocation movement of destitute children and unloaded at various train stations for inspection by couples who might want to adopt sturdy children to help them work the farms, we can be sure that children will be suffering through the current recession along with their parents.

The media—the instruments of the cultural commonsense of the social—are structural features of capitalist society and thus part of society's social practices and as such must be linked to larger historical developments linked to wider social forces and relations. Seen in this light, it becomes clear that the media supports those institutions that undercut the collective needs, rights, and causes of workers and sully any fertile ground in which social struggles might take root that can challenge capital on behalf of labor and the global working-class. In other words, the corporate media normalize the social division of labor and the ruthless exploitative practices needed to keep this division in place. Different blocs of capital must expand in order for capitalism to survive, and this means extracting the most profit possible. This essentially determines what gets produced, how, and by whom. It accounts for why one in six children worldwide are child laborers, and why corn and sugar are now often produced in the so-called Third World not to feed the hungry but to provide biofuels for advanced capitalist countries. This is why education and healthcare systems in the United States are in tatters.

As racism became the torch of hope for the electoral victory of the Republican Party, millions of Americans decided that the juggernaut of hate riding on a crest of bile was too much for the American public and a groundswell of support for Obama—largely made possible by the organizing skills of the antiwar movement and the popular left— was just enough to change the tide of history. To what extent the left can keep the pressure on the Obama presidency to focus on the unemployed at least as much as on the beleaguered industries remains to be seen. And even if it managed to keep the pressure on, there is no guarantee their voices will be heard as Obama has shifted center-right since his election victory and seems bent on getting US troops further bogged down in Afghanistan. Regular "America at War" features on media outlets are sure to be there as long as US capital seeks to impose its will on foreign markets and serve as the alpha male for the transnational capitalist class.

And what about race? Since people of color still lag well behind whites in almost every major social, economic, and political indicators, Eduardo Bonilla-Silva (2008) asks whether Obama will contest the new system of racial practices—what Bonilla-Silva calls "the new racism"— that is, costructured by a new racial ideology called "color-blind racism." In other words, is Obama a postcivil rights minority politician (i.e., an antiminority minority Republican or postracial Democrat) who is successful because he does not directly challenge the white power structure? Bonilla-Silva argues that social movement politics and not electoral politics is the vehicle for achieving racial justice. And he notes that Obama's policies on healthcare, immigration, jobs, racism, the war in Iraq, and the Palestinian question are not radical, that he has made a strategic move toward racelessness and that he has adopted a postracial persona and political stance. Obama doesn't like to talk about racism (and when he does he likes to remind people he is half white) and unlike black leaders unpopular with whites (such as Jesse Jackson, Maxine Waters, and Al Sharpton) even suggests that America is beyond race. Bonilla-Silva writes that Obama works as a "Magic Negro" figure:

> Obama also became, as black commentator David Ehrenstein has argued, the "Magic Negro"—a term from film studies that refers to

black characters in movies whose main purpose is to help whites deal with their issues. In this case, voting for Obama allowed many whites feel like they were cleansing their racial soul, repenting for their racial sins, and getting admission into racial heaven! Obama became whites' exceptional black man—the model to follow if blacks want to achieve in Amerika!

For many nonwhites, particularly for blacks, Obama became a symbol of their possibilities. According to Bonilla-Silva (2008),

> He was indeed, as Obama said of himself, their Joshua—the leader they hoped would take them to the Promised Land of milk and honey. They read in between the lines (probably more than was/is there) and thought Obama had a strong stance on race matters. For the old generation desperate to see change before they die (Jackson crying, John Lewis, etc.), and for many post-Reagan generation blacks (will.i.am from The Black Eyes Peas) and minorities who have seen very little racial progress during their life, Obama became the new Messiah following on the footsteps of the leaders they did not see such much as Martin and Malcolm.

But as Bonilla-Silva remarks, Obama's policies on race matters are not that much different from Hillary's, he is the darling of the Democratic Leadership Council, his economic and healthcare programmes are modest, he wants to expand the military by **90,000**, intends to redeploy troops from Iraq to Afghanistan, is a big supporter of free-market capitalism and his policies on Cuba, Venezuela, North Korea, and Palestine are no better than Hillary's. But many Obama voters believed (and many continue to believe) that "these are tactical positions Obama needed in order to get elected" and many of his positions are temporary, and Obama will suddenly turn left when he takes office. Obama's really a "stealth candidate"—a revolutionary about to announce a far shift to the left that will have both Liberals and Conservatives quaking in their boots. The fear that Bonilla-Silva (2008) raises—that "the voices of those who contend that race fractures America profoundly may be silenced" in Obamerica—are real, and that Obamerica may bring us closer to the racial structure of many Latin American countries:

> We may become like Brazil, Cuba, Mexico, Belize, or Puerto Rico—nation-states that claim to be comprised of "one people" but where various racial strata receive social goods in accordance to their proximity to "whiteness." And like in Latin American countries, Obama's

nationalist stance ("There's not a black America and white America and Latino America and Asian America; there's the United States of America") will help close the space to even talk about race. Hence, in Orwellian fashion, we may proclaim "We are all Americans!" but in Obamerica, some will still be "more American than others".

And while clearly racial justice has been retreating to its lowest point since the Kerner Commission Report announced 40 years ago that "Our nation is moving toward two societies, one black, one white—separate and unequal," the election of Obama is unlikely to signal a permanent reversal of this trend.

Can Obama take on the military establishment? The corporate structure? Sheldon Wolin notes that we live in an "inverted totalitarianism" in which the entertainment industry via spectacles and diversions is able to keep the citizenry politically passive, as long as there exists a reasonable standard of living. Even if there are more popular protests due to the economic crisis, the media will ignore them. In my view, we need more Battle of Seattle, in every city, simultaneously![1]

III

RK: In your work Capitalists and Conquerors, you argue that schools teach students skills that are required by capital and even their dreams are limited to the sphere of capital. The desire to transcend the rule of capital is suppressed through the mechanics of school. This also invokes the Althusserian idea of ideological state apparatuses. How does one counter this suppression?

PM: I have tried to give you the basics of this answer in my discussion of Glenn Rikowski's path-breaking work on teaching for an anticapitalist future. I have had trouble, myself, taking on the ideological apparatuses of the state, especially after a right-wing group in 2006 launched an attack on me and my fellow leftist professors at UCLA, placing me as the number one figure in their Dirty Thirty list, as the most dangerous professor at UCLA. Steve Best, Tony Nocella, and I have just finished editing a book on academic repression. In the introduction we discuss right-wing pundits such as David Horowitz, who has penned an Academic Bill of Rights. The introduction to the book describes the Academic Bill of Rights as "a thinly veiled Trojan horse that threatens the core values and very life of academia. Horowitz's clever tactic is to use liberal/left discourse to advance an extreme right-wing agenda that strips professors—or any professor not a totally brainwashed product of American society and its capitalist values—of their right to publish, teach, and act as citizens as they wish. What the Academic Bill of Rights attempts to do is to give the already advantaged and overprivileged more power than the surplus stock it already holds. "Intellectual diversity" and such phrases are merely code words for empowering right-wing ideologies. Its call for "balance" is really a ploy for imbalance, for a pre-'60s sterile groupthink, conformist environment dominated by conservative thought without any diversity among faculty, programs, courses, and intellectual life (if there would be one at all). Unable to think outside of the corporate box and utilitarian model of education, they have no idea what real education is, a mission that includes encountering and engaging differing viewpoints; students would be denied this opportunity. It is healthy and vital for conservative students to hear radical perspectives, as it is for progressive students to hear conservative perspectives."

The truth of the matter is the stranglehold of corporate power on the universities is choking the life out of whatever remains of the university's role as a vehicle for the advancement of public life. Some of us are directly involved in fighting for academic freedom, and resisting the capitalist and imperialist values that the universities are coming to enshrine through curricula, business partnerships, and the like. Our battle in the schools of education, housed in universities, is through the advancement of critical pedagogy. Critical pedagogy is under ideological assault, both here and elsewhere, such as Australia. Bill Ayers, the distinguished leftist at the University of Illinois, Chicago, who was a member of the Weather Underground in the 1960s, was demonized recently by the Republican Party during the Presidential election, since Ayers and Obama knew each other as fellow community activists in Chicago. So, the demonization of Ayers has also spread to a demonization of so-called "critical" educators in general, some of whom who are tarred with the same brush as being anti-American and proterrorist. These are tough times for the educational left. Very tough times.

RK: The resistance to this suppression becomes furthermore difficult when one finds, what you call "reproletarianisation" of teachers. Given this situation we encounter certain problems, as in the case of India. There are teachers who are employed till the age of "retirement" with different kinds of benefits and their unionization is limited to demands for salary raise. On the other hand, there are teachers who are employed on contract with meagre salary (in many cases as low as $20) by government. In a sense while there is a "teaching aristocracy" that does not consider itself as workers and on the other a pauperized teaching labor force, which is nonunionized. The role of the left forces in these cases has been dismal. Where does resistance begin in such cases?

PM: Yes, the same is true here. Teaching assistants in universities in many cases do the bulk of the teaching yet they get little compensation and protection. Many students want a few waivers so they can go to school while they teach and not pay tuition. Budgets are currently being slashed, and tuition fees are rising dramatically. Historically, it has been a tough battle to get academic student-employee unions recognized. Universities, no longer protected from the market, as they once were through funding by the state, are relying more and more on corporate funding that invests in technology-based research, research that can make the corporations more effective and help to make them dominant in the neoliberal capitalist economy. Professors—especially those in the hard sciences—put as much, if not more, effort in getting research funding and doing research than teaching, and of course the class sizes are ever-increasing and there is a decrease in the number of full-time, tenured professors teaching classes and there is the necessity for more cheap intellectual part-time labor in the form of teaching assistants. So strong union movements are needed to protect teaching assistants, since they face a difficult task. Clearly, the labor aristocracy needs to be challenged. There needs to be joint efforts between tenured professors and teaching assistants, they have to form a united front and work together with the unions to take on the universities. This type of united front is needed, and it should have a common purpose of saving the university from becoming just another subsector of the economy. All of this revolves around developing an understanding of how social institutions need to reorganize themselves—in tandem with the reorganization of society as a whole—to fight the capitalization and commodification of subjectivity, to fight universities whose mission is to educate labor-power for capital, and such a valorization process can only lead to structured hierarchies of power and privilege that serve the few, and bring misery to the many.

RK: This crisis is augmented by the increasing significance of a nonpolitical, anticapital, anticlass gang of people (also called activists) who do not approach the problems under capitalism such as the issue of displacement of millions of Indians (caused by "developmental" projects) as by-products of a system that needs to be overthrown to prevent such callous and insensitive treatment of the masses. The World Social Forums or the Narmada Bachao Andolan (movement against a big dam

on river Narmada because it displaced millions) have been criticized on such lines. Where does one place the role of such an "opposition"?
PM: Well, clearly we need to insist on the priority of affiliation—political commitments based on the basis of moral and political judgement—rather than a politics of filiation, or ethnic belongingness. But this mandates that activists examine critically social relationships in their totality, that is, in the context of their relationship to the greatest totalizing force history has ever known—capitalism.

The 1999 battle of Seattle summoned a collective "ya basta!" that saw the closure of a meeting of the World Trade Organisation (WTO) and since that time the WTO, World Bank and IMF have been forced to conduct their business behind police barricades. Initially, the WSF forum succeeded in creating an antihierarchical and nonvanguardist space for the grassroots left to give collective voice to a critique of global capitalism and its attendant abuses. But it soon became taken over by established political parties of a leftist bent, who promoted reformism and various forms of accommodation to capitalist accumulation and the law of value, and also gave way to the glamour politics of major celebrity speakers. The question that has been posed to the WSF by James Petras and others is: "To what extent does WSF dissent become a fashionable guerrilla apostasy and to what extent does its work actually threaten the interests of global capital"? The fundraisers, after all, set the agenda. And many of the sponsors of the WSF are hardly radical institutions. What is heartening is the recent declaration of the Assembly of Social Movements at the recent WSF in Belem, Brazil, 2009. Here the social movements—which are in solidarity with the efforts by feminist, environmentalist and socialist movements—maintain promisingly that the current global crisis "is a direct consequence of the capitalist system and therefore cannot find a solution within the system." They write: "All the measures that have been taken so far to overcome the crisis merely aim at socialising losses so as to ensure the survival of a system based on privatising strategic economic sectors, public services, natural and energy resources and on the commoditisation of life and the exploitation of labour and of nature as well as on the transfer of resources from the Periphery to the Centre and from workers to the capitalist class." An important consensus has been reached—that a radical alternative is necessary that would do away with the capitalist system.

- Nationalizing the banking sector without compensations and with full social monitoring;
- Reducing working time without any wage cut;

- Taking measures to ensure food and energy sovereignty;
- Stopping wars, withdrawing occupation troops, and dismantling military foreign bases;
- Acknowledging the peoples' sovereignty and autonomy, ensuring their right to self-determination;
- Guaranteeing rights to land, territory, work, education, and health for all;
- Democratizing access to means of communication and knowledge.
- Here, we can appreciate the fact that forms of ownership that favor the social interest are supported and advanced: small family freehold, public, cooperative, communal, and collective property.

But all of this is a cautionary tale: The mass movements and trade unions can always be co-opted by center-left regimes or even center-Right regimes. As critical educators, we must work tirelessly to broaden our political project to include the support of social movements seriously challenging the distribution of public wealth and the destruction of local habitat and economies by multinational corporations. As Petras argues, social movements must work toward developing national cadre structures so that they have a chance to take state power—without state power little can be done to seriously challenge the power of the transnational capitalist class. Needed more than ever, Petras argues, are concrete organizations of struggle rooted among radical youth and among "employed" as well as "informal workers" in a broad effort at socialist revival and renewal that will ensure socialist organizations make stronger organic links with everyday anticapitalist struggles. Direct intervention of conscious socialist-political formations deeply inserted in everyday struggles capable of linking economic conditions to political action is, according to Petras, the only way forward. That is the point at which we must secure our opposition to the rule of capital.

RK: It is significant to talk of such categories of "opposition" because at a certain plane, their acts have furthered the idea of education as autonomous in itself. Hence, we find thousands of "alternative" schooling systems, which rarely link the flaws and fallacies in education system to the rule of capital. The dialectics of labor and capital, or system and education machinery is missed out by such experiments and so is the simultaneity of reform and revolution. How do you see resistance to capitalism and its education system coming up?

PM: Yes, there is danger in presenting education as autonomous, as unconnected to the totality of capitalist social relations. Here in the United States, we have charter schools, and alternative schools, but very few of them, to my knowledge, teach from an anticapitalist perspective. Such schools assume, ideologically, left liberal (i.e., reformist) positions but at the level of practice they amount to a left neoliberalism, since by not challenging the law of value in capitalist societies, they implicate themselves in the widening economic gap between the rich and the poor.

RK: Lastly, you argue that schools should become "sites for production of both critical knowledge and sociopolitical action". How do you see this happening given the complex relationship of schools, system (run by private capital), and pauperizing mass of people? What direction should the analysis of educational ills take?

PM: Well, I believe that my previous answers have mainly addressed your final question, and I can only add the following point—whatever strategies we adopt in our analysis of education, they need to have a transnational reach. Which is why it is important that we have conversations such as this, since we are in the process of charting out a transnational anticapitalist agenda on the part of educational workers, global citizens who fight both locally and globally for bringing about a socialist future? Now the first step is to become aware of the perpetual pedagogies at work that normalize the rule of capital—the corporate media, the new computer and communication technologies, and all of the ideological state apparatuses that serve to legitimize capitalist social relations. We need to become critically literate about how all of these media function through multiple literacies, and how the new technologies work in the process of self and social formation. Once we know how they work in the process of ideological production, we can develop ways to interrupt their efforts and counter them. Our classrooms, community organizations, alternative media, and social movements can become sites for the creation of a counterpublic sphere in which we can strengthen and coordinate our efforts to build national and transnational cadres—but this requires that we work to exercise state power responsibly and protagonistically by transforming the institutional structures of society and working to change the state from the bottom up in participatory, democratic, and revolutionary ways.

Note

1. This section derives a great deal, while making the argument, from book *The Phenomenon of Obama and the Agenda for Education: Can Hope Audaciously Trump Neoliberalism?* by Paul R. Carr, Bradley J. Porfilio.

Contributors

Curry Stephenson Malott is an assistant professor in the department of professional and secondary education at West Chester University of Pennsylvania (WCU). He is cofounder of the Critical Theories in the Twenty-First Century conference (ct21st.org) at WCU. He has published works on critical theories and is interested in democratic, global, socialism for the twenty-first century. His recent authored/ coedited works include *Critical Pedagogy in the Twenty-First Century: A New Generation of Scholars* (Information Age Publishing, 2011); *Policy and Research in Education: A Critical Pedagogy for Educational Leadership* (Peter Lang, 2010)

Dave Hill is professor of education at Middlesex University, London, and is also visiting professor of critical education policy and equality studies at the University of Limerick, Ireland, and visiting professor at the University of Athens, Greece. He has coauthored and coedited eighteen books and written over seventy chapters and refereed journal articles. His recent authored/coedited works (2009–2010) include *Revolutionizing Pedagogy: Education for Social Justice Within and Beyond Global Neo-Liberalism* (Palgrave Macmillan); *Equality in the Primary School: Promoting Good Practice across the Curriculum* (Continuum); *Class in Education: Knowledge, Pedagogy, Subjectivity* (Routledge), as well as four books in the *Education and Neoliberalism Series* (Routledge). He is founder editor of online international refereed *Journal of Critical Education Policy Studies*, which has had three quarters of a million downloads, and coorganizer of the annual International Conference on Critical Education. He is a political and trade union activist, and has fought ten elections, at European Parliament, British Parliament, and municipal levels.

David Hursh is an associate professor at the University of Rochester in Rochester, NY, USA. His recent book is *High-Stakes Testing and the Decline of Teaching and Learning: The Real Crisis in Education*

(Rowman & Littlefield). He has also published in numerous journals, including *American Educational Research Journal*, *Educational Researcher*, and *Race, Ethnicity and Education*. His most recent teaching is in schools in sub-Saharan Africa where he has developed and implemented a curriculum on energy use and environmental health. His forthcoming book, coauthored with Camille A. Martina, is *Teaching Environmental Health to Children: An Interdisciplinary Approach*, which will be published in fall, 2011.

Faith Agostinone-Wilson is an associate professor of education at George Williams College of Aurora University in Williams Bay, Wisconsin. She is a member of the Rouge Forum collective and has been published in *JCEPS*, *Radical Notes*, and *Public Resistance*. She lives in Waukegan, IL and her research interests include education policy and practices, built environment / social justice issues, and counterhegemonic research methodologies. Her latest book is *Marxism and Education Beyond Identity: Sexuality and Schooling* (Palgrave, 2010).

Mike Cole is Mike Cole is emeritus professor in education and equality at Bishop Grosseteste University College, Lincoln, UK. He has written extensively on equality issues. Recent books include *Marxism and Educational Theory: Origins and Issues* (Routledge, 2008); *Critical Race Theory and Education: A Marxist Response* (Palgrave Macmillan, 2009); *Equality in the Secondary School: Promoting Good Practice Across the Curriculum* (Continuum, 2011); *Racism and Education in the U.K. and the U.S.: Towards a Socialist Alternative* (Palgrave Macmillan, 2011); and *Education, Equality and Human Rights: Issues of Gender, "Race," Sexuality, Disability and Social Class* (3rd Edition, Routledge, 2011). He is the coeditor (with Curry Malott) of *Teaching Marx Across the Curriculum: The Socialist Challenge* (Information Age Publishing, forthcoming, 2012)

Paresh Chandra is an Mphil candidate in English at the University of Delhi. His essay, "Through and Beyond: Identities and Class Struggle" was published in the volume, *The Heart of the Matter: Development Identity and Violence—Reconfiguring the Debate* edited by Ravi Kumar (Aakar Books, 2010). His areas of interest include Marxism, critical theory, students' politics, novel studies, and Modernism. He is the coconvenor of "Correspondence," a political group active in New Delhi, and is a regular contributor to *Radical Notes*, an internet journal (www.radicalnotes.com).

Peter McLaren is a professor in the division of urban schooling, the Graduate School of Education and Information Studies, University of California, Los Angeles (UCLA). He is the author and editor of 45 books and hundreds of scholarly articles. Professor McLaren's writings have been translated into 20 languages. Four of his books have won the Critic's Choice Award of the American Educational Studies Association. One of his books, Life in Schools, was chosen in 2004 as one of the 12 most significant education books in existence worldwide, by an international panel of experts instituted by The Moscow School of Social and Economic Sciences and by the Ministry of Education of the Russian Federation. McLaren was the inaugural recipient of the Paulo Freire Social Justice Award presented by Chapman University, CA. The charter for La Fundación McLaren de Pedagogía Critica was signed at the University of Tijuana in July, 2004. La Catedra Peter McLaren was inaugurated in Venezuela on September 15, 2006, as part of a joint effort between El Centro Internacional Miranda and La Universidad Bolivariana de Venezuela. In 2006, during the Bush administration, Professor McLaren made international headlines when he was targeted by a right-wing extremist organization in the United States and put at the top of the "Dirty Thirty" list of leftist professors at UCLA. His written/edited/coedited works include *Pedagogy and Praxis in the Age of Empire*, *Academic Repression: Reflections from the Academic Industrial Complex* (San Francisco: AK Press, 2010), *Life in Schools* (5th edition, New York: Allyn & Bacon, 2005), *Capitalists and Conquerors: Critical Pedagogy Against Empire* (Lanham, MD: Rowman and Littlefield, 2005), *Teaching Against Global Capitalism and the New Imperialism. A Critical Pedagogy* (Lanham, MD: Rowman and Littlefield, 2005), *Che Guevara, Paulo Freire, and the Pedagogy of Revolution* (Lanham, MD: Rowman and Littlefield, 2000).

Ravi Kumar is associate professor at the department of sociology, South Asian University. He has a doctorate in Sociology from Jawaharlal Nehru University. His authored/coedited/edited works include *The Heart of the Matter: Development, Identity and Violence: Reconfiguring the Debate* (Aakar Books, 2010); *Ghetto and Within: Class, Identity, State and Politics of Mobilisation*, (Aakar Books, 2010); *Global Neoliberalism and Education and its Consequences*, (Routledge, 2009); *The Crisis of Elementary Education in India* (Sage Publications, 2006); *The Politics of Imperialism and Counterstrategies* (Aakar Books, 2004). He is coeditor of a series on *Social Movements, Dissent and Transformative Action* (Routledge). He has published extensively on education, media, and social movements. He is coeditor of *Radical Notes* (www.radicalnotes.com)

Rich Gibson is a an emeritus professor at San Diego State University, a cofounder of the activist Rouge Forum, and a California advisor to the Student March 4th Movement which seeks to "Rescue Education from the Ruling Classes." He is a former iron foundry worker and union organizer. His recent works include *Neoliberalism and Education Reform* (coedited, Hampton Press, 2007).

Savyasaachi is associate professor at the department of sociology, Jamia Millia Islamia, New Delhi. He has worked in the fields of political ecology, indigenous people, development, social movements, and conservation architecture. His works included *Dissent, Self Determination and Resilience: Social Movements in India* (coedited, Delhi: Intercultural Resources, 2010); *Between the Earth and the Sky: The Penguin Book of Forest Writings* (edited, New Delhi: Penguin, 2005). He has published in *Economic and Political Weekly*, *Social Action*, and *Radical Notes,* among other journals.

Index

abstract democracy, 47–49
Abu Ghraib, 115–16, 123
Academic Council (AC), 161–62
  see also Executive Council (EC)
Afghanistan, 41–42, 47, 55, 115, 126, 232–33
Agostine-Wilson, Faith, 10, 113–32, 242
Agropatria, 192
Al Qaeda, 42
Aleman, George III, 121–24
Allman, Paula, 210, 215, 226
Althusser, Louis, 77, 83, 234
antiwar movement, 43, 45, 48, 56–57, 88, 116, 232
Apple, Michael, 82, 91, 209
Apter, Bob, 59
Arbenz, Jacobo, 46
Armed Forces Recruiter Access to Students and Student Recruiting Information, 117
Armed Services Vocational Aptitude Battery (ASVAB), 120, 125, 130
Ayers, Bill, 45, 56, 235

Bakan, Joel, 17–18
Baker, D., 19
Balfanz, Robert, 124–25
bankruptcy, 127, 131
Barsamian, David, 35
Bauman, Zygmant, 209
Berry, Thomas, 103
Biden, Joe, 33

Binh, Pham, 125–27
Blackwater: The Rise of the World's Most Powerful Mercenary Army (Scahill), 121
Blair, Tony, 202
Boff, Leonardo and Clodovis, 35
Bolivarian Revolution, 190, 192, 194–95, 200–2
Bologna Agreement, 156, 168
Bolshevism, 44–45
Bombay Plan, 158
Bonilla-Silva, Eduardo, 232–33
Brahmin caste, 136
Brandt, Deborah, 84
Brenner, Neil, 102
Bretton Woods, 18
Brissenden, John, 7–8
Brown, Gordon, 81
Bush, George W., 21, 32, 42–43, 58, 102, 104, 107, 212, 230–31

Caffentzis, George, 166
Calcare, 61
Campaign of Resistance (CoR), 87
Capital (Marx), 23, 25
capitalism
  commodity fetishism and, 50–51
  controlling workers, 81
  current crisis of, 64–72
  education and, 70–72
  explained, 49–54
  growth of national and global inequalities, 67–70
  reification and, 51–52

capitalism—*Continued*
  responses to current economic crisis, 79–81
  revolution and, 54–61
  social class exploitation and, 72–75
  social democracy and, 81–82
  as system of exploitation, 49–50
Capitalism and Freedom (Chomsky), 31
capitalist democracy, 49
Castro, Fidel, 34, 47
Central Intelligence Agency (CIA), 47–48, 220
Chandra, Paresh, 10, 153–68, 243
Chávez, Hugo, 11, 189–94, 196, 200–2, 204, 220, 228
Cheney, Dick, 129
Cherry, Eugene, 122, 126
China, 30, 33, 46, 54, 66, 105
Chomsky, Noam, 17–18, 31, 34–35, 38, 82
Cleaver, Harry, 166–67
Clinton, Bill, 130
Clinton, Hillary, 48, 233
Cole, Mike, 11, 16, 74–75, 82, 91, 189–203, 210, 215, 226, 242
Collins, Michael, 46
colonialism, 15, 33, 81, 213, 215–17
commodification, 5, 7–8, 28, 30, 50–51, 55, 71, 81, 105–6, 108, 146, 149, 224, 236–37
Commonwealth Games, 141, 154–55, 167
Communism, 43–45, 58, 75, 142, 161, 164–65, 205, 212
Concurrent Admissions Program manual, 120
Correo Del Orinico International, 203
critical education for economic and social justice, 83–86
  overview, 83
  radical left principles for education systems, 85–86
  revolutionary critical pedagogy, 84–85
  role of intellectuals and politics of educational transformation, 84
critical pedagogy, 9, 22, 34–37, 60, 74, 83–85, 209, 211, 216, 224–27, 235
Cuba, 15, 34, 192, 233
cultural capital, 65
Cunningham, Randy "Duke," 48, 58

Davis, Mike, 107–8
Day X, 87
Deep Economy: The Wealth of Communities and the Durable Future (McKibben), 108
Delhi University Teachers' Association (DUTA), 155
DeMint, Jim, 117
democracy, 45–48
Democratic Party, 45
Deserter's Tale, A (Key), 122
Diop, Cheikh Anta, 22–23
Dorling, Danny, 68–69
Dumenil, Gerard, 4–6, 64, 91
Dunayevskaya, Raya, 212, 228
Durkheim, Emile, 28–30, 38
Dussel, Enrique, 213, 215

Ebert, Teresa, 210
Edison Schools, 32
education
  arenas for resistance, 86–90
  business of, 78–79
  capitalist agendas and, 78–81
  commodification of, 71–72
  critical education for economic and social justice, 83–86
  cuts to funding, 78
  growth of educational inequality, 70–71
  media and, 76–78
  neoliberalism and, 6–8, 104–6, 108–10
  radical left principles for, 85–86

INDEX

restructuring of, 78
role of intellectuals and politics of educational transformation, 84
state and, 73
undemocratic accountability, 71
Education as Enforcement (Saltman and Goodman), 114
Egypt, 15, 20, 22–23, 89, 205
Eighteenth Brumaire of Louis Napoleon, The (Marx), 75
Ellis, Edward, 196, 198, 204
Engels, Frederick, 4, 22–25, 58, 72–73, 75, 205
England, Lyndie, 123
entrepreneurialism, 4, 10, 101, 104–6, 140, 144, 228
European Bank (EB), 76
European Union (EU), 66
Executive Council (EC), 161–62
  see also Academic Council (AC)
Exiled in the Land of the Free (Lyons, Oren, and Mohawk), 36

Fannie Mae/Freddie Mac, 219
Fanon, Frantz, 217
Faramandpur, Ramin, 3–4, 74, 84–85
fascism, 17, 45, 55–56, 142
Fertinitro, 192
Flaubert, Gustave, 47
Ford, 6
Foreign Educational Institutions (FEI) bill, 160
Fourth International, 89
FOX News, 231
Freire, Paulo, 3, 34–35, 84, 197–98, 202, 205, 211, 213–14
Friedman, Milton, 31–34, 36, 38
Friedman, Thomas, 103–4, 107

Gandhi, Mahatma, 135, 148
Gasper, Phil, 124
Gates, Bill, 125
Gaza, 42
General Agreement on Trade in Services (GATS), 66, 71

General Motors, 6, 128
generalization, 10, 154–55, 163–68
Generation Debt (Kamenetz), 128
Gerardo, 192, 196–97, 199–200
Gerson, Jack, 125
GI Bill, 130
Gibson, Rich, 9, 41–61, 120, 244
Giroux, Henry, 4, 115–16, 209
Glass-Steagall Act, 102
Globalism: Market Ideology Meets Terrorism (Steger), 103
globalization
  capitalism and, 63
  education and, 101–10
  hijacking to serve neoliberalism, 103–4
  overview, 101–3
  poverty gap and, 70
  wealth and, 19
Gramsci, Antonio, 3, 190, 203–4
Great Depression, 4, 15, 18, 219, 231
Greece, 15, 19–20, 22, 44, 48, 50–51, 65, 76–77, 80, 86, 205, 220
Greenspan, Alan, 102
Greider, W., 19
Griffiths, Tom, 194–95, 201
Grinde, Donald A., 36
Grosfoguel, Ramon, 213, 215, 217
Guevara, Che, 46
Gutiérrez, Gustavo, 35

Halpin, D., 71
Hamas, 47
Harman, Susan, 59
Harvey, David, 82, 102, 110, 144, 148, 219
health care, 42, 52, 65, 78–79, 82, 109, 121–25, 132, 191, 199, 232–33
Hearse, P., 66–67, 86, 90–92
Hegel, G.W.F., 57, 168, 212, 228
Hill, Dave, 9, 63–90, 210, 215, 226, 241–42
Hirtt, N., 71

historical revisionism, 10, 63, 231
Hrutkay, Matt, 126
Hudis, Peter, 212, 228
Hurricane Katrina, 42, 74
Hursh, David, 7, 10, 101–10, 242
Hutchinson Amendment, 117

imperialism, 15, 43, 55–57, 81, 84, 115, 193–94, 201, 213–15, 222, 235
India, education and
  neoliberalism and, 138–40
  understanding educational process, 135–38
Indian Institute of Technology (IIT), 147–48
Indian Institutes of Management (IIMs), 148
inflation, 65, 69, 81, 113, 121, 130–31
Inhofe, Jim, 117
Injustice: Why Social Inequality Persists (Dorling), 68
Inner London Education Authority (ILEA), 201–2
International Action Center, 123–24, 127, 129
International Finance Corporation, 80
International Monetary Fund (IMF), 70, 76, 107, 237
Iraq, 41–42, 47, 55, 57, 69, 88, 113, 115–16, 121, 123, 126, 129, 232–33
IRAs (individual retirement accounts), 131
Israel, 42
Iyer, Krishna, 158, 169

J30, 88–89
Jameson, Frederic, 157
Johnson, Chalmers, 59, 115
Joint Action Body (JAB), 156, 162–63
Judge Judy, 43, 56

Junior Reserve Officer Training Corps (JROTC), 116–17, 119, 129

Kamenetz, Anya, 128–32
Key, Joshua, 122, 129
Keynes, John Maynard, 66, 80, 136, 140, 148
Kilpatrick, Kwame, 48
Klein, Naomi, 68
Kohn, Alfie, 32
Kosik, Karel, 211–14
Kozol, Jonathon, 48, 68
Krantikari Yuva Sangathan (KYS), 154–55
Kshatriya caste, 136, 179
Kumar, Ravi, 1–11, 135–51, 209–39, 243
Kyoto protocols, 102, 107

Legters, Nettie, 124–25
Leitner, Hilga, 104
Lenin, Vladimir, 44, 204
Leslie, Larry, 106
Levy, Dominique, 4–6, 64
Libya, 15, 89
Lippman, Walter, 34, 36, 38
Loach, Ken, 89
Long March, 46
Lynch, Jessica, 123

Maldonaldo-Torres, Nelson, 213
Malott, Curry Stephenson, 6, 9, 15–38, 241
Manifesto of the Communist Party (Marx and Engels), 22, 24–25, 75
Maringanti, Anant, 104
Mariscal, Jorge, 118–20
Martín-Baró, Ignacio, 217
Marxism
  arenas for resistance and, 86–87
  capitalism and, 1, 49–54, 115, 168
  capitalist democracy and, 49

Chávez and, 190, 200
critical pedagogy and, 209–12, 214–15, 219, 222–29
education and, 8, 135–36
generalization and, 166
labor and, 17, 73, 157
militarism and, 114–15
neoliberalism and, 4, 64–65
passion and, 46, 57–58, 60
post-Marxism, 1–4
postmodernist analyses of social class and, 74–75
reason and, 46
resistance to neoliberal capital and, 81–83
social class and, 22–30, 33, 36, 38, 74–75, 205–6
structuralist neo-Marxism, 82–83
Trotskyism and, 89–90
Venezuela and, 200, 203
McCain, John, 43, 48
McDonnell, John, 87
McKibben, Bill, 103, 108
McLaren, Peter, 3–4, 8, 11, 74, 84–85, 209–39
Mencken, H.L., 47
metanarratives, 2, 75
Mignolo, Walter, 213
miltarism
 compulsory volunteerism, 121–27
 economy and, 113–14, 127–32
 as public policy, 115–16
 schools and, 114–21
Miller, Steven, 125
Mission Barrio Adentro, 199
Mongardini, C., 141
Monroe Doctrine, 34
moral law, 41–43
Morales, Evo, 220
Mouffe, Chanatal, 2, 11
Murdoch, Rupert, 65
Murphy, Dick, 48
Myers, A., 69

National Assessment of Educational Progress, 70
National Coalition of Homeless Veterans, 126
National Commission on Skills in the Workplace, 125
National Council for Education Research and Training (NCERT), 174
National Council for the Social Studies, 60
National Endowment for Democracy, 47
National Rural Employment Guarantee Act (NREGA), 161
National Shop Stewards Network (NSSN), 87–88
National Union of Students, 87
Native Americans, 34–36
neoconservatism, 9, 63, 81
neoliberal capitalism, 5–7, 9–10, 15, 17, 145–46, 149, 151, 209, 215, 219, 230, 236
 explained, 65–66
 impacts of, 67
neoliberalism
 destruction of common good and, 107–8
 education and, 6–8, 104–6, 108–10, 140–43
 evolution of, 4–6
 globalization and, 101–3
 hijacking globalization to serve, 103–4
 Milton Friedman and, 31–34
 politics of capital, 138–40
New Deal, 231
New Orleans, Louisiana, 74, 113
new public managerialism (NPM), 66
Nixon, Richard, 124
No Child Left Behind (NCLB), 32, 42, 51, 59, 61, 70, 105, 117–18, 124

Obama, Barack, 20–21, 33, 42–43, 48, 55–56, 81, 102, 228–29, 231–35
organized action, 47
Orr, David, 103
Oxfam, 143

Pakistan, 55, 71
Palestine, 232–33
Paris Commune, 29
Parsons, Talcott, 1
Participatory Action Research (PAR), 199, 205
passion, 46–47
Pedagogy of the Oppressed, 35
Pell Grant, 130–31
Perino, Dana, 21
Peru, 15, 35
Petras, James, 237
Pilger, John, 68
Pinker, Steven, 114
Pizzigati, S., 66, 69
Plato, 30
Pollan, Michael, 109
post-traumatic stress disorder (PTSD), 126–27
Poverty of Philosophy, The (Marx), 75
Power, S., 71

Queen, Greg, 120
Quijano, Anibal, 213, 215–16

race/racism
  Abstract Democracy and, 56–57
  capitalism and, 20
  education and, 42, 58–59, 105
  globalization and, 216–17
  militarism and, 124, 128
  morality and, 222
  neoliberalism and, 67–68
  reification and, 52
  social class and, 72, 81, 91
  U.S. politics and, 42–43, 55–56, 228, 232–34
  Venezuela and, 201–2, 204, 206
Rasmus, Jack, 121–22

Reagan, Ronald, 80, 91, 101, 124, 192, 233
reason, 47
Recruiting Operations Manual, 117, 119, 123
Reich, Wilhelm, 58
Representing Capital (Jameson), 157
revisionism
  see historical revisionism
Rhoades, Gary, 106
Right to Work (RtW) campaign, 87
Rikowski, Glenn, 8, 71, 73, 75, 210, 215, 222–27, 234
Robinson, William I., 213, 215–16
Romero, Oscar, 35
Romney, Mitt, 58
Ross, E. Wayne, 120
Roubini, Nouriel, 219
Rouge Forum, 47, 57, 60–61
rule of law, 53
Russia, 30, 42, 55, 204

Sallie Mae, 131
Savyasaachi, 10, 171–87, 244
Scahill, Jeremy, 121
Schmidt, George, 116
School Recruiting Handbook, 117–20, 129
Sempre Fi Act, 117–18
Shame of the Cities (Steffens), 48
Sharma, Vijender, 160
Sheppard, Eric S., 104
Sibal, Kapil, 156, 160
Slaughter, Sheila, 106
"slowdown of accumulation," 5
Smith, Adam, 17
social class
  competing conceptions of, 16–22
  critical pedagogy and, 34–36
  Durkheim and, 28–31
  exploitation of, 72–75
  knowledge production within capitalism, 22–28
  Marxist and postmodern analyses of, 74–75
  overview, 15–16

INDEX

Solomon Amendment, 116–17
Soviet Union, 34, 204
Spitzer, Elliot, 58
St. Stephens College, 159, 165
Stalin, Joseph, 44, 192, 204
Steffins, Lincoln, 48
Steger, Manfred, 103
Stobart, Luke, 192
Suggett, James, 197
Sun Tzu, 41
Syria, 15, 89
Sziarto, Kristin, 104

Tabb, William, 220–21
Tagore, Rabindranath, 135
Taliban, 42, 49
tax cuts, 66, 230
Taylor, Frederick Winslow, 175
Thatcher, Margaret, 80, 91, 101, 192, 202
Theodore, Nicholas, 102
Tillman, Pat, 123
Tooley, James, 143–44
Troops-to-Teachers program, 118

United Auto Workers (UAW), 6, 48
University Community for Democracy (UCD), 154–55

Valéry, Paul, 220
Venezuela
 Barrio Pueblo Nuevo, 195–96
 community and, 198–200
 education and, 11, 193–95, 197–98
 globalization and, 15
 socialism and, 189–93, 196–97, 200–3
Venoco, 192
Veterans Affairs (VA), U.S. Department of, 126–27, 130
Victor, Maria Paez, 190–92
Vidal, Gore, 219
Vinson, Kevin, 120

Wal-Mart, 115, 128
Walter Reed Army Medical Center, 127
Weber, Max, 16, 215
Whitty, G., 71
Wilcox, Richard, 115
Williams, Jo, 194–95, 201
Wind That Shakes the Barley, The, 89
World Bank, 80, 107, 142, 237
World is Flat, The (Friedman), 103
World Social Forum (WSF), 56, 237

Yashpal Committee, 145, 160–61
Yates, M., 69

Ziemba, Rynn, 130

GPSR Compliance

The European Union's (EU) General Product Safety Regulation (GPSR) is a set of rules that requires consumer products to be safe and our obligations to ensure this.

If you have any concerns about our products, you can contact us on

ProductSafety@springernature.com

In case Publisher is established outside the EU, the EU authorized representative is:

Springer Nature Customer Service Center GmbH
Europaplatz 3
69115 Heidelberg, Germany

www.ingramcontent.com/pod-product-compliance
Lightning Source LLC
LaVergne TN
LVHW051913060526
838200LV00004B/131